Communications
in Computer and Information Science   1478

More information about this series at https://link.springer.com/bookseries/7899

Pablo H. Ruiz · Vanessa Agredo-Delgado ·
André Luiz Satoshi Kawamoto (Eds.)

Human-Computer Interaction

7th Iberoamerican Workshop, HCI-COLLAB 2021
Sao Paulo, Brazil, September 8–10, 2021
Proceedings

 Springer

Editors
Pablo H. Ruiz ⓘD
Corporación Universitaria Comfacauca
Unicomfacauca
Popayán, Colombia

Universidad del Cauca
Popayán, Colombia

Vanessa Agredo-Delgado ⓘD
Corporación Universitaria Comfacauca
Unicomfacauca
Popayán, Colombia

Universidad del Cauca
Popayán, Colombia

André Luiz Satoshi Kawamoto ⓘD
Universidade Tecnológica Federal do Paraná
Curitiba, Brazil

ISSN 1865-0929 ISSN 1865-0937 (electronic)
Communications in Computer and Information Science
ISBN 978-3-030-92324-2 ISBN 978-3-030-92325-9 (eBook)
https://doi.org/10.1007/978-3-030-92325-9

This Springer imprint is published by the registered company Springer Nature Switzerland AG
The registered company address is: Gewerbestrasse 11, 6330 Cham, Switzerland

Preface

The seventh edition of the Iberoamerican Workshop on Human-Computer Interaction (HCI 2021), was organized by the Universidade Presbiteriana Mackenzie, Brazil. The event has been held in different parts of the world, and as time has passed it has attracted more support. Despite the COVID-19 pandemic, and the workshop being held virtually this year, many people still participated both in terms of submitting papers and attending the various keynote talks and paper presentations covering a range of topics on human-computer interaction (HCI).

HCI is the discipline that studies how people interact with computers and to what extent computers are developed to interact with people, which consists of three components: users, computers, and the interaction between them. HCI is defined as the understanding, design, evaluation, and implementation of interactive systems for use by humans. In this sense, given that the evolution of computers has resulted in computerized systems being purely interactive, there is a real need for the new generation of such systems to incorporate the concepts established by this discipline, providing users with all the benefits of utility and usability (easy to learn, easy to use), lower costs and fewer errors made by users, effectiveness, efficiency, motivation, and acceptance, to increase productivity (individual and organizational) and the security of both the system and the users, ensuring that both elements are appropriately integrated into the organizational setting.

HCI research seeks to increase the satisfaction of end-users and reduce their effort to perform the tasks they must perform on the computer, without this diminishing the ability of users to develop their activities and interactive processes with the computer system. To this end, this book brings together a set of works related to HCI on specialized topics such as: emotional interfaces, usability, video games, computational thinking, collaborative systems, IoT, software engineering, ICT in education, augmented and mixed virtual reality for education, gamification, emotional interfaces, adaptive instruction systems, accessibility, use of video games in education, artificial intelligence in HCI, among others.

The call for papers at the VII HCI Iberoamerican Congress (HCI-COLLAB 2021) resulted in 68 submissions, of which 19 were accepted to be part of this book. Each submission was reviewed by at least three national and international reviewers. In addition, the EasyChair system was used to manage and review the papers.

We thank the members of our Program Committee for their work and contribution to the success of our workshop, the authors for their submissions, the organizers, and Springer for allowing us to put together the best works in this book.

October 2021

Pablo H. Ruiz
Vanessa Agredo-Delgado
André Luiz Satoshi Kawamoto

Organization

Academic Committee President

Valéria Farinazzo Martins   Universidade Presbiteriana Mackenzie, Brazil

Program Committee President

César Alberto Collazos   Universidad del Cauca, Colombia

Program Committee Chairs

Pablo H. Ruiz — Corporación Universitaria Comfacauca
and Universidad del Cauca, Colombia
Vanessa Agredo-Delgado — Corporación Universitaria Comfacauca
and Universidad del Cauca, Colombia
André Luiz Satoshi
Kawamoto — Universidade Tecnológica Federal do Paraná, Brazil

Program Committee

Adriana Vivacqua	Universidad Federal de Río de Janeiro, Brazil
Adriana Lopes	Universidade Federal do Amazonas, Brazil
Agustin Lagunes Dominguez	Universidad Veracruzana, Mexico
Alberto Raposo	Catholic University of Rio de Janeiro, Brazil
Alejandra Beatriz Lliteras	Universidad Nacional de la Plata, Argentina
Alejandro Fernández	Universidad Nacional de la Plata, Argentina
Alejandro Benito Santos	Universidad de Salamanca, Spain
Alessandra Reyes-Flores	Universidad Veracruzana, Mexico
Alexandre Cardoso	Universidade Federal de Uberlândia, Brazil
Alfredo Garcia	Benemérita Universidad Autónoma de Puebla, Mexico
Alfredo Mendoza-González	Instituto Nacional de Estadística y Geografía, Mexico
Alicia Mon	Universidad Nacional de La Matanza, Argentina
Alicia García-Holgado	University of Salamanca, Spain
Ana Carolina Bertoletti De Marchi	Universidat Pompeu Fabra, Spain
Ana Isabel Molina Díaz	University of Castilla-La Mancha, Spain
Anas Abulfaraj	King Abdulaziz University, Saudi Arabia
André Luiz Satoshi Kawamoto	Universidade Tecnológica Federal do Paraná, Brazil
André Freire	Universidade Federal de Lavras, Brazil
André Constantino Da Silva	Instituto Federal de Educação, Ciência e Tecnologia São Paulo, Brazil

Andrea Vázquez-Ingelmo	University of Salamanca, Spain
Andréia Formico	University of Fortaleza, Brasil
Andrés Solano	Universidad Autónoma de Occidente, Colombia
Angelo Jesus	Instituto Federal de Educação, Ciência e Tecnologia, Brazil
Anna Beatriz Marques	Universidade Federal do Ceará, Brazil
Antonia Huertas	Universitat Oberta de Catalunya, Spain
Antonio Silva Sprock	Universidad Central de Venezuela, Venezuela
Arturo Moquillaza	Pontificia Universidad Católica del Perú, Peru
Beatriz Beltran	Benemérita Universidad Autónoma de Puebla, Mexico
Beatriz Pacheco	Universidade Presbiteriana Mackenzie, Brazil
Blanca Nydia Perez Camacho	Benemerita Universidad Autónoma de Puebla, Mexico
Bruno Gadelha	Universidad Federal del Amazonas, Brazil
Bruno Azevedo Chagas	University of Rio de Janeiro, Brazil
Carina Gonzalez-González	Universidad de La Laguna, Spain
Carla Denise Castanho	Universidade de Brasília, Brazil
Carlos Vaz de Carvalho	Instituto Superior de Engenharia do Porto, Portugal
Carlos Eric Galván Tejada	Instituto Tecnológico y de Estudios Superiores de Monterrey, Mexico
Carlos Henrique da Santos	Instituto Federal de Educação, Ciência e Tecnologia São Paulo, Brazil
Caroline Queiroz Santos	Universidad Federal de Vales do Jequitinhonha e Mucuri, Brazil
Cecilia Camacho	Colegio Mayor del Cauca, Colombia
Cecilia Sanz	Universidad Nacional de la Plata, Argentina
Celmar Guimarães Da Silva	University of Campinas, Brazil
Cesar A. Collazos	Universidad del Cauca, Colombia
Christian Sturm	Applied Science University, Bahrain
Claudia González Calleros	Benemerita Universidad Autónoma de Puebla, Mexico
Clodis Boscarioli	Western Paraná State University, Brazil
Cristian Rusu	Pontificia Universidad Católica de Valparaiso, Chile
Cristina Manresa-Yee	University of the Balearic Islands, Spain
Daniela Quiñones Otey	Pontificia Universidad Católica de Valparaíso, Chile
Daniela Marques	Instituto Federal São Paulo, Brazil
Daniela Quiñones	Pontificia Universidad Católica de Valparaíso, Chile
Delano M. Beder	Federal University of São Carlos, Brazil
Diego Torres	Universidad Nacional de la Plata, Argentina
Diego Dermeval	Federal University of Alagoas, Brazil
Eduardo Hideki Tanaka	Eldorado Research Institute, Brazil
Elaine H. T. Oliveira	Universidade Federal do Amazonas, Brazil
Elena Navarro	University of Castilla-La Mancha, Spain
Erika Martínez	Benemérita Universidad Autónoma de Puebla, Mexico
Esteban Clua	Universidade Federal Fluminense, Brazil
Eva Villegas	La Salle University, Spain
Eva Cerezo	Universidad de Zaragoza, Spain

Fernando Figueira Filho	Federal University of Rio Grande do Norte, Brazil
Fernando Moreira	Universidade Portucalense, Portugal
Francisco Javier Álvarez Rodríguez	Universidad Autónoma de Aguascalientes, Mexico
Francisco José García Peñalvo	University of Salamanca, Spain
Francisco Luis Gutiérrez Vela	University of Granada, Spain
Freddy Paz	Pontificia Universidad Católica del Perú, Peru
Gabriel Avila	Institución Universitaria Politécnico Grancolombiano, Colombia
Germán Ezequiel Lescano	Universidad Nacional de Santiago del Estero, Argentina
Guillermina Sánchez Román	Benemérita Universidad Autónoma de Puebla, Mexico
Gustavo Rossi	Universidad Nacional de la Plata, Argentina
Gustavo Eduardo Constain Moreno	Universidad Nacional Abierta y a Distancia, Colombia
Hamurabi Gamboa-Rosales	Universidad Autonoma de Zacatecas, Mexico
Héctor Cardona Reyes	Centro de Investigación en Matemáticas A.C, Mexico
Huizilopoztli Luna-García	Universidad Autonoma de Zacatecas, Mexico
Ingrid Monteiro	Pontifícia Universidade Católica do Rio de Janeiro, Brazil
Isabela Gasparini	Université de l'État de Santa Catarina, Brazil
Ismar Frango Silveira	Universidade Presbiteriana Mackenzie, Brazil
Jacques Duílio Brancher	University of East London, London
Jaime Muñoz-Arteaga	Universidad Autónoma de Aguascalientes, Mexico
Jaime Díaz	Universidad de La Frontera, Chile
Javier Jaen	Universidad Politécnica de Valencia, Spain
Jeferson Arango Lopez	Universidad de Caldas, Colombia
Jesús Gallardo Casero	Universidad de Zaragoza, Spain
Joan Arnedo-Moreno	Universitat Oberta de Catalunya, Spain
Joao Soares de Oliveira Neto	Universidade Federal do Recôncavo da Bahia, Brazil
Jorge I. Galván-Tejada	Universidad Autónoma de Zacatecas, Mexico
Jorge Luis Pérez Medina	University of East London, London
Jose García-Alonso	University of Extremadura, Spain
Jose Aires de Castro Filho	Universidade Federal do Ceará, Brazil
José Antonio Pow-Sang	Pontificia Universidad Católica del Peru, Peru
José Antonio Macías Iglesias	Universidad Autónoma de Madrid, Spain
José Guadalupe Arceo Olague	Universidad Autónoma de Zacatecas, Mexico
Jose Maria Celaya Padilla	Universidad Autónoma de Zacatecas, Mexico
Josefina Guerrero Garcia	Benemerita Universidad Autónoma de Puebla, Mexico

Juan Manuel Gonzalez Calleros	Benemerita Universidad Autónoma de Puebla, Mexico
Juan Manuel Murillo Rodríguez	University of Extremadura, Spain
Juan Ruben Delgado Contreras	Tecnologico de Monterrey, Mexico
Kamila Rios H. Rodrigues	University of São Paulo, Brazil
Klinge Villalba-Condori	Universidad Nacional de San Agustín and Universidad Católica de Santa María, Peru
Laura Aballay	Universidad Nacional de San Juan, Argentina
Laura Cortés-Rico	Universidad Militar Nueva Granada, Colombia
Leander Oliveira	Universidade Tecnológica Federal do Paraná, Brazil
Leonardo Ramon Nunes De Sousa	Universidad Federal de Piauí, Brazil
Lesandro Ponciano	Pontifical Catholic University of Minas Gerais, Brazil
Lourdes Moreno	Universidad Carlos III de Madrid, Spain
Luciana Zaina	Universidade Federal de São Carlos, Brazil
Luciana Salgado	Universidade Federal Fluminense, Brazil
Luciana Alvim Santos Romani	Universidade Estadual de Campinas, Brazil
Luis Freddy Muñoz Sanabria	Fundacion Unversitaria de Popayan, Colombia
Manuel Ortega Cantero	University of Castilla-La Mancha, Spain
Marcelo de Paiva Guimarães	Federal University of São Paulo, Brazil
Marcelo Da Silva Hounsell	Université de l'État de Santa Catarina, Brazil
Maria Villegas	Universidad del Quindío, Colombia
Maria Eliseo	Universidade Presbiteriana Mackenzie, Brazil
Maria Clara Gomez Alvarez	Universidad de Medellín, Colombia
Mario Rossainz	Benemerita Universidad Autónoma de Puebla, Mexico
Mario Chacon	Instituto Tecnológico de Costa Rica, Costa Rica
Miguel Redondo	University of Castilla-La Mancha, Spain
Milene Silveira	Pontifícia Universidade Católica do Rio Grande do Sul, Brazil
Natalia Padilla-Zea	Universidad Internacional de la Rioja, Spain
Natasha Malveira Costa Valentim	Universidade Federal do Paraná, Brazil
Nuria Medina Medina	University of Granada, Spain
Oscar Carrillo	INSA Lyon, France
Oscar Alberto Henao Gallo	Technological University of Pereira, Colombia
Oscar David Robles Sanchez	Universidad Rey Juan Carlos, Spain
Pablo Torres-Carrion	Universidad Tecnica Particular de Loja, Spain
Pablo Santana Mansilla	Universidad Nacional de Santiago del Estero, Argentina
Pablo Ruiz	Unicomfacauca, Colombia

Contents

Combining Two Inspection Methods: Usability Heuristic Evaluation and WCAG Guidelines to Assess e-Commerce Websites

Afra Pascual-Almenara(✉) [ORCID] and Toni Granollers-Saltiveri(✉) [ORCID]

Departament d'Informàtica i Enginyeria Industrial, Universitat de Lleida, Lleida, Spain
{afra.pascual,toni.granollers}@udl.cat

Abstract. The usability and accessibility of 8 e-commerce websites (from five different sectors such as food, sports, fashion, electronics and DIY) were analysed by thirty-two evaluators. The assessment was done using the heuristic evaluation technique for usability and the Web Content Accessibility Guidelines (WCAG) 2.1 for accessibility. The results show higher levels in usability (an overall average of 73.80%) than in accessibility (an overall average of 64.00%). In terms of quality, we noticed a similarity between the accessibility problems of the e-commerce websites belonging to the study and the most problematic criteria according to others accessibility studies. Additionally, as we are interested in linking both attributes (usability and accessibility), a new index was proposed and, as a proof of concept, calculated using the data obtained in the study. We called the new index as *"UsabAccessibility"* and, summarizes the levels of usability and accessibility of any evaluated website in a single value. Finally, although we have created an index that unifies usability and accessibility, this is only a first approximation, we are aware that it is still necessary to mature both the concept and the way of calculating it.

Keywords: Usability evaluation · Heuristic evaluation · Accessibility evaluation · WCAG guidelines · Web usability · Web accessibility

1 Introduction

In 2020, e-commerce in the B2C (Business to Consumer) sector grew by 20% [1]. These results are significant, and with the global health crisis derived from the Covid-19 pandemic that people from all around the planet are experiencing, this kind of business model has accelerated, and by 2021 it is expected to grow by around 24%. In this scenario, it is essential that the websites of companies in relevant and essential economic sectors such as food, sports, fashion, and DIY, offer usable and accessible websites to facilitate the use and access of all users to online shopping.

In addition, between 15–20% of the world's population lives with some form of disability [2] and these people have the fundamental right of access to the Web, to participate actively in society like any other citizen [3]. E-commerce is an essential aspect for this type of user as there are many benefits of shopping online compared

© Springer Nature Switzerland AG 2021
P. H. Ruiz et al. (Eds.): HCI-COLLAB 2021, CCIS 1478, pp. 1–16, 2021.
https://doi.org/10.1007/978-3-030-92325-9_1

to going to a physical shop. However, a non-accessible website excludes people with disabilities from these needs.

Usability is an internal quality of interactive systems defined as "the ability of software to be understood, learned, used and appealing to the user, under specific conditions of use" [4]. Web accessibility is the practice that ensures that websites, technologies and tools are designed to be usable by people with disabilities [5].

The purpose of this article is to analyse the level of usability and accessibility of some significant e-commerce websites of the main Spanish food, electronics, sports, fashion and DIY companies with the objective of provide a separately and combined point of view.

The article is organised as follows: first the context of the study is presented, followed by the methodology and results obtained in the evaluation. The final part presents future work and conclusions.

2 Study Context

A total of 8 e-commerce websites of the most relevant Spanish companies (according to the employer's association of manufacturers and distributors, AECOC[1]) have been evaluated. Various sectors were considered: food, sports, fashion, electronics, DIY. Table 1 shows the list of websites that were part of the study.

Table 1. List of websites evaluated

Id	Companies	URL
1	Carrefour	https://www.carrefour.es/
2	CorteIngles	https://www.elcorteingles.es/
3	Decathlon	https://www.decathlon.es/es/
4	LeroyMerlin	https://www.leroymerlin.es/
5	Mango	https://shop.mango.com/
6	MediaMark	https://www.mediamarkt.es/
7	Mercadona	https://www.mercadona.es/
8	Zara	https://www.zara.com/es/

Some aspects of UX quality have been analyzed [6] such as usability and accessibility to obtain results from two different but complementary perspectives: on the one hand, to obtain a result related to the usability of the system and on the other hand, to obtain results related to the accessibility of the website of the 8 websites.

In 2020, a usability evaluation study with heuristic evaluation was carried out on a total of 7 websites with relevant information related to the covid-19 pandemic. The result of this study indicated that the level of usability of the total number of websites

---

[1] Association of Spanish manufacturers and distributors: https://www.aecoc.es/.

evaluated is good, with an average value of *Usability Percentage* (following Granollers proposal [7]) of 71,78%.

According to a WebAIM survey [8] which annually (since 2019) analyses the accessibility of a total of 1,000,000 homepages of the most important companies worldwide, a total of 97.4% of these websites show weaknesses that are automatically detectable by the WCAG guidelines [9]. In addition, a recent European Commission report [10] indicates that less than 10% of European websites are accessible. It is significant data to take into account. However, even if a website complies with the WCAG guidelines this does not guarantee full website accessibility [11, 12].

3 Methodology

In the following, the implementation of the study, the usability evaluation methodology and the accessibility evaluation methodology are presented.

The outline of the results report is also presented. It has been organized to include the conclusions of all the evaluations carried out by the work teams.

3.1 Launching the Study

The evaluation of the e-commerce websites was carried out during March-April 2021. It was carried out in the context of the Web Design subject[2] of the 2nd academic course of the Bachelor's Degree in Design and Creative Technologies[3] of University of Lleida.

A specific scenario was proposed: the students belonged to a web design consultancy and had to evaluate a website and obtain the strengths and weaknesses regarding usability and accessibility of various e-commerce websites.

They were organized in working groups in which each one played a different role: project manager, coordinates and supervises the evaluation of the website; usability manager, coordinates heuristic evaluation and summarizes the results; accessibility manager, performs accessibility evaluation of WCAG 2.1 guidelines and synthesizes the results and finally the assistant to make support tasks. The working groups consisted of 4 people and a total of 8 websites were evaluated, giving a total of thirty-two participants (4 people x 8 websites = 32 participants). Each group of 4 participants evaluates only one single website.

Previously to participate on the project, every student made two activities: a heuristic evaluation and the evaluation of the WCAG guidelines form an online flower shop. These activities were scoring to the final mark of the Web Design subject.

3.2 Usability Evaluation

The usability evaluation was carried out following one of the best known and used methodologies, the heuristic evaluation. An inspection methodology where a group of

---

[2] Course guide for Web Design: http://guiadocent.udl.cat/pdf/es/102184.

[3] Bachelor's degree in Digital Desing and Creative Technologies: http://www.graudissenydigital itec.udl.cat/.

experts 1314 assess the quality of an interactive interface in relation to its ease of learning and use by a given user group and in a given context of use [15]. In the evaluation of e-commerce websites, a new proposal of heuristic principles was used, resulting from analysing and synthesising J. Nielsen's Heuristic Usability Principles for User Interface Design and B. Tognazzini's Interface Design Principles [16]. This proposal consists of a total of [15] heuristic principles on the basis of answering 60 specific questions, which provides a final result value called *Usability Percentage*[4]. It gives an overall idea of the level of usability of the analysed interface. In addition, this evaluation methodology has a template[5] which eases the experts' job.

The members of each working group individually observed the aspects related to the heuristic evaluation and then met to analyse the individual results. At the end, each group agreed on the results of the individual heuristic evaluation in a single data set for each heuristic [17, 18].

Although there is a list of heuristic criteria specifically designed for the evaluation of e-commerce [19, 20], only the general heuristic set was considered for inclusion as it assesses the usability of the website in a more generic way.

3.3 Accessibility Evaluation

The accessibility evaluation was carried out following the Web Site Accessibility Conformance Assessment Methodology (WCAG-EM) [21] developed by the Web Accessibility Initiative (WAI) [22]. This methodology guides in the development process of accessibility evaluation and proposes in addition to the evaluation of the WCAG guidelines, optionally to evaluate the website with assistive technologies or to involve users with disabilities.

The WCAG guidelines evaluation [9] was carried out only on the homepage of each of the websites included in the study and used the template[6] proposed by the Web Accessibility Observatory (OAW). The template also calculates an average score for the accessibility of the website, which is a numerical value, and corresponds to the weighting of the result of the compliant or non-compliant criteria of the evaluated website. This score has been transformed into a percentage, becoming the *Accessibility Percentage*, and thus equating to the above-mentioned *Usability Percentage* value.

To facilitate the WCAG 2.1 guidelines evaluation process, the students developed a wiki[7] on the UdL Virtual Campus prior to the start of the study of e-commerce websites.

The wiki contained information corresponding to the principles, guidelines and criteria obtained from the technical guides offered by the Web Accessibility Observatory (OAW) for each of the principles: Perceptible [23], Operable [24], Understandable [25]

---

[4] A percentual value that, according to every evaluator, provides an idea about the level of usability of the evaluated user interface.

[5] Ms Excel Template for Heuristic Evaluation: http://mpiua.invid.udl.cat/wp-content/uploads/2018/04/Evaluaci%C3%B3n-Heuristica-v2018-OK.xlsx.

[6] Accessibility review templates for public sector bodies. https://administracionelectronica.gob.es/pae_Home/pae_Estrategias/pae_Accesibilidad/implantacion-rd-1112-2018/revisiones_accesibilidad.html#INFORMESREVISION.

[7] Wiki of accessibility https://cv.udl.cat/wiki/site/102184-2021/home.html.

and Robust [26]. Each student included a total of 2–3 criteria from the WCAG 2.1 guidelines in the wiki. The criteria to each student was randomly assigned. The explanation associated with each criterion was developed based on the information that an evaluator should consult to analyse each of the accessibility criteria. For each criterion, 4 aspects were indicated: a) the objective of the criterion, b) an example of what the evaluator should observe on the website; c) the support tools to carry out the evaluation and, d) the references to the WCAG 2.1 guidelines corresponding to that criterion. The information corresponding to the examples was divided into two: an accessible example with a figure, an explanation and the source URL of the example; and a non-accessible example with a figure, an explanation and the source URL of the example. The information in sections c and d came from the OAW reports discussed above. Figure 1 shows a screenshot of the information provided on the wiki.

3.4 Report of Results

The data obtained from the usability and accessibility evaluations were added to the results reports that collected all the observations of the working teams. Additionally, every group presented their results to the rest (around 15 min presentations summarising the most important data).

The following is the general outline that the students followed in their presentations. This schema has been derived by combining relevant aspects of the report - Common Industry Format (CIF) for Usability [27] and of the report proposed by the WCAG-EM methodology [28].

1. Introduction
1.1 Executive Summary
1.2 Full product description
1.3 Test objectives
1.4 Evaluations carried out

2. Usability evaluation
2.1 Description of the process
2.2 Participants
2.3 Methodology followed
2.4 Quantitative results
2.5 Qualitative results

3. Accessibility evaluation
3.1 Description of the process
3.2 Participants
3.3 Methodology followed
3.4 Quantitative results
3.5 Qualitative results

4. Results and recommendations
4.1 Interpretation of the results

4.2 Usability proposals and recommendations
4.3 Proposals and recommendations for accessibility

5. Conclusions
5.1 Synthesis of usability evaluation results
5.2 Synthesis of accessibility evaluation results
5.3 Proposals for joint improvement considering usability and actual accessibility of the system 5.4 Proposals for joint improvement considering usability and actual accessibility of the system

APPENDICES:
A1. Evaluation documents
Heuristic Evaluation Results Sheets
WCAG Guidelines Evaluation Results Sheets

4 Results

The results are organised according to quantitative data and qualitative data. The quantitative data are obtained from the detailed data of the evaluations and are synthesised in the *Usability Percentage* obtained from the heuristic evaluation and the *Accessibility Percentage* obtained from the WCAG guidelines evaluation.

The qualitative data were obtained from the comments and observations made by the work teams involved in the experimentation and collected in the results reports.

4.1 Qualitative Data

Quantitative data from the usability and accessibility evaluation are shown below.

Usability Evaluation. Table 2 shows the average scores for each heuristic as assessed for each website. In this table, the important values are those in the bottom row, which correspond to the *Usability Percentages*. The range of values for the Usability Percentage is set between the highest value of 83% and the lowest value of 60%, with an average of 73.8%. Analysing these results, we can observe that, in general terms, the evaluated websites have a good level of usability.

Fig. 1. Screen of the wiki with concrete information on an accessibility criterion.

The values corresponding to the "average" column of Table 2 have been presented in the graph in Fig. 2. This graph shows (in black) the average value of each principle obtained in the evaluation of each website. It also shows (in grey) the maximum value that each principle could reach. However, the maximum value may vary according to the evaluator's answer and depends on whether all the questions can be applied in the evaluation, are or are not a problem on the website or are "warnings" impossible to check. In all these cases, the score is 0 points (although for the final percentage value, the questions ranked as a warning or as a not a problem are eliminated); questions that are completely fulfilled are given a score of 1; questions that some cases are missing 0.66, and the questions that not always are fulfilled, are given a score of 0.33. Although this is a result, we know that this maximum value needs to be better adjusted to suit the particular answers of each principle.

The graph in Fig. 3 shows the average value of the *Usability Percentage* obtained in the evaluation of each website, obtained from the last row of Table 2.

Table 2. Results of the average evaluation of all evaluators on each website

Heuristic Criteria	Carrefour	Corteingles	Decathlon	LeroyMerlin	Mango	MediaMark	Mercadona	Zara	Average
HC1- Visibility and system state	5,00	4,37	4,66	2,99	5,00	4,26	3,49	2,66	4,05
HC2 - Connection between the sustem and the real world, metaphor usage and human objects	3,66	3,92	3,92	3,49	3,66	3,59	3,66	2,20	3,51
HC3 - User control and freedom	1,58	2,75	2,92	1,66	1,58	2,33	1,66	2,63	2,14
HC4 - Consistency and standards	3,82	5,75	5,00	4,33	3,82	5,32	5,32	3,37	4,59
HC5 - Recognition rather than memory, learning and anticipation	4,67	3,87	4,41	2,99	4,67	4,73	4,16	2,36	3,98
HC6 - Flexibility and efficency of use	2,00	3,33	3,41	1,91	2,00	2,99	2,91	2,07	2,58
HC7 - Help users recognize, diagnose and recover form errors	2,83	2,17	2,91	2,75	2,83	3,26	0,17	2,75	2,46
HC8 - Preventing errors	2,25	2,04	2,41	2,08	2,25	2,80	0,66	1,25	1,96
HC9 - Aesthetic and minimalist design	3,41	3,75	3,49	3,16	3,41	4,75	3,92	2,25	3,52
HC10 - Help and documentation	3,99	4,63	5,00	4,33	3,99	4,59	3,99	3,58	4,26
HC11 - Save the state and protect the work	2,00	2,08	0,58	2,17	2,00	2,53	0,00	1,62	1,62
HC12 - Color and readability	1,82	3,08	2,32	2,32	1,82	2,77	3,41	1,83	2,42
HC13 - Autonomy	2,92	1,54	1,08	1,41	2,92	2,53	0,66	2,45	1,94
HC14 - Defaults	2,00	0,46	0,25	0,75	2,00	2,53	0,08	0,17	1,02
HC15 - Latency reduction	2,00	0,75	0,17	0,67	2,00	1,00	0,17	0,25	0,85
Usability Percentage	79,93%	82,87%	77,77%	63,96%	76,75%	83,30%	65,2%	60,7%	73,8%

Accessibility Evaluation. Regarding the quantitative results of the WCAG guidelines, Tables 3 and 4 together with Tables 5 and 6 show the detailed values of each e-commerce website accessibility assessment of levels A and AA. Guideline 1.1-Alternative text fails on all websites; Guideline 1.2-Multimedia content does not apply to any website; and Guideline 1.3-Adaptable and 1.4-Distinguishable have different results (pass or fail) depending on the website content. Regarding Guideline 2.1-Accessible keyboard, 50% of the websites meet this criterion; Guideline 2.2-Sufficient time, has a great diversity of results; Guideline 2.3-Epileptic seizures generally does not apply or passes; Guideline 2. 4-Navigation, except for the first criterion 2.4.1 which has a more varied result, the rest of the criteria are fulfilled, except for 2.4.3, 2.4.6 and 2.4.6 corresponding to the order and visualisation of the focus and labelling of headings appropriately which has more problems. Regarding Guideline 2.5: Input modalities, criteria 2.5.1 and 2.5.2 are practically fulfilled on all websites. However, criteria 2.5.3 and 2.5.4 present more problems. Regarding Guideline 3.1- Legible, criterion 3.1.1 has a higher compliance than criterion 3.1.2; Guideline 3.2-Previsible, there is good compliance in the websites, both in the criteria corresponding to level A and level AA; Guideline 3.3 Data entry assistance, the websites have deficiencies in correctly communicating the type of data to be entered in the form fields. Finally, Guideline 4.1 Compatible, only one website meets all criteria 4.1.1, 4.1.2 and 4.1.3.

Furthermore, in addition to the pass/fail results assessed for each accessibility criterion, the *Accessibility Percentage* has been obtained, which can be consulted in the graph in Fig. 4.

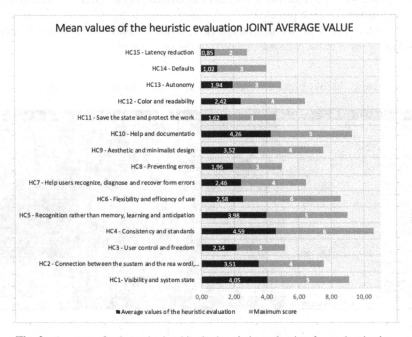

Fig. 2. Average of values obtained in the heuristic evaluation for each criterion.

Joint Quantitative Results. The *Usability Percentage* and *Accessibility Percentage* values, obtained by evaluating the websites with the heuristic criteria evaluation templates and WCAG guidelines, have been observed jointly (see Table 7).

The websites with the three highest scores were: "Mango", "Decathlon" and "Media-mark". The website with the highest *Usability Percentage* was "Mediamark" (83.30%). The website with the highest *Accessibility Percentage* was "Mango" (85.40%). However, the "Decathlon" website obtained more balanced percentages: 77.77%–75.60% corresponding to the *Usability Percentage* and *Accessibility Percentage* respectively. It is also important to highlight that only the "Mango" website obtained a higher *Accessibility Percentage* with respect to the *Usability Percentage*. And in general, all the websites

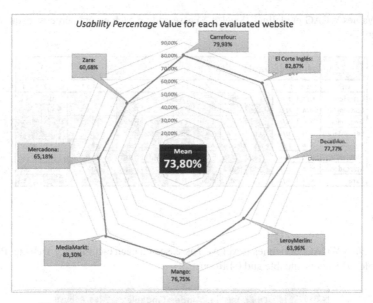

Fig. 3. *Usability Percentage* value obtained for each website.

Table 3. Results of the evaluation of the WCAG guidelines (level A). Principles: 01.Perceptible, 03.Understandable and 04.Robust

A	01. Perceivable									03. Understandable					04. Robust	
WEB	1.1.1	1.2.1	1.2.2	1.2.3	1.3.1	1.3.2	1.3.3	1.4.1	1.4.2	3.1.1	3.2.1	3.2.2	3.3.1	3.3.2	4.1.1	4.1.2
Carrefour	Fail	N/A	N/A	N/A	Fail	Pass	Pass	Fail	Pass	Pass	Pass	Pass	Pass	Pass	Fail	Fail
CorteIngles	Fail	N/A	N/A	N/A	Fail	Pass	Pass	Fail	N/A	Fail	Pass	N/A	Fail	N/A	Fail	N/A
Decathlon	Fail	N/A	N/A	N/A	Pass	Pass	Pass	Pass	Pass	Pass	N/A	Pass	Fail	Pass	Pass	Pass
LeroyMerlin	Fail	N/A	N/A	N/A	Pass	Fail	Fail	Fail	N/A	Fail	Fail	Pass	Fail	Fail	Fail	Fail
Mango	Fail	N/A	N/A	N/A	Pass	Fail	Pass	Pass	N/A	Pass	Pass	Pass	Pass	Pass	Pass	Pass
MediaMark	Fail	N/A	N/A	N/A	Fail	Pass	Fail	Fail	N/A	Pass	Pass	Fail	N/A	Pass	Fail	Pass
Mercadona	Fail	N/A	N/A	N/A	Fail	Fail	Pass	Pass	N/A	Pass	Pass	Fail	Fail	Pass	Fail	Fail
Zara	Fail	N/A	N/A	N/A	Pass	N/A	Pass	Pass	N/A	Pass	Pass	N/A	Pass	N/A	N/A	Fail

Table 4. Results of the evaluation of the WCAG guidelines (level A). Principle: 02.Operable

A	02. Operable													
WEB	2.1.1	2.1.2	2.1.4	2.2.1	2.2.2	2.3.1	2.4.1	2.4.2	2.4.3	2.4.4	2.5.1	2.5.2	2.5.3	2.5.4
Carrefour	Fail	Pass	Fail	Fail	N/T	N/A	Fail	Pass	Pass	Pass	Pass	Pass	Pass	Fail
CorteIngles	Pass	Pass	Fail	N/A	N/A	N/A	N/A	Pass	Pass	Pass	Pass	Fail	Fail	N/A
Decathlon	Fail	Fail	N/A	N/A	Pass	Pass	Fail	Pass	Pass	Pass	Pass	Pass	Pass	Fail
LeroyMerlin	Pass	Pass	N/A	Pass	Pass	Pass	Pass	Pass	Fail	Pass	Pass	Pass	Fail	N/A
Mango	Pass	Pass	N/A	N/A	Fail	Pass	Pass	Pass	Pass	Pass	Pass	Pass	Pass	Fail
MediaMark	Pass	Pass	N/A	N/A	Fail	Pass	Fail	Pass	Pass	Pass	Pass	Pass	Fail	N/A
Mercadona	Fail	Pass	N/A	N/A	Fail	Pass	Fail	Pass	Fail	Pass	N/A	Pass	Fail	N/A
Zara	Fail	Pass	Fail	N/A	N/A	N/A	Pass	Fail	Fail	Pass	Pass	Pass	Fail	Fail

Table 5. Values WCAG guidelines (level AA) assessed on each e-commerce website. Principle 01. Perceptible

AA	01. Perceivable										
WEB	1.2.4	1.2.5	1.3.4	1.3.5	1.4.3	1.4.4	1.4.5	1.4.10	1.4.11	1.4.12	1.4.13
Carrefour	N/A	N/A	Pass	Pass	Pass	Pass	Pass	Pass	Fail	Fail	Fail
CorteIngles	N/A	N/A	Pass	Pass	Pass	Pass	Fail	Pass	Fail	Fail	Pass
Decathlon	N/A	N/A	Pass	Pass	Fail	Fail	Pass	Pass	Pass	Pass	Pass
LeroyMerlin	N/A	N/A	Pass	N/A	Pass	Fail	Pass	Pass	Fail	Pass	Pass
Mango	N/A	N/A	Pass	Pass	Fail	Pass	Pass	Fail	Pass	Pass	Pass
MediaMark	N/A	N/A	Pass	Pass	Pass	Pass	Pass	Pass	Pass	Fail	Pass
Mercadona	N/A	N/A	Pass	Pass	Pass	Pass	Pass	Pass	Pass	N/A	Fail
Zara	N/A	N/A	N/A	Fail	Fail	N/A	Pass	Fail	Pass	Pass	Pass

Table 6. Values WCAG guidelines (level AA) assessed on each e-commerce website. Principles 02. Operable, 03.Understandable and 04.Robust

AA	02. Operable			03. Understandable					04. Robust
WEB	2.4.5	2.4.6	2.4.7	3.1.2	3.2.3	3.2.4	3.3.3	3.3.4	4.1.3
Carrefour	Pass	Pass	Fail	Fail	Pass	Pass	Pass	N/A	Fail
CorteIngles	N/A	Fail	Pass	Fail	N/A	N/A	Fail	N/A	N/A
Decathlon	Pass	Pass	Fail	Pass	Pass	Pass	Pass	N/T	Fail
LeroyMerlin	Pass	Fail	Fail	Fail	Fail	Fail	Pass	N/A	N/A
Mango	Pass	Pass	Pass	Pass	Pass	Pass	Pass	N/A	Pass
MediaMark	Pass	Pass	Fail	Fail	Pass	Pass	N/A	N/A	Fail
Mercadona	Fail	Fail	Pass	Pass	Pass	Pass	Fail	N/A	Fail
Zara	Pass	Pass	Pass	Pass	Pass	Fail	N/A	N/A	Fail

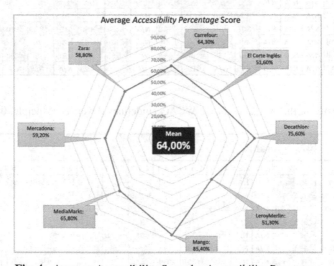

Fig. 4. Average Accessibility Score by *Accessibility Percentage*

obtained a higher level of *Usability Percentage* than *Accessibility Percentage*. In addition, we can observe that the difference between both percentages is very significant for the "El Corte Inglés" website, being more than 3 points.

Table 7. *Usability* and *Accessibility Percentages* of evaluated websites

Web site	Usability percentage	Accessibility percentage
Carrefour	79,93%	64,30%
Corte Inglés	82,87%	51,60%
Decathlon	77,77%	75,60%
Leroy Merlin	63,96%	51,30%
Mango	76,75%	**85,40%**
MediaMark	**83,30%**	65,80%
Mercadona	65,18%	59,20%
Zara	60,68%	58,80%
Mean values	*73,80%*	*64,00%*

4.2 Qualitative Analysis

The following are the qualitative results observed in the usability and accessibility evaluation that the working teams collected in the results reports. After analysing all the reports received, the main qualitative aspects to be highlighted are organized first with the results of heuristic evaluations and then the results according to the WCAG 2.1 guidelines.

Observations Corresponding to the Heuristic Evaluations. The most salient and general observations obtained in the website evaluations are shown (likewise, the Heuristic Criterion, HC, to which they refer is included):

– Websites follow the same patterns in terms of consistency and design standards, which facilitate user actions. In general, the same actions lead to the same results (HC4, HC1).
– All the websites evaluated have the logo and title (HC1) in a homogeneous place. The "Mercadona" website shows two different pages between the homepage and the shopping page, it has direct impact on its heuristic criteria scores.
– In general, all menus are extensive (HC1). It should be noted that on the "Carrefour" website the main menu is in a "hamburger" icon, a symbolic representation for describing drop-down menus, and this makes it difficult to find the product categories. In addition, on some websites there are access to ghost pages. For example, on the "Decathlon" website, there are menus with 8 sections and a multitude of sub-sections which, when selecting a higher category, open a page with no information or products.

- All the websites evaluated offer search functionality, and in all cases the search produces a result, although there are typographical or spelling errors when entering the product to be searched for (HC8).
- In general, links are not well defined, and standard colours are not used (HC12).
- Text fonts displayed on the websites generally are too small and do not have adequate contrast (HC12). This can be seen on the website of "Decathlon", "Zara" or in the help section of "Carrefour".
- All websites designs are responsive (HC6), except the shopping website of "Mercadona", which does not adapt to the screen resolution.
- The shopping cart functionality had some problems on the "Carrefour" website as it was inconsistent (the user selects a product, but the cart remains empty and is not updated) (HC11, HC13).
- Only on the "Mercadona" website, it was necessary to register to start the shopping process, all the others could start filling the shopping cart, as the registration was done when the order was going to be processed (HC13).
- Users tend to look in the footer of the page for information related to the page contact and even if the link is at the top, they do not find it (HC1). On some websites the interface word for the same functionality was "Customer Service" (in "El Corte Inglés" and "Mercadona". In addition, on the "Mango" website, the contact information is hidden inside the "Help" page. (HC10).

Observations Corresponding to the WCAG Guideline Evaluations. Only the most outstanding and generalized observations are shown in the websites in terms of accessibility evaluation. The number of the WCAG 2.1 criterion to which they refer is also included:

- All the pages evaluated have problems with the labelling of content related to images. What has been observed on the sites evaluated is that the images do not have the "ALT" attribute or that the text added to the image is not suitable as alternative text. (WCAG 1.1.1)
- Websites do not display videos on their homepage. Therefore, this criterion was not applied in the evaluation (WCAG 1.2 Guidelines).
- None of the websites have keyboard traps (WCAG 2.1.2), and therefore keyboard navigation does not present any difficulties.
- Half of the websites do not have a good header structure (WCAG 1.3.1) or do not have a proper title (WCAG 2.4.6).
- There is good compliance with the new criteria corresponding to the guideline version (WCAG: 2.5.1 and 2.5.2) but there are more failures, or the guideline does not apply to the criteria (WCAG: 2.5.3 and 2.5.4).
- No site evaluated has found flashes that may cause problems for people with epilepsy (WCAG 2.3.1).
- Not all websites have mechanisms for skipping blocks of information (WCAG 2.4.1).
- All websites have a page title describing their purpose (WCAG 2.4.2).
- 5 of the 8 evaluated websites have text and elements without good contrast (WCAG 1.4.3 and WCAG 1.4.11).

– Almost all websites define the language in the header of the page (WCAG 3.1.1), there is less compliance when the language must be defined when content appears in a language other than the main language of the website (WCAG 3.1.2).
– All the evaluated pages have important HTML code validation errors (using with the W3C validation service) (WCAG 4.1.1).
– The form and button fields corresponding to the search functionality do not have appropriate labels (attribute "label") (WCAG 4.1.2).

5 Conclusions

A total of 8 Spanish e-commerce websites have been evaluated. The level of usability has been evaluated with heuristic evaluations and the level of accessibility with the WCAG 2.1 guidelines. From the data presented in this article, several conclusions are analysed.

Firstly, even that it is difficult to compare, the e-commerce websites evaluated have a higher usability index than accessibility. This is an aspect that can be intuited in any website, but thanks to the data obtained in the study, it has been confirmed. In general, the e-commerce websites evaluated have a medium-high usability level (an average *Usability Percentage* of 73,80%), however, the level of accessibility is lower (average *Accessibility Percentage*: 64,00%). This data clearly shows how e-commerce companies do not take accessibility into account in the process of designing and publishing content and products. This aspect can limit to a great extent the actions that users with disabilities can carry out on the website.

Another relevant point that needs to be analysed is related to the accessibility problems obtained in the evaluated websites. There is a similarity between the accessibility problems of the e-commerce websites belonging to the study and the most problematic criteria according to the WebAIM study 8. This fact is relevant as it indicates that in general all websites have the same problems, mainly due to the lack of training in the area of accessibility of content developers or editors or due to the lack of tools necessary to create accessible websites.

It is important highlight that two inspection methods used on the evaluation (heuristic evaluation and WCAG guidelines) have different structures and different goals and it is necessary adapt results to compare data.

6 Future Work

As future work, and as a result of the observation of the indexes obtained in terms of the *Usability Percentage* from the heuristic evaluation and the *Accessibility Percentage* from the WCAG guidelines evaluation, it is proposed to unify them into a single value. This new index, which we will provisionally call UsabAccessibility index, summarizes the level of usability and accessibility of an evaluated website. A formula is presented to obtain this value:

$$UsabAccesibilidad = \frac{Usability\ Percentage + Accessibility\ Percentage}{2}$$

In addition, and as a proof of concept, the index has been calculated from the data obtained in the study. The graph in Fig. 5 shows the calculated UsabAccessibility value for each website. The website with the lowest value for this index is the "LeroyMerlin" website (57.6%).

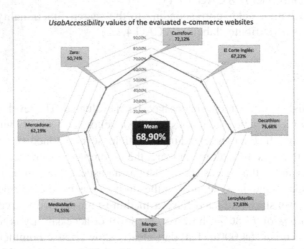

Fig. 5. Graph with UsabAccessibility values (*Usability percentage* and *Accessibility percentage* shown together).

However, this is early data and a thorough and detailed analysis of what a certain UsabAccessibility index value indicates is needed: What could a UsabAccessibility value of 81.07% of the Mango website mean? And the same with all other possible values of the same index. Also, there is one important limitation with the calculus of UsabAccessibility: there are usability aspects covered by heuristic evaluation that also cover aspects related to WCAG. It is important so, prior to comparing two percentages, it is necessary to identify how they intersect or not (that do not seem to be easy).

From the work done throughout the study, different needs emerge. In the short term, to extend the current evaluation by including a user test with different groups of participants running basic functionalities of an e-commerce website: searching for products, shopping, and contacting the company. The user test will allow us to collect data related to usability and to know how people feel when interacting with a product and their perception when using it, i.e. to obtain the level of user experience (User eXperience, UX)4. Related to this, including people with disabilities in the test to evaluate the Accessibility User Experience (AUX) will allow us to observe how accessibility is integrated into UX design and to evaluate digital experiences so that they are satisfactory for everyone, regardless of their ability. [29, 30].

Acknowledgments. Special thanks to all the students of the Web Design course of the Bachelor's degree in Digital Design and Creative Technologies of the 2020/21 academic year at the Universitat de Lleida for carrying out the evaluations and obtaining the data necessary to carry out this study.

References

1. Cramer-Flood, E.: Global Comercio-e Update 2021. https://www.emarketer.com/content/global-comercio-e-update-2021
2. World Health Organization: Disabilities (2021). https://www.who.int/topics/disabilities/
3. United Nations: Universal Declaration of Human Rights (2021). https://www.un.org/en/about-us/universal-declaration-of-human-rights
4. ISO/CD 9241-11. Ergonomics of human-system interaction–Part11: Guidance on usability (1998). http://www.iso.org/iso/catalogue_detail.htm?csnumber=63500
5. Introduction web accessibility (2021). https://www.w3.org/standards/webdesign/accessibility
6. Masip, L., Oliva, M., Granollers, T.: User experience specification through quality attributes. In: Campos, P., Graham, N., Jorge, J., Nunes, N., Palanque, P., Winckler, M. (eds.) INTERACT 2011. LNCS, vol. 6949, pp. 656–660. Springer, Heidelberg (2011). https://doi.org/10.1007/978-3-642-23768-3_106
7. Granollers, T.: Usability evaluation, coronavirus as an example (2020). https://mpiua.invid.udl.cat/usability-evaluation-coronavirus-as-an-example/
8. The WebAIM Millionv (2021). https://webaim.org/projects/million/
9. Web Content Accessibility Guidelines 2.1 (WCAG). World Wide Web Consortium (W3C) (2021). http://www.w3.org/TR/WCAG21/
10. European Commission. Accessibility: essential for some, useful for all (2021). https://digital-strategy.ec.europa.eu/en/library/accessibility-essential-some-useful-all
11. Deshmukh, M., Phatak, D., Save, B.: User experience for person with disabilities. Int. J. Comput. Appl. **180**, 6–11 (2018). https://doi.org/10.5120/ijca2018917141
12. Termens, M., Ribera, M., Porras, M., Boldú, M., Sulé, M., Paris, P.: Web content accessibility guidelines: from 1.0 to 2.0. In: Proceedings of the 18th International Conference on World Wide Web, WWW 2009, pp. 1171–1172 (2009). https://doi.org/10.1145/1526709.1526912
13. Sears, A., Jacko, J.: The Human-Computer Interaction Handbook: Fundamentals, Evolving Technologies, and Emerging Applications (Human Factors and Ergonomics Series). L. Erlbaum Associates Inc., USA (2007)
14. Cockton, C.: "Usability Evaluation". The Encyclopedia of Human-Computer Interaction, 2nd edn. Chapter 15 (2020). https://www.interaction-design.org/literature/book/the-encyclopedia-of-human-computer-interaction-2nd-ed/usability-evaluation
15. Nielsen, J.: 10 Usability Heuristics for User Interface Design [Online Resource]. https://www.nngroup.com/articles/ten-usability-heuristics/
16. Granollers, T.: Usability Evaluation with Heuristics, Beyond Nielsen's List. (2018). https://www.thinkmind.org/articles/achi_2018_4_10_20055.pdf
17. Lores, J., Gonzalez, M.P., Pascual, A.: Evaluación Heuristica (2006) Libro AIPO. https://aipo.es/libro/pdf/15-Evaluacion-Heuristica.pdf
18. Granollers, T., Gonzales, M.: Taller: Evaluacion de usabilidad heurística [Video] (2020). https://www.youtube.com/watch?v=YAwrCpVaw6I&t=15s
19. Granollers, T.: Validación experimental de un conjunto heurístico para evaluaciones de UX de sitios web de comercio-e. In: IEEE 11th Colombian Computing Conference (CCC), pp. 1–8 (2016). https://doi.org/10.1109/ColumbianCC.2016.7750783
20. Díaz Rodríguez, E.S.: Elaboración y validación de métricas para la evaluación de usabilidad de sitios Web de Comercio Electrónico (2020). http://hdl.handle.net/20.500.12404/18622
21. W3C. Website Accessibility Conformance Evaluation Methodology (WCAG-EM 1.0) (2014). https://www.w3.org/TR/WCAG-EM/
22. W3C. Web Accessibility Initiative (2021). https://www.w3.org/WAI/ER/tools/

23. Technical guide to the Perceptible principle. Web Accessibility Observatory (2021). https://administracionelectronica.gob.es/pae_Home/dam/jcr:ec04c677-64b1-4be2-a51f-1352144e4 556/Guia_Tecnica_-_Principio_Perceptible.pdf
24. Technical guide to the Operable principle. Web Accessibility Observatory (2021). https://administracionelectronica.gob.es/pae_Home/dam/jcr:ffb08d21-f9bf-4258-b111-246504fca 67e/Guia_Tecnica_-_Principio_Operable.pdf
25. Technical guide to the Understandable principle. Web Accessibility Observatory (2021). https://administracionelectronica.gob.es/pae_Home/dam/jcr:0218c154-89cf-4a2f-937d-74b 57f0a41e9/Guia_Tecnica_-_Principio_Comprensible.pdf
26. Technical guide to the Robust principle. Web Accessibility Observatory (2021). https://administracionelectronica.gob.es/pae_Home/dam/jcr:2c13789f-3f56-463b-89f6-9ac75a2ffb45/ Guia_Tecnica_-_Principio_Robusto.pdf
27. ISO. ISO/IEC 25066:2016. Systems and software engineering—Systems and software Quality Requirements and Evaluation (SQuaRE)—Common Industry Format (CIF) for Usability—Evaluation Report (2016). https://www.iso.org/standard/63831.html
28. Template for Accessibility Evaluation Reports (2002). https://www.w3.org/WAI/test-eva luate/report-template/
29. Oswal, S.K.: Breaking the exclusionary boundary between user experience and access: steps toward making UX inclusive of users with disabilities. In: Proceedings of the 37th ACM International Conference on the Design of Communication, SIGDOC 2019, pp. 1–8 (2019). https://doi.org/10.1145/3328020.3353957
30. Graham, G., Chandrashekar, S.: Inclusive process and tool for evaluation of Accessible User Experience (AUX). In: Antona, M., Stephanidis, C. (eds.) UAHCI 2016. LNCS, vol. 9737, pp. 59–69. Springer, Cham (2016). https://doi.org/10.1007/978-3-319-40250-5_6

Considering the Older Adults' Perceptions of IoT for Designing IoT Technologies

Sandra Souza Rodrigues[1,3](✉) ⓘ, Débora Maria Barroso Paiva[2] ⓘ,
and Renata Pontin de Mattos Fortes[3] ⓘ

[1] University Paulista, São Carlos, SP, Brazil
[2] Federal University of Mato Grosso do Sul, Campo Grande, MS, Brazil
debora.paiva@ufms.br
[3] ICMC, University of São Paulo, São Carlos, SP, Brazil
ssrodrigues@usp.br, renata@icmc.usp.br

Abstract. Technologies for the Internet of Things (IoT) have reached different sectors of the economy due to the growing number of connected objects. At the same time, the global number of older adults is increasing dramatically and is expected to more than double, reaching more than 1.5 billion by 2050. We advocate that older people can benefit from IoT technologies to achieve a better quality of life and healthy aging if the developers of these applications consider Usability. This study aimed to understand better seniors' main concerns and perceptions about IoT technologies to see the implications for the design of these technologies. We interviewed 11 Brazilian older adults (aged 60+) to identify their needs and, based on this, we developed and evaluated a prototype to support older people with forgetfulness problems. Finally, it was possible to analyze the narrations of the interviewees' speeches and obtain their perceptions about the IoT.

Keywords: Internet of Things · Older adults · Usability · Accessibility

1 Introduction

The dissemination and massive use of Information and Communication Technologies (ICTs) have significantly improved people's quality of life. Given the computational advancement, popularization of mobile devices, and increased access to the Internet, new services have emerged, increasing the efficiency of systems and processes, and providing more intelligent ways to live, work, teach and learn. A new computational paradigm called the Internet of Things (IoT) has allowed various objects in our routine to communicate with each other. Kevin Ashton [3] introduced this concept in 1999, and the basic idea of IoT is that several things can identify and interact with each other to achieve common goals [4].

Technologies with the Internet of Things (IoT) have reached different economic sectors due to the growing number of connected objects. IoT features are increasingly available in the consumer market and are gaining strength to be available in everyday objects. The number of IoT devices worldwide is forecast to almost triple and reach

© Springer Nature Switzerland AG 2021
P. H. Ruiz et al. (Eds.): HCI-COLLAB 2021, CCIS 1478, pp. 17–31, 2021.
https://doi.org/10.1007/978-3-030-92325-9_2

more than 25.4 billion IoT devices in 2030, as predicted by [26]. This rapid growth has accompanied population aging. The global number of older adults is increasing drastically and is expected to more than double, reaching more than 1.5 billion in 2050 [30]. An estimated condition is that the global population aged 65 and over will increase to 16.0 percent in 2050 [29]. In Brazil, the population aged 65 or over will reach 25.5% (58.2 million older adults). In comparison, in 2018, this proportion was 9.2% (19.2 million), according to the Brazilian Institute of Geography and Statistics (IBGE) [13]. Aging presents challenges and requires more research that addresses the needs of older people.

As people age, they face some declines in their abilities due to the aging process, making it difficult to use technologies [31]. Older adults can benefit from IoT technologies to achieve a better quality of life, well-being, and healthy aging [7]. For this, IoT applications need to be adequately designed to minimize problems such as high perceptual and cognitive demand due to increased interactivity and the infinity of devices in intelligent environments. Other benefits ensured by these new environments include the possibility of task delegation to the environment and its agents, which can reduce physical and cognitive strain, as well as the breadth of applications and services that will be available, addressing a wide variety of domains that are critical for the disabled and older users [8]. Thus, it is required to understand the demands, preferences, feelings, and the impact that IoT solutions can cause for those who have not grown up with technology in their lives.

According to Ashraf et al. [2], researchers have investigated elements that may affect the perception and attractiveness of widespread technology through a typical user. These studies have centered on encouraging acceptance via enhancing the usability of technology for older adults. Kowalski et al. [15] highlighted four key needs to older adults: (a) understanding technology and receiving feedback; (b) accessible design with low barrier of entry, unlike regular computers; (c) seamless incorporation into everyday life, as the participants liked the idea of being able to accomplish specific tasks using only speech not only because they might have difficulties moving; and (d) control and assurance of security. We can also reinforce a need to investigate the development of IoT solutions considering older adults. Indeed, older adults can benefit from the potential of IoT solutions if they are user-friendly.

Our study aimed to get the main concerns and perceptions of older adults about IoT technologies to identify implications for the design of these technologies. In addition, we seek to explore the experience of these users with connected smart devices and see the impact that these new technologies can have on their lives. For this, we conducted interviews with 11 Brazilian older adults aged 60 or over to identify their needs. We have developed a prototype and evaluated it considering the Human-Centred Design (HCD) approach [14]. According to scientific research, we have defined the following Research Question:

- "What are the older adults' concerns about IoT technologies, which should be considered during their design to make them attractive and well-accepted by those users?"

Based on our analysis results, we developed an IoT app to support seniors with forgetfulness issues. The contributions of this research are also: (a) an investigation into ideas for applying IoT technologies to support the daily routines of older adults, (b) the development of a prototype (named *"Perdi?"*) based on the identified needs of older adults during in the interviews, (c) usability and accessibility evaluations of the *"Perdi?"*, and (d) refinement of the prototype.

The remainder of the paper is organized as follows: Sect. 2 presents the related research. Next, Sect. 3 describes the development of an IoT application and its evaluation. Section 4 outlines the discussion, and in Sect. 5, we discuss future directions for IoT research in HCI and our conclusion.

2   Related Work

Since it is essential to investigate older adults' concerns for developing IoT applications for them, we need to understand their needs and functionalities that these users would expect. Different studies have investigated the development of IoT applications taking into account those users [12, 15]. Other studies regarding older adults have discussed special issues addressing these people [1, 10], but their concerns had different context of use, so they would not be appropriate to new IoT demands because they had as their goal an unique app at one device. However, the design and development of intelligent environments have specific needs and are more complex than conventional systems [27]. In addition, few studies have been investigating approaches, tools, and methodologies to assist designers and developers in developing intelligent systems [5, 19].

The TROUVE Project aimed to develop an assistive technology to help older adults with cognitive impairment to find personal items lost at home [17]. The proposal was implemented as a device and involved users during development. Our proposal, in turn, was to get the expectations of older adults and to develop an application for smartphones and smartwatches considering usability and accessibility issues regarding the older people's concerns. Another study had investigated basic ideas around a tracking system for small personal items, such as glasses, keys, wallets, etc. belonging to people with mild memory problems [21]. This study did not present evaluations of the proposal and did not consider aspects of usability and accessibility.

Other studies applied the universal design and user-centered design in the development of prototypes and mobile applications for the IoT to visually impaired people and people with dyslexia, such as Schulz *et al.* [24]. The study found that the application of these approaches allows identifying interaction problems that would not be found only by using the accessibility guidelines. The study proposed general recommendations and the presence of an accessibility specialist, which may represent a high cost in the project. The application of a user-centered methodology to develop intelligent environments aimed at helping people with Down's Syndrome was reported by Augusto *et al.* [5]. The proposed methodology still needs to be investigated for application in other domains.

In this context, Lopes *et al.* (2014) proposed an IoT architecture specific for people with disabilities. The researchers investigated two use cases to study the IoT technologies and their applications that can be used mainly by disabled people. The architecture still needs to be tested, and suitability checked for the other IoT application domains with similar requirements. The proposed HELIX approach aimed to provide accessibility to the visually impaired through the Internet of Things concepts [11]. This project integrates hardware, firmware, and software capabilities in the perspective of an IoT infrastructure. Another study, conducted by Velasco et al., 2016, presented an architecture, system components, applications, and interfaces of a Web of Things (WoT) framework to support users with chronic diseases. This study investigated a new approach to a WoT eHealth that is still under development.

A survey performed by Stara *et al.* [25] investigated the factors that may influence the perceptions and expectations of 306 Italian older adults (average age = 74 years) regarding smart home technology. The results showed that about half of the respondents had a positive interest in technology. However, their attitudes towards technology were involved by practical means, such as utility, facility, security, and privacy. Aspects such as aesthetics, size, and weight were not crucial for participants. Researchers also highlight other issues, such as the relevance of gender and education in the acceptance of technology.

Tsuchiya *et al.* [9] carry out a study to understand the needs and problems encountered by older users in computer systems familiar to them and, from there, implement new control systems for their homes. A focus group was performed with people over 60 who had some experience with computers and smartphones. The main findings evidenced an interest in the use of technologies. However, they have reported some concerns about the dependability, reliability, and cost of such applications.

3   Development of an IoT Application

During this research, an IoT application was developed. We have based this development on the HCD approach, which means *"approach to systems design and development that aims to make interactive systems more usable by focusing on the use of the system and applying human factors/ergonomics and usability knowledge and techniques"* [14]. Following, we describe the procedures used: the interviews, use scenario, the proposed architecture, prototype, and its evaluation. It's worth to notice that all these procedures had been made focusing on the older adults' requirements.

3.1   Understanding and Ideation

At this stage, interviews were conducted with older people to identify their needs and requirements. From the results, we have designed a use scenario to assist in the development of the prototype.

Interviews. The study aimed to investigate ideas for applying IoT technologies to support older adults' daily routines. We recruited participants from the educational program of the of the University of the Third Age in the University of São Paulo (UATI/USP), in the town of São Carlos, São Paulo, Brazil. Eleven participants aged 60 or older participated in the study. They were six men and five women, with an average age of 66.5 years.

Participants had some experience with the Internet, smartphones, and computers. When asked to indicate their education level, 45.4% of the respondents reported having an undergraduate degree. Most participants reported having Wi-Fi Internet access in their homes. Almost two-thirds of the participants (63.6%) said that the frequency of Internet use per day was between 1 h and 4 h. Table 1 shows a summary of this data.

Table 1. Participant demographic data and Internet usage.

Participant	Age	Gender	Highest level of education	Wi-fi at home	Daily time of Internet usage
1	78	Male	Undergraduate	Yes	$1 \leq t \leq 4$ h
2	65	Male	Undergraduate	Yes	$t > 4$ h
3	61	Male	High school	Yes	$1 \leq t \leq 4$ h
4	62	Male	Undergraduate	Yes	$1 \leq t \leq 4$ h
5	66	Male	Elementary school	No	$1 \leq t \leq 4$ h
6	70	Male	High school	Yes	$t < 1$ h
7	73	Female	Undergraduate	Yes	$1 \leq t \leq 4$ h
8	67	Female	Undergraduate	Yes	$1 \leq t \leq 4$ h
9	64	Female	Elementary school	Yes	$1 \leq t \leq 4$ h
10	63	Female	Graduate degree	Yes	$t > 4$ h
11	62	Female	Postgraduate	Yes	$t > 4$ h

The face-to-face semi-structured interviews were conducted at laboratory of the Institute of Mathematics and Computer Sciences at the University of São Paulo (ICMC/USP). Participation was voluntary, and all participants were asked to read and sign the informed consent form before starting the research. After a short description of the purpose of the study, the interview was divided into the following parts: demographic data, Internet usage, and familiarity with IoT devices. We provided the participants with questions and a fictional scenario and asked them to identify smart things that could assist their routines. The interview period was approximately four weeks (October to November 2018). We registered all the interviews with written notes and audio recordings. They totaled 5.12 h, and the average time spent in each session was 28.2 min (SD = 7.04 min).

By the end of the interview period, all responses were considered valid answers. We transcribed the audio recordings using the oTranscribe[1]. Next, transcripts of records were entered in MAXQDA Analytics Pro[2] for analysis. We analyzed the transcriptions using a thematic analysis [6], inspecting the contents and identifying the underlying ideas or concepts that emerged.

---

[1] https://otranscribe.com.
[2] https://www.maxqda.com.

Based on their comments, we observed that older adults are interested in things to help them not forget anything. Participants reported difficulty remembering when to take medication, forgetting the wallet when leaving the house, and forgetting where the house or the car keys were. Also, participants reported the need for a smart kitchen cabinet to communicate with a smart refrigerator to help them control and manage food and smart cars. Following, we transcribe some remarks by participants concerning the research:

"Something that reminds me to take and manage my medicines, it's difficult,… a vitamin that I have to take and I forget, and then I'll see, I took? Did not I?"

"It would be interesting to remind me: are you carrying your wallet? A smart car warns you when the part is wearing. For example, it is time to change the oil…"

"A kitchen cabinet that checks the expiration date of the food. It would be a dream."

Although we had not carried out a pilot study with end-users, this research was approved by the Research Ethical Committee (CEP) of the university - study protocol 02896318.2.0000.5390. All the data collection for this research proceeded with the participants' consent for using their answers, and the complete anonymity of participants was assured. Also, participants in our study were 60 years or older, in conformity with article 1 of the Statute of the Elderly (Brazilian Law 10.741). According to the Law, the Brazilian elders are persons aged 60 years or over [22].

Use Scenario. From the results of the interviews, we decided to create an application to help older users regarding their forgetting complaints. The aging process affects the ability to remember facts and tasks [18]. Older adults face more difficulty concentrating and keeping attention on activities for extended periods [16].

In this context, imagine the following scenario: a 67-year-old widow (Maria) who lives alone in a condominium far from downtown. Her children have moved in to be close to their jobs. By spending a lot of time alone at home, Maria takes advantage of the various activities offered by her condominiums, such as gymnastics, ballroom dancing, and volleyball. Maria is an older woman full of energy. However, she has recently begun to face the decline of some cognitive skills, such as altered memory, attention, and concentration due to the aging process. In the past month, she often forgot the condo club key at home. The forgetfulness causes problems for Maria and leaves her in unpleasant situations. Mrs. Maria is a very independent woman, and she likes to feel useful, so forgetfulness has left her discouraged. This kind of situation causes emotional problems in older adults, reinforcing the sense of worthlessness. In this scenario, we find the possibility of applying IoT technologies to help these users to remind them of these objects. Therefore, an IoT application can alert older adults when they forget any item at home, such as keys, access cards, wallets, among others. This app can track objects that have been registered through a beacon. Thus, the system can identify objects that are out of reach.

3.2 Designing and Prototyping

Based on the results of the interviews and usage scenario, we designed two architectural ideas. Three researchers in the HCI area held meetings to see what the most suitable architecture would be implemented. The final architecture was refined based on two discussions with the researchers.

Architecture. The proposed IoT architecture from a technical perspective is shown in Fig. 1. It is divided into three layers. The components and their functionalities are summarized as follows:

- **Presentation smartphone:** this component presents all the resources available to the user, such as interface, notifications, Beacon information, and beacon manager. Beacon information is related to all this device information available in the application. In addition, it relates to the Beacon manager, which is responsible for managing all things connected to the application.
- **Communication smartphone:** it is responsible for retrieving the signal from the beacon and identifying it. If it is a known beacon, obtain information from it with the Beacon Physical Entity (BPE). Once the BPE has the answer, it sends a request to the Service Component. In addition, all beacons that were used must be previously registered. The central component is responsible for the communication between the other parts, enabling the interaction between things: personal objects with beacons and smartwatches, for example. Thus, the basic software and the central modules of the application are installed on the smartphone.
- **Service:** this component acts as a back-end. Therefore, all Database and Web Service features are located here. Once the beacon information is available, it will be stored in the database. The beacon manager, located in the next component, can access the Web Service to add or delete any information.

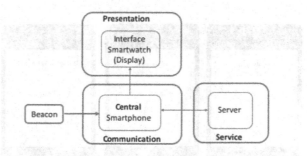

Fig. 1. Architecture proposed.

All three components are divided by the devices used in the application. In this architecture, at least one beacon, smartphone, and smartwatch are required. The smartwatch is fully connected to the smartphone. Thus, there is a central component where all data is collected and used. If something is lost, the smartwatch must send a notification.

Prototype. Based on the architecture presented in the previous topic, we developed the prototype using the Justinmind tool[3]. In this prototype, the smartphone and smartwatch work in a particular way. Figure 2 and Fig. 3 show the two devices involved in this simulation, a smartphone, and a smartwatch, each one with its interface and functionality, as described as follows.

- **Smartphone:** It works as a central component, where the user can see and edit all the monitored things. Figure 2 illustrates its three screens: main screen, list screen, and add screen. On the main screen, all the available features are shown. Next, in the list screen, all the monitored things are shown, and in the add screen, the user can add a thing.

Fig. 2. Smartphone screens

- **Smartwatch:** It works as an extension of the smartphone, where the user can activate notifications, as shown in Fig. 3.

Fig. 3. Smartwatch screens

---

[3] https://www.justinmind.com.

3.3 Evaluation and Refinement

The evaluation of the prototype considered two criteria of software quality [14]: accessibility and usability. We developed the prototype to help older people to avoid forgetting their personal belongings. So, it was necessary to check its ease of use and how accessible it was for these target users. We provide the necessary files for the simulation of the prototype in the Justinmind tool for evaluations.

Usability Evaluation. Four experts conducted the Heuristic Evaluation (HE) [20] to identify usability problems in the prototype that involved the interfaces of two devices, the smartphone, and the smartwatch. One senior undergraduate student, one master's student, one Ph.D. candidate, and one post-doctoral researcher, all with more than three years of usability experience. The undergrad student had previous training guided by the Ph.D. candidate about usability evaluations. The experts used ten Nielsen's Heuristics [20] described in Table 2 to guide user interface inspections.

Each participant was asked to individually inspect the prototype following predefined tasks that we provide them. The tasks were performed in the following sequence:

1. *Visualize all monitored objects:*

   a. *Visualize monitoring status;*
   b. *Visualize object description;*

2. *Visualize object Bag 1 settings:*

   a. *Visualize object status;*
   b. *Change cursor distance;*
   c. *Visualize object description.*

3. *Add home key monitoring:*

   a. *Select sensor type;*
   b. *Fill inputs;*

      i. *Add monitored object name;*
      ii. *Add an image.*

4. *Visualize home key*
5. *Delete the home key.*

For each problem found, each expert pointed out its location on the interface, assigned a level of severity to it, described the violated heuristics and possible solutions. All this information was recorded in spreadsheets by the evaluators. In the end, all experts met remotely and reviewed the problems identified in the individual evaluations, and created a consolidated report. The evaluations lasted a week, and each one lasted about forty minutes.

After the evaluations, the data were grouped according to the evaluated interface. We have grouped into problems related to smartphone screens and those related to smartwatch screens. Then, the analysis consisted of verifying the relationship between the number of problems found and their levels of severity. With that, it was possible to analyze which problems were more recurrent, their levels of severity, and the heuristics violated.

A total of 29 usability problems were found in the prototype. The majority of the problems encountered were related to Task 3 ("add home key monitoring"). The experts complained about the organization of the information, the use of the term sensor, problems in the exclusion message, and some simulation failures. Another common complaint was the lack of a "back button," although the Android button is functional. Table 2 shows the number of violations about each heuristic. The three most violated heuristics were H1, H2, and H5.

Table 2. The number of violations of ten Nielsen's heuristics found in the prototype.

Nielsen's heuristics	Number of violations
H1 - Visibility of system status	5
H2 - Match between system and the real world	8
H3 - User control and freedom	2
H4 - Consistency and standards	4
H5 - Error prevention	9
H6 - Recognition rather than recall	3
H7 - Flexibility and efficiency of use	1
H8 - Aesthetic and minimalist design	1
H9 - Help users recognize, diagnose, and recover from errors	0
H10 - Help and documentation	0

Accessibility Evaluation. The conformance review was conducted to identify accessibility problems in the prototype. Three experts, two master's students, and one Ph.D. candidate, all with more than three years of accessibility experience, performed the conformance review with some WCAG 2.1 success criteria [32]. We have selected some WCAG success criteria for this evaluation, only those that apply to mobile apps and older users. For this, we elaborated a checklist with the success criteria chosen to guide the specialists in evaluating the prototype.

The results of the conformance review showed that six of the eight success criteria considered for evaluation were violated, as shown in Table 3. In addition, we observed that the prototype does not satisfy the Level A Success Criteria (the minimum level of conformance) due to violations of Success Criteria 1.1.1, 1.4.1, and 2.4.2. Therefore, the evaluation performed showed that the prototype is not in conformance with WCAG 2.1.

The main problems identified were the inappropriate contrast between text and background colors, inadequate font size, absence of alternative text for non-textual content, and language difficult to understand. The application does not use other visual means besides colors to show the information, and finally, the prototype does not have titles that describe topic or purpose.

Table 3. WCAG 2.1 success criteria violated in prototype, according to conformance review.

WCAG 2.1 success criteria applied in the evaluation	Violation
Success Criterion 1.1.1 – Non-text Content	X
Success Criterion 1.4.1 – Use of Color	X
Success Criterion 1.4.3 – Contrast (Minimum)	X
Success Criterion 1.4.5 – Images of Text	X
Success Criterion 1.4.8 – Visual Presentation	–
Success Criterion 2.4.2 – Page Titled	X
Success Criterion 3.1.3 – Unusual Words	X
Success Criterion 3.1.4 – Abbreviations	–

Based on HE and accessibility's evaluation results, we made a refinement and improvements to the prototype. Sequentially, we have developed the application following the proposed architecture (Fig. 1), and what do we name *"Perdi?"* (in Portuguese). We developed an open-source application whose source code is hosted in the GitHub repository: https://github.com/abe2602/Beacon_Application. The technical report documenting the *"Perdi?"* application is available at: https://repositorio.usp.br/item/002 981232. Although evaluations with specialists are necessary to identify problems, it is essential to conduct tests with older adults using this application.

4 Discussion

All participants in the interview have experience with computers and smartphones and use the Internet every day. In addition, there was a gender balance, and most of the participants were undergraduates. It is essential to consider the cultural differences of the elderly involved in the studies, especially concerning education level, professional experiences, and others. Our results reaffirm a positive interest of older adults in IoT technologies, as verified in [25, 28]. Some participants demonstrated enthusiasm and identified ideas of things that could be smart and help their individual needs. They reported that these technologies could provide economy and prevention, time organization, and security. However, other participants pointed to a low acceptance of IoT technologies. They also reported that they would not want to be controlled just because they are elderly and retired.

From the interviews conducted in the study of potential use scenarios for IoT, one of the open questions asked the participants to describe the desirable use and assist them in everyday situations. The stories were transcribed, and we analyzed that there would be a variety of applications that could be developed with IoT technologies. We grouped the words of all the scenarios to obtain an overview of the expectations of these interviewees. Figure 4 shows the word cloud obtained, considering only the words mentioned repeatedly more than four times. It is worth mentioning that all participants are Brazilian; therefore, we reproduce the terms with the fidelity of the native language.

It can be observed, at first glance, that the standing out words: "people", "thing" / "things", "everything", "to do", and "intelligent" were the most recurrent, which suggest a tendency of favorable issues that were idealized or desirable by them.

During the interview, we asked participants to also speak about how much they knew or heard about the most common IoT devices and what impression or reasons for using them or not. Similarly, we obtained several responses and grouped the words mentioned to obtain an overview of the perceptions of these participants. Figure 5 shows 3-word clouds, considering only the words mentioned repeatedly more than three times. We reproduce the terms in Portuguese, again, with the fidelity of the native language.

Of these word clouds, the most standing out ones show a certain positive receptivity regarding IoT devices.

Fig. 4. Word cloud based on the described answers by interviewed participants, during their narration of possible scenarios of IoT.

Fig. 5. Three word clouds based on what were mentioned by interviewed participants, during their description of devices of IoT: in the middle, the word cloud from all participants, and on the left and right sides, there are 2 examples of clouds from 2 participants.

It is essential to study the older adults' concerns around IoT technologies [25], given the projections of the aging of the world population [13, 30], and the exponential increase in the number of devices connected to IoT in the coming years [26]. Given the rapid aging of the population, the largest proportion of future users of smart applications will be older adults. These users face difficulties in perceiving the technologies due to the limitations caused by the aging process. The interaction with various devices simultaneously and complex interfaces and sensors can introduce a considerable mental workload and generate a complicated and frustrating experience for these users.

In this research, a detailed study involving the collection of requirements from interviews with end-users was essential to allow the identification of the real needs of older adults in relation to the use of IoT. In fact, as presented by [23], requirements engineering is a fundamental activity of the development process, and it is related to global software quality.

5   Conclusion and Future Work

The Internet of Things is a new paradigm-changing people's everyday lives and how they interact with technologies. IoT applications have the potential to provide support and assistance to older adults. However, if IoT technologies are not designed to consider these users' concerns, perceptions, and values, they may not be adopted by this rapidly growing population.

This paper presented an investigation on the main concerns and perceptions of older adults about IoT to find implications for the design of these technologies. We interviewed 11 older Brazilian respondents (60+) and the results reinforced previous studies identifying interest in IoT technologies use. The data analysis showed that most of these people have a significant interest in things to help them not forget anything, paying particular attention to tasks based on day-to-day experiences. We could also analyze the narrations from the interviewed speeches. Their most used words suggest a tendency of favorable issues idealized or desirable and a certain positive receptivity regarding IoT devices.

When planning the research, COVID-19 did not influence our initial study design since we previously had conducted interviews, developed the prototype, and evaluated with experts. However, pandemic influenced our decision to evaluate the application with older adults, the end-users. The performance of user tests is essential to evaluate the experience of use of the target users. But at this point, we chose to do it later due to the challenges with the in-person study. Despite the limitations of this study, we believe that our findings can contribute to research on older people and the IoT.

The small number of participants limited our findings. We recruited older adults who attended the educational program and already had experience with the Internet, smartphones, and computers. Therefore, interviews may have captured older adults who have more experience and interest in technology than the general population. Additionally, we only interviewed participants from a specific region of Brazil in an urban center. Our participants' experiences may differ from those living in other regions of the country and rural areas. We recommend that future studies include focus groups with a more representative sample of older adults from other regions and who are not experienced with the Internet. In another future work, we will conduct user tests with older adults to investigate the interactions, user experience, and acceptance of the application *Perdi?*.

Acknowledgments. This study was financed partially by the Coordenação de Aperfeiçoamento de Pessoal de Nível Superior - Brasil (CAPES) - Finance Code 001.

References

1. Al-Razgan, M.S., Al-Khalifa, H.S., Al-Shahrani, M.D.: Heuristics for evaluating the usability of mobile launchers for elderly people. In: Marcus, A. (ed.) DUXU 2014. LNCS, vol. 8517, pp. 415–424. Springer, Cham (2014). https://doi.org/10.1007/978-3-319-07668-3_40
2. Ashraf, A., et al.: Aging population perception and post adoption behavior about the usability of smart home technology of Pakistani culture (2020). https://doi.org/10.1145/3379247.337 9248
3. Ashton, K.: That 'Internet of Things' thing. RFID J. **22**(7), 97–114 (2009)
4. Atzori, L., et al.: The Internet of Things: a survey. Comput. Netw. (2010). https://doi.org/10. 1016/j.comnet.2010.05.010
5. Augusto, J., Kramer, D., Alegre, U., Covaci, A., Santokhee, A.: The user-centred intelligent environments development process as a guide to co-create smart technology for people with special needs. Univ. Access Inf. Soc. **17**(1), 115–130 (2017). https://doi.org/10.1007/s10209-016-0514-8
6. Braun, V., Clarke, V.: Using thematic analysis in psychology. Qual. Res. Psychol. **3**(2), 77–101 (2006). https://doi.org/10.1191/1478088706qp063oa
7. Burzagli, L., et al.: Intelligent environments for all: a path towards technology-enhanced human well-being. Univ. Access Inf. Soc. **1**, 3 (2021). https://doi.org/10.1007/s10209-021-00797-0
8. Constantine Stephanidis, C., et al.: Seven HCI grand challenges. Int. J. Hum.-Comput. Interact. **35**, 1229–1269 (2019). https://doi.org/10.1080/10447318.2019.1619259
9. Diniz Tsuchiya, L., et al.: A study on the needs of older adults for interactive smart home environments in Brazil. **8** (2018). https://doi.org/10.1145/3218585.3218592
10. Ferreira, F., et al.: Elderly centered design for Interaction – the case of the S4S Medication Assistant. Procedia Comput. Sci. **27**, 398–408 (2014). https://doi.org/10.1016/j.procs.2014. 02.044
11. Garcia, C., et al.: A proposal based on IoT for social inclusion of people with visual impairment. In: WebMedia 2017 Proceedings of the 23rd Brazillian Symposium on Multimedia and the Web (2017). https://dl.acm.org/doi/10.1145/3126858.3126864
12. Geeng, C., et al.: Who's in control? Interactions in multi-user smart homes. In: CHI 2019: Proceedings of the 2019 CHI Conference on Human Factors in Computing Systems (2019). https://dl.acm.org/doi/abs/10.1145/3290605.3300498
13. Instituto Brasileiro de Geografia e Estatística: Projeção da População 2018: número de habitantes do país deve parar de crescer em 2047. Agência IBGE Notícias 1–7 (2018)
14. ISO 9241-210:2019 - Ergonomics of human-system interaction—Part 210: Human-centred design for interactive systems (2019). https://www.iso.org/standard/77520.html. Accessed 28 May 2021
15. Kowalski, J., et al.: Older adults and voice interaction: a pilot study with Google home (2019). https://doi.org/10.1145/3290607.3312973
16. Kurniawan, S.H.: Ageing. In: Harper, S., Yesilada, Y. (eds.) Web Accessibility: A Foundation for Research, pp. 47–58. Springer, London (2008). https://doi.org/10.1007/978-1-84800-050-6_5
17. Lopes, P., et al.: Co-conception Process of an Innovative Assistive Device to Track and Find Misplaced Everyday Objects for Older Adults with Cognitive Impairment: The TROUVE Project | Elsevier Enhanced Reader. IRBM (2016). https://doi.org/10.1016/j.irbm.2016. 02.004

18. Malone, L.A., Bastian, A.J.: Age-related forgetting in locomotor adaptation (2015). https://doi.org/10.1016/j.nlm.2015.11.003
19. Mora, S., et al.: RapIoT toolkit: rapid prototyping of collaborative Internet of Things applications. In: Proceedings - 2016 International Conference on Collaboration Technologies and Systems, CTS 2016, pp. 97–114 (2018). https://doi.org/10.1109/CTS.2016.0083
20. Nielsen, J.: Heuristic evaluation. Usability inspection methods (1994)
21. Oestreicher, L.: Finding keys for people with mild dementia – not just a matter of beeping and flashing. In: Schmorrow, D.D., Fidopiastis, C.M. (eds.) AC 2014. LNCS (LNAI), vol. 8534, pp. 315–324. Springer, Cham (2014). https://doi.org/10.1007/978-3-319-07527-3_30
22. Planalto. LEI No 10.741, DE 1° de outubro de (2003)
23. Preece, J., et al.: Interaction Design: Beyond Human-Computer Interaction. Wiley, Hoboken (2019)
24. Schulz, T., et al.: A case study for universal design in the Internet of Things. Assistive Technol. Res. Ser. 45–54 (2014). https://doi.org/10.3233/978-1-61499-403-9-45
25. Stara, V., Zancanaro, M., Di Rosa, M., Rossi, L., Pinnelli, S.: Understanding the interest toward smart home technology: the role of utilitaristic perspective. In: Leone, A., Caroppo, A., Rescio, G., Diraco, G., Siciliano, P. (eds.) ForItAAL 2018. LNEE, vol. 544, pp. 387–401. Springer, Cham (2019). https://doi.org/10.1007/978-3-030-05921-7_32
26. Statista. Number of Internet of Things (IoT) connected devices worldwide 2019 to 2030 (2021)
27. Taivalsaari, A., Mikkonen, T.: A roadmap to the programmable world: software challenges in the IoT era. IEEE Softw. 34(1), 72–80 (2017). https://doi.org/10.1109/MS.2017.26
28. Tsuchiya, L.D., et al.: A study on the needs of older adults for interactive smart home environments in Brazil 33–40 (2019). https://doi.org/10.1145/3218585.3218592
29. United Nations - World Population Prospects Population Division (2019). https://population.un.org/wpp/. Accessed 28 May 2021
30. United Nations (UN). World Population Ageing 2020 Highlights (2020)
31. Vines, J., et al.: An age-old problem: examining the discourses of ageing in HCI and strategies for future research. ACM Trans. Comput.-Hum. Interact. 22(1), 2:1–2:27 (2015). https://doi.org/10.1145/2696867
32. W3C. Web Content Accessibility Guidelines (WCAG) 2.1 (2018)

Control of a Robotic Hand Through Voice Commands and Biosignals

Nicolas Viniegra[1,2]([⊠]) [iD] and Jorge Ierache[1,2] [iD]

[1] Institute of Intelligent Systems and Experimental Teaching of Robotics, Morón, Argentina
[2] ESIICA University of Morón, Morón, Argentina
{nviniegra,jierache}@unimoron.edu.ar

Abstract. In this work an experimental architecture is developed that allows the control a robotic hand through voice commands recognition and biosignals by applying a brain-computer interface (BCI). The voice commands control is implemented by a voice recognition module, that allows saving voice commands and recognizing them and is used to control the hand. On the other hand, the biosignals control works through a BCI that returns the brain activity of the user, that brain activity is given in metadata, such as blinking frequency, attention and relaxation. The blinking frequency of the eyes is applied to the hand control. The user has the possibility to switch between one control and another whenever he/she wishes. The movements that the robotic hand can do are constructed through a software whose development is within the scope of the project. Finally, the tests carried out are described. The work was carried out within the framework of the subject Degree Thesis, Final Integrative Project.

Keywords: Robotics · Hand · Voice recognition · Brain-computer interface

1 Introduction

Technological prostheses are a field that is constantly growing, since, with constant technological innovation, better tools are created that allow us to develop better prostheses. There are various prostheses for different parts of the body, but the most developed is the hand prostheses. There are many ways to control a robotic hand, it can be controlled through voice commands, through myoelectric control and through brain computer interface. This work's objective is to develop an experimental architecture that allows the control of a robotic hand, through voice commands and biosignals acquired by a brain computer interface. Today's artificial hands are made mostly with 3D printing, which can be opened and closed like a real hand [1]. But there are also developments that go further and increase the complexity and technology of the hand to add mobility, and it is here where a wide range of possibilities opens up for the development of robotic hands and their control ways [2]. Techniques such as BCI (Brain Computer Interface), both invasive and non-invasive, automatic speech recognition techniques and myoelectric control are used. In the brain-computer interfaces field, devices that can translate neural information from specific areas of the brain into data are developed that can be

© Springer Nature Switzerland AG 2021
P. H. Ruiz et al. (Eds.): HCI-COLLAB 2021, CCIS 1478, pp. 32–43, 2021.
https://doi.org/10.1007/978-3-030-92325-9_3

controlled by external hardware or software [3]. BCIs are often used as devices to assist people with motor or sensory disabilities, video games, in particular to control robots [4, 5] explored the potential of the equipment by obtaining the bioelectrical signals of the users, generated by the activity patterns of the facial muscles, the eyes and the brain. In recent works, the potential of BCI is exploited to capture different emotional readings in virtual and real contexts [6, 7].

In Sect. 2 the related works are enunciated, in Sect. 3 the challenge that the problem represents is presented, in Sect. 4 the proposed solution, accompanied by the architecture used for development, in Sect. 5 the results of the tests carried out with the robotic hand for both control modes and finally in Sect. 6 the conclusions, future lines of work and research are presented.

2 Related Works

In particular, the construction of hand prostheses with 3D printers had a significant contribution, Gino Tubaro, an Argentinian inventor, creates robotic hand prostheses with 3D impressions, for people who lost the whole hand, or those who lost only the fingers [1]. Developments with the use of non-invasive brain computer interface (BCI) use electrodes to detect electrical activity that is generated through specific brain areas. This activity is processed and signal data (alpha, beta, delta, theta) and metadata such as blinking, relaxation, attention, among others, are returned. Currently there are robotic hands that are controlled by "non-invasive" BCI, through myograms (facial gestures) and others that are controlled by EEG signals [3, 4]. Other developments employ voice commands, in particular an artificial hand called "InMoov" that was developed in 2013, an Arduino module capable of making voice recognition was incorporated [8]. The hands developed so far can make simple movements, they can close and open the fingers and move the wrist. Giving them more advanced movements such as moving the fingers in directions other than closing and opening, represent a functional improvement in search of being able to replicate the best possible movements that a real hand can make. The present work proposes the combination of non-invasive BCI control and voice command recognition control in order to allow greater functionality and adaptation to the user.

3 Problem Definition

To help address this problem, an experimental architecture is developed for the control of a robotic hand with voice command control and biosignals (blinks) controls. A series of objectives to be met were defined, which are the following: a) Develop an experimental architecture that allows the control of a robotic hand through voice commands and brain signals captured by a BCI, b) Generate a flexible interaction that allows the user to freely choose the hand control by voice or biosignals, c) controls construction, both the voice command recognition system, and the BCI use. d) allow to add, modify or delete movements to the robotic hand, and assign these movements to voice commands and brain signals.

4   Proposed Solution - Experimental Architecture of the Robotic Hand

The experimental architecture allows to control a robotic hand through recognition of voice commands and biosignals (blink). The architecture offers at all times, the possibility of changing from one control to another. The control by voice commands was implemented through a voice recognition module that allows saving voice commands and recognizing them, which is used to control the hand. On the other hand, the biosignal control, which is carried out through BCI (Neurosky Mindwave) [9, 10] returns the user's brain activity, in particular the blink rate, which is applied to control the robotic hand. The architecture contains a logical interface that runs on an Arduino Nano microcontroller. The information it receives from the speech recognition module and the BCI, will be interpreted based on its stored commands, and will be used to order the hand to perform a specific movement. An interface is contemplated with a system that allows creating new movements for the hand, modifying and eliminating them. The construction of new movements is carried out from the basal movements of the project. The basal movements are the most basic movements that the hand can perform, and by combining them, more complex movements can be built. A conceptual model of the experimental architecture is presented in Fig. 1. It contemplates the control of the robotic hand by voice commands, through a microphone and the capture of the user's blinks through the use of a BCI (Neurosky). There will only be one active input at a time, which corresponds to the selected control.

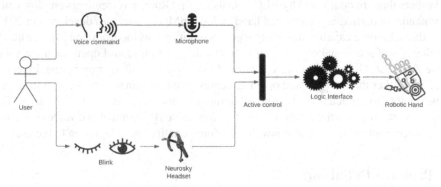

Fig. 1. Conceptual model of experimental architecture

Figure 2 presents the classes diagram corresponding to a movement, which is related to a voice command and a biosignal through an action. The Action class is related to a Movement, a Command and also has the amount of necessary blinks to execute the action. A Movement basically consists of a movement for each motor of the hand. Putting together all the movements, the desired position of the hand for the global movement is achieved, for which an identifier and a name are saved. The Action class is the one that relates the movement to the voice command and the corresponding number of blinks. Besides, it contains a name and an identifier. Command is the class that stores each voice command, it contains the name of the command and an identifier. Signal is the class that saves the strength that the user used on a blink.

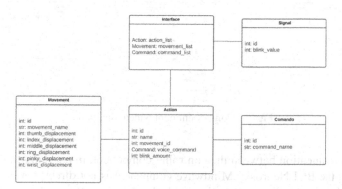

Fig. 2. Class diagram

The interface makes use of various physical components to fulfill all its functionalities. Figure 3 shows the deployment diagram of the components that are used, which are described below. The controller component is made up of: a) Arduino Nano [11] microcontroller where the interface is executed and which controls the rest of the components, the Arduino Nano through the interface, activates or deactivates the controls, and sends the commands to the effector component of the robotic hand, to make the movements, b) Bluetooth module [12] dedicated to receiving the information emitted by the BCI component, c) voice recognition module [13], it has a built-in microphone, the module stores, manages and recognizes the user's voice commands, d) Buzzer [14]: it is a module that allows to emit beeps to assist the user in the control by biosignals in the selection of movements, e) led: it is a component to assist the user that indicates which control is active, if the led is on, the active control is voice recognition, otherwise the active control is biosignals (blinks), through the use of the BCI.

The BCI component (Neurosky Mindwave): It is the brain machine interface used to obtain the blinking force, metadata used for biosignal control, it communicates with the controller component using a notebook that acts as a gateway for bluetooth communications. The structure of the data that it registers is the following: PC_DATE, TEST_NAME, TEST_COMMENT, PORT, ROW_TIME, POORSIGNAL, ATTENTION, RELAXATION (also called Meditation), EEGPOWER, EegPowerDelta, EegPowerThetha, EegPowerAlphaguerPetalPower2, EegPowerAlphagetalPetal2Pamma2, EephagPowerAlphag2AlphagP2, EephagPowerAlphag2AlphagP2 Blinking.

The robotic hand component: It's made up of six servo motors, each motor controls a different part of the hand (five motors, one for each finger) and a motor for turning the wrist [15]. When the interface commands the hand to perform a movement, each servo motor rotates, and together, all the servo motors make up the movements of the hand.

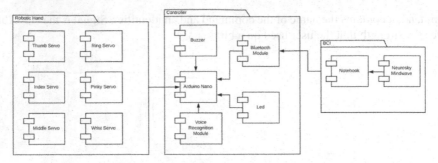

Fig. 3. Component deployment diagram

The communication between the controller component, in particular the Bluetooth module, and the BCI Neurosky Mindwave component is not direct. On the one hand, the notebook makes a first connection with the Arduino Bluetooth module. On the other hand, it also connects via Bluetooth with the BCI. This happens because the headset model used supports Bluetooth connections with devices that are only PC's or notebooks. Figure 4. This is only contemplated for the experimental architecture, the replacement is currently being studied (eg Raspberry pi or another, which will allow direct communication, without resorting to a notebook that acts as a communications gateway.

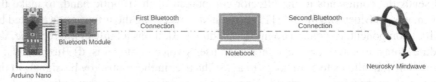

Fig. 4. Communication diagram between Notebook, Neurosky Mindwave and Bluetooth Module

Figure 5 shows an image of the robotic hand component already connected to the controller component - voice recognition module, and to the BCI component next to it, the led on indicating that the active control is the voice commands control. The black plate on the right is the handheld portable power supply. The other components (microcontroller, servo motors, bluetooth module and buzzer) are inside the forearm of the hand. Figure 6 shows an image where you can see the inside of the robotic hand's forearm. On the right you can find the five servo motors corresponding to the fingers, the wrist motor is hidden right in the wrist. In the middle the controller component is set, its microcontroller module is covered by all the cables of the different components.

4.1   Biosignals Control

A Neurosky Mindwave BCI was used to capture the user's eye blinks. When blinking, a person does so with a certain intensity and the BCI can obtain that intensity, and returns it in Hz, which makes it possible to associate actions of the robotic hand with a number

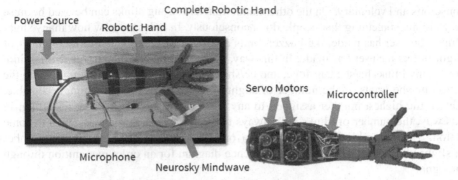

Fig. 5. Robotic hand with connected controls and working correctly

Fig. 6. Robotic hand with exposed forearm

Table 1. Range of values for blinking intensities

Intensity level	Range of values
Slight	Between 30 and 45 Hz
Normal	Between 45 and 75 Hz
Strong	Between 75 and 220 Hz

of blinks. The blinks were divided into three ranges of force, which are shown in Table 1. The ranges obtained depend on each user in particular, so, in order to use this blinking control mode, a previous calibration is required for a custom configuration.

A blink is considered as the sequence of: open eye - closed eye - open eye. In other words, having the eye open, close it, and open it again. A slight blink is a very delicate blink, done with very little force. A normal blink is the one that people do unconsciously. A strong blink is one that is done with more force than normal. The control works in the following way, a unique amount of slight blinks is associated to each action to differentiate the way to activate them. After that comes one strong blink that confirms the activation, all movements have a strong blink at the end. The normal blinks were not taken into account because they are the blinks that we perform unconsciously, and they do not contribute to the control of the hand since the control has to be something completely conscious and voluntary, On the other hand, light and strong blinks can be used because they are not something that people do unconsciously. In order to know how many slight blinks the user has made, the buzzer emits a number of beeps equal to the number of slight blinks the user has made. In this way, as the user blinks, the buzzer will tell him how many blinks he/she has done, and he/she can know how many are left to get to the action he/she wants. If the number of slight blinks exceeds the maximum acceptable, that is, the highest number assigned to any action, it will return to one, restarting. In this way, the number of blinks will always be kept at values that are assigned to some action. The strong blink is applied to perform the selected movement by the number of slight blinks. Figure 7 shows the sequence diagram for an order recognition through biosignals.

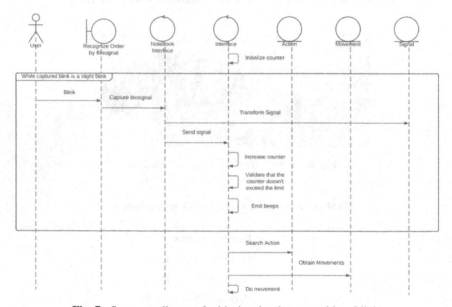

Fig. 7. Sequence diagram for biosignal order recognition (blink)

4.2 Voice Commands Control

The command corresponding to a movement are stored in the voice recognition module. The way to store them in the module is through an open source software [13], this code is executed in the Arduino module of the controller component. To register a voice command associated with a new movement in the module, the administrator has to repeat the voice command twice near the microphone to be recognized correctly. The sequence diagram to recognize an order by voice command, applied to the control of movements is presented in Fig. 8.

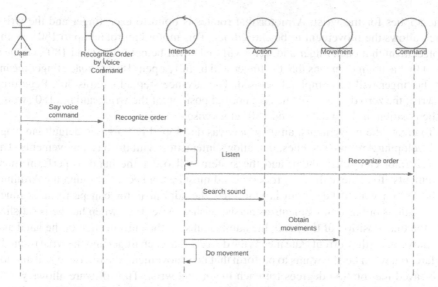

Fig. 8. Sequence diagram recognition of orders by voice command

4.3 Movements Creation

Basal movements were defined, which represent basic functionalities that the hand can perform, which by combining them can lead to more complex movements. Figure 9 shows the basal movements.

Open and close a finger

Open and close hand

Open and close more a finger

Open and close more hand

Turn wrist

Close hand in half

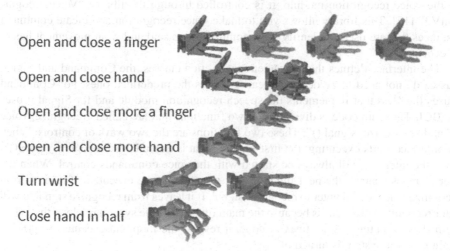

Fig. 9. Basal movements

Each basal case involves a basic movement of the hand, that movement can contain the movement of a single finger or all fingers together a certain number of degrees, the same applies for the wrist. A motor that rotates is bond to each finger and the wrist, which allows the movement to be carried out. This motor can rotate up to 180°, so the displacement that each finger and wrist will make will be between 0 and 180°. Grade 0 (zero) for each finger means that the finger will be fully open. 180° for each finger means that the finger will be completely closed. The advance step adopted is 30°. Regarding the wrist, the zero degree indicates the normal position of the wrist, and the 180° would be the position of the wrist rotated 180° clockwise.

To create the movements, an interface was developed in C++, the default language for developing Arduino sketches, that allows interaction with the basal movements. The administrator can select them, and the system will order the hand to perform those movements. To achieve this, the robotic hand must be connected, through the Arduino, to the PC on which the admin is working. The administrator can perform as much combinations of basal movements as he/she wishes. After that, when he/she is satisfied with the final position of the hand, the admin can save the current state of the hand as a new movement (the current state means the degrees that each finger and the wrist rotated). So, later on, when he/she wants to perform that new movement, the interface will already have saved the rotation degrees for each finger and wrist. The software allows you to add new movements, modify existing ones and also delete them. Due to the number of physical components used, there was no space left on the Arduino to connect a persistent memory module, so movements cannot be saved directly in the Arduino. Instead, they are saved in a text document which can be consulted. The administrator has to access this document and manually upload the movements in the interface.

To communicate the Arduino with the BCI, the physical port of the Arduino is occupied by the Bluetooth module through the library "SoftwareSerial" [16]. That allows to control the module and send and receive messages. When the physical port is occupied by the voice recognition module, it is controlled through the library "VoiceRecognitionV3" [17]. This library allows you to make voice recognition and create command instances that are used to identify what command was said and what movement has to be executed.

The interface defines the Movement and Action classes, the Command and Signal classes do not need to be defined because it uses the predefined ones. For Command it uses the class that implements the speech recognition module and for Signal it uses the BCI. The main code is divided into two functions that are called "recognize_voice ()" and "recognize_signal ()". These two functions are the two ways of controls. When the interface starts executing, the first function that is executed is "recognize_voice()", since the interface will always be started with the voice commands control. When the user changes control, the next function will immediately be executed. If it exits from recognize voice, it will enter to recognize signal. If it leaves from recognize signal, it will enter recognize voice, this is because the main function of the system is a loop that when it finishes executing all the lines of code, it restarts the loop and executes everything again until the system is turned off.

When the interface has the biosignal control active, it is constantly listening to the Bluetooth communication channel that you established with the notebook. When the notebook sends a message, the interface reads it and makes a decision based on the blink force contained in the message. The counter used to identify the amount of slight blinks that were made, is implemented within the recognize signal function. When the interface receives a message with a strong blink, it will look for the action that is assigned the number of slight blinks corresponding to the counter value, and it will execute that action.

In the voice command control, the interface uses the instance "MyVR" of class "VR". This class is defined in the speech recognition library that is imported into the sketch and allows voice recognition of what the user says through the voice recognition module. When it recognizes a command, the class will return the id corresponding to that command, and the interface will look for the action assigned to that voice command. To configure the speech recognition module, the module's configuration software is programmed in C++ to be executed by an Arduino.

To move the fingers and wrist, the "Servo" library [18] was used, which allows creating and assigning logical instances to the physical motors that are connected to the Arduino and giving orders to move them.

5 Tests Performed with the Robotic Hand

First, tests were carried out on the basal cases to evaluate their correct functioning. Each one was run to check that it makes the correct hand movement, details can be seen in the video posted on [19]. In Fig. 10 the hand can be seen after trying to close it with one of the basal cases. Once these tests were finished, tests were carried out on the functionalities for creating movements. The functionality of adding new movements was mainly evaluated. For this functionality it was mandatory that the basal cases worked well, that's the reason of the tests order, details can be seen in the video posted on [20]. Tests were also made on the functionalities of modifying and deleting existing movements. Using the movements creation, basal cases were combined to get to new and more complex movements, for example, closed hand with raised thumb, Fig. 11, various movements created can be observed in Fig. 12.

Fig. 10. Basal movement: closed hand   **Fig. 11.** Created movement: closed Hand thumb up

Tests were made on the interface and controls. For the voice commands control, the precision with which the voice recognition module recognizes the saved commands was evaluated, resulting in perfect precision. On the other hand, the failure rate of the module was evaluated, this means, the frequency with which the module confuses the saved words with other similar words. Tests were also made with the hand-connected control to assess its overall performance, details can be seen in the video posted on [21] For the calibration of the biosignal control, tests were carried out to determine the Hz

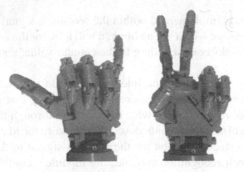

Fig. 12. Various movements created

returned by the BCI for a given blink, testing with different blink intensities and thus be able to establish a range of values in Hz for a given blink force. Tests were made with the biosignal control connected to the hand to evaluate its operation as a whole, and later the global operation of the architecture was evaluated, alternating between voice commands control and biosignals control, both being connected to the hand, the details can be seen in the video published in [22].

6 Conclusions and Future Work and Research Lines

An experimental architecture for the control of a robotic hand with voice commands and biosignals could be successfully developed and implemented. This project contributes to the prosthetic hands development to help those people who lost an arm, providing a new solution. As future lines of work, the replacement of the controller is considered to integrate direct communication with the BCI, without having to apply a notebook, as well as having a greater capacity to incorporate a persistent memory module and being able to store the movements directly and not have to manually load them with a txt file. Extend the number of field tests with the robotic hand, explore construction with 3D printing. In the framework of future research lines, it is contemplated to extend the experimental work in order to exploit metadata attention, relaxation and its correlation with the eyes blinking to improve the use of the robotic hand. In this order, it is intended to experiment with control with brain-machine interfaces superior to the one used, contemplating myograma, osculogram, and EEG signals, emotional metadata.

References

1. Gino Tubaro - Inventor. http://www.ginotubaro.com/. Accessed 17 Dec 2020
2. Ramaswamy, C., Deborah, S.: A survey of robotic hand-arm systems. Int. J. Comput. Appl. **109**(8), 26–31 (2015)
3. Hamadicharef, B.: Brain-computer interface (BCI) literature-a bibliometric study. In: 10th International Conference on Information Science, Signal Processing and Their Applications (ISSPA 2010), pp. 626–629 (2010)

4. Ierache, J., Pereira, G., Iribarren, J.: Navigation control of a robot from a remote location via the internet using brain-machine interface. In: Kim, J.-H., Matson, E.T., Myung, H., Xu, P., Karray, F. (eds.) Robot Intelligence Technology and Applications 2. AISC, vol. 274, pp. 297–310. Springer, Cham (2014). https://doi.org/10.1007/978-3-319-05582-4_26
5. Ierache, J.S., Pereira, G., Sattolo, I., Irribaren, J., Suiffet, N.: Robot control on the basis of bio-electrical signals. In: Kim, J.H., Matson, E., Myung, H., Xu, P. (eds.) Robot Intelligence Technology and Applications 2012, vol. 208, pp. 337–346. Springer, Heidelberg (2013). https://doi.org/10.1007/978-3-642-37374-9_33
6. Ierache, I., Ponce, G., Nicolosi, R., Sattolo, I., Chapperón, G.: Assessment of the degree of attention in classroom contexts with the use of the brain-computer interface (2019)
7. Ierache, J., Sattolo, I., Chapperón, G.: Framework multimodal emocional en el contexto de ambientes dinámicos. Rev. Ibérica Sist. E Tecnol. Informação **40**, 45–59 (2020)
8. Hand prothesis control by voice, Hacedores.com, Maker Community. https://hacedores.com/protesis-de-mano-y-antebrazo-controlado-por-voz/. Accessed 04 Nov 2020
9. Neurosky. EEG - ECG - Biosensors. http://neurosky.com/. Accessed 28 Sept 2020
10. NeuroSky Developer – Docs, Developer Toolkit, NeuroSky Developer Program. http://developer.neurosky.com/docs/doku.php?id=thinkgear.net_sdk_dev_guide_and_api_reference. Accessed 29 Sept 2020
11. Arduino Nano, Arduino Online Shop. https://store.arduino.cc/usa/arduino-nano. Accessed 30 July 2020
12. HC-06 BlueTooth Module, Arduino Store, Arduino Store and Electronic Items Prometec.net. https://www.prometec.net/bt-hc06/. Accessed 31 July 2020
13. Voice Recognition, Arduino Online Shop, Arduino Store and Electronic Items Prometec.net. https://www.prometec.net/reconocimiento-voz/. Accessed 20 July 2020
14. Buzzers, Arduino Online Shop, Arduino Store and Electronic Items Prometec.net. https://www.prometec.net/buzzers/. Accessed 05 Aug 2020
15. Robotic Hand, ArduMaker. https://www.ardumaker.com/mano-antebrazo. Accessed 28 Mar 2021
16. SoftwareSerial, Arduino Home. https://www.arduino.cc/cn/Reference/SoftwareSerial. Accessed 30 July 2020
17. Voice Recognition V3 GitHub, elechouse/VoiceRecognitionV3: Arduino library for elechouse Voice Recognition V3 module, GitHub. https://github.com/elechouse/VoiceRecognitionV3. Accessed 21 Aug 2020
18. Servo, Arduino Home. https://www.arduino.cc/reference/en/libraries/servo/. Accessed 15 Aug 2020
19. Baseline cases tests [Video]. Nicolas Viniegra. YouTube. https://www.youtube.com/watch?v=vghAfrq8r7M. Accessed 24 May 2021
20. Movements construction [Video]. Nicolas Viniegra. YouTube. https://www.youtube.com/watch?v=4THLYflVrv4. Accessed 24 May 2021
21. Voice commands control test [Video]. Nicolas Viniegra. YouTube. https://www.youtube.com/watch?v=uG3YXqRRFxg. Accessed 24 May 2021
22. Biosignals control test [Video]. Nicolas Viniegra. YouTube. https://www.youtube.com/watch?v=X7vCwmAut-4. Accessed 24 May 2021

Desktop Application for Water Quality Prediction and Monitoring System Using ISO 9241-210 and Machine Learning Techniques

Maximiliano Guzman-Fernandez[1]($\boxtimes$) , Huizilopoztli Luna-García[1] ,
Cesar A. Collazos[2] , Wilson J. Sarmiento[3] , Jorge I. Galvan-Tejada[1] ,
Hamurabi Gamboa-Rosales[1] , Carlos E. Galvan-Tejada[1] ,
Jose M. Celaya-Padilla[1] , Misael Zambrano-de la Torre[1] ,
and J. Guadalupe Lara-Cisneros[1]

[1] Universidad Autónoma de Zacatecas, Zacatecas, México
{maxguzman,hlugar,gatejo,hamurabigr,ericgalvan,jose.celaya,
zambranot1,jglara}@uaz.edu.mx
[2] Universidad del Cauca, Popayán, Colombia
ccollazo@unicauca.edu.co
[3] Universidad Militar Nueva Granada, Bogotá, Colombia
wilson.sarmiento@unimilitar.edu.co

Abstract. Water is one of the main natural resources for humanity and it is important for countries to be aware of the water quality. The physical, chemical and biological parameters provide information on the current condition of surface waters used for municipal, industrial and agricultural water supply. Thus, the design and development of equipment used for water quality monitoring and analysis are essential to avoid dangerous situations. Feedback sources from the monitoring equipment are the main interface between the study area and the specialists. This equipment must have the necessary features and tools to achieve an optimal water quality analysis. This study proposes a desktop application design to support the management of water quality monitoring equipment. The design was developed based on the methodology and stages of User Centered Design from the ISO 9241-210-2019 standard. The evaluation of the prototype was done using the question technique and task assignment. The results showed a quick adaptability and easy navigation by users. In addition, the implementation of a Machine Learning algorithm showed preliminary results of water quality prediction.

Keywords: User-Centered Design (UCD) · Surface waters · Logistic regression

1 Introduction

The efficient use, conservation, protection, and access to water is fundamental for humans, and several countries consider it to be a national security resource [1]. Due to the importance of this natural resource, the concept of water security has been discussed and defined by several institutions, such as the United Nations Water Group

© Springer Nature Switzerland AG 2021
P. H. Ruiz et al. (Eds.): HCI-COLLAB 2021, CCIS 1478, pp. 44–57, 2021.
https://doi.org/10.1007/978-3-030-92325-9_4

(UN-Water) [1, 2], the Global Water Partnership (GWP) [1, 3], the Economic Commission for Latin America and the Caribbean (ECLAC) [4], among others. The use of water from rivers, wells, and lagoons is important as they are the main sources of water supply in municipalities and states for various uses, such as human consumption and industrial demand [5]. Water quality is an important factor to be considered, as it can be at high levels of contamination and directly impact food, hygiene, health and economy [6].

The National Water Commission (CONAGUA) is an administrative agency of Mexico, responsible for managing, regulating, controlling and protecting the country's national waters. CONAGUA performs, through the National Water Quality Measurement Network, the monitoring of the main water sources in the country, both surface and groundwater [7]. Some of the parameters considered to determine water quality are: Biochemical Oxygen Demand at five days (BOD5), Chemical Oxygen Demand (COD), Total Suspended Solids (TSS), Fecal Coliforms (FC), Escherichia coli, (E_COLI), Enterococci (ENTEROC), Oxygen Saturation Percentage (DO%), Toxicity (TOX), hydrogen potential (pH), including others [7, 8].

Water quality measurements are commonly acquired by taking samples in the study area and then moved to a laboratory for chemical, physical and biological analysis of the sample. This conventional method of collecting samples from the study area and analyzing them in the laboratory requires considerable time, which involves from several hours to months [9]. Therefore, it is an opportunity to design a system for real-time monitoring of water quality parameters and develop a desktop application to visualize and collect the measurements. In addition, generating robust and efficient models using artificial intelligence would help predict water quality by using parameters that are easy to measure in the study area.

To achieve an efficient and safe application design, human-computer interaction is important in proposing methods to design and evaluate the systems. This enhances the user experience and supports them in their activities using communication and information technologies. This can contribute to make easier the work of specialists and stakeholders in the analysis of water quality in different study areas.

2   Related Works

There have recently been developments in water quality monitoring systems using IoT technology to help reduce the time to collect and analyze water samples [10, 11]. Mobile and desktop applications are used for real-time monitoring of water quantity and quality, both in the environment and in pipelines [10–12]. In addition, the implementation of artificial intelligence through machine learning, data mining and analysis has been a trend in previous work, using algorithms for water quality prediction in different monitoring areas [13].

Monitoring systems involving different indicators and study zones have been proposed, for example, a monitoring system with a sensor network implemented in drinking water distribution pipes. The sensors measure temperature, conductivity, pH and pressure in the flow of water through the pipeline. The values of these parameters are transmitted via GSM/GRPS from the cellular network, and are displayed and stored on a server in the cloud. The device is notable for being a self-regenerating energy device, using the flow of water in the pipeline to drive a turbine and charge a battery module [10].

Another paper presents a wireless sensor network for monitoring water quality, measuring pH, dissolved oxygen, turbidity, conductivity and temperature parameters. The connection to the cloud is made via WI-FI to store, visualize and analyze the values on a server. A neural network is implemented to predict water quality from the data stored by the system [11].

Similarly, a wireless sensor network has been proposed to monitor water quality from temperature, pH, turbidity and total dissolved solids (TDS). Data collected in a river are transmitted by GSM/GPS and stored on an external server. Subsequently, the data are analyzed using two stages, the first one reduces the size of the training data and the second step is the classification of water quality by K-Nearest Neighbors (KNN), Support Vector Machine (SVM), Bayesian classifier (BC) and decision trees (DT) algorithms [12]. However, the monitoring systems of these works in which the values are displayed, stored and analyzed are not designed according to the needs of the users using international standards.

Derived from the above, an opportunity is identified to design and develop a prototype desktop application for water quality monitoring system. The design and development of desktop applications using international standards is important because it facilitates the user's understanding, manipulation and compliance with the user's needs. There are several methodologies and international standards and one of them is User-Centered Design (UCD). UCD focuses on knowing the needs of users. User-Centered Design is an approach to developing interactive systems that specifically focuses on making systems usable and safe for their users. These User-Centered Design have benefits such as increased productivity, improved quality of work, reduced training costs, and increased user safety [14].

This paper presents the design and evaluation of a prototype desktop application for water quality prediction and monitoring system using the methodology and stages of User-Centered Design (UCD) from the ISO 9241-210-2019 standard [14, 15]. In addition, preliminary results of implementing the machine learning algorithm, logistic regression, for water quality prediction that were shown in the desktop application are presented.

3   Materials and Methods

The methodology used for this work consists of the implementation of the user-centered design for a prototype desktop application for water quality prediction and monitoring system. From the UCD stages, electronic devices for water quality monitoring are identified and machine learning techniques are implemented for water quality prediction. This is shown in Fig. 1.

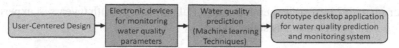

Fig. 1. Process for prototype of a desktop application for water quality prediction and monitoring system.

3.1 User-Centered Design

User-Centered Design represents a design and development cycle that takes into account the specific users who will use the system. Using this process helps to design and develop more user-friendly systems and improve performance. In this way, preventing complications and confusion when using the product. UCD is based on ISO 9241-210: 2019 [15], which establishes 4 stages as guidelines for system design and development shown in Fig. 2.

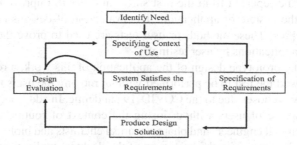

Fig. 2. Stages of User-Centered Design [15].

Specification Context of Use

In this stage, the users who will use the product, the use they will make of it and the context in which it will be used are identified [14]. To complete this stage, virtual surveys were conducted with users involved in the chemical area and in the chemical analysis of water. The survey consisted of questions from education level and age to experience in the use of specialized equipment and software.

In addition, information was collected about the work environment in the laboratory. Google Forms was the platform used to send the questions and collect the feedback [16]. After the answers were collected and analyzed, a common profile of the users was generated using the "personas" technique to have the target user profile [17, 18]. This helps to identify and take into account the characteristics of the users in the design process.

Specification of Requirements

In this stage, user needs and motives are identified, in addition to the functional requirements of the product [14]. An area of the survey was designed to focus on questions related to user requirements in the use of measurement software. These questions were designed with the support of specialists in the areas of chemistry with a degree in chemical engineering with 2 years of experience and a PhD in biology with 6 years of experience, involving their participation as stakeholders.

Produce Design Solution

After analyzing the information obtained in the two previous stages, the prototypes are designed. The prototypes designed in this stage are a first contact with the final system, allowing to simulate the operation scenarios and facilitate the users involved in the design of the system. The design and development of the prototype was created in the Pencil Project software. Pencil facilitates the creation of free and open source GUI prototypes that people can easily install and use to create mockups on desktop platforms [19].

Design Evaluation

Once the prototype is finalized, at this stage the designs are evaluated with the objective of compliance with the requirements and context of use of the users. The process is completed if this evaluation is satisfactory, and if the requirements are not satisfied, the process must be repeated from the first stage, in order to improve the design and development of the system or application. The evaluation of designs can be done by several methods [20]. These methods or user tests are used to prove the usability and processes of the applications by user testing.

To evaluate the prototype design of the application of this work, a remote test was used, which allowed the test to be performed without moving the users to a laboratory. The remote test was chosen due to the COVID-19 pandemic. In addition, remote testing facilitates the capture of users without losing the context of routine use. The users evaluated are chemical engineers and pharmaceutical chemists and biologists. A .pdf file was provided to the users with the prototype of the desktop application. The question protocol [21] was used, in which the prototype of the desktop application was provided to the users and a scenario of tasks to be executed. Users were required to complete the tasks. In addition, they were asked direct questions about how to complete tasks and explain what they were thinking as they were working with the application.

3.2   Machine Learning Techniques for Water Quality Prediction

Machine learning is about using the appropriate functions to create the correct models that accomplish the desired tasks [22]. Tasks can be described and represented by input and output data points or features. This representation or model is produced as the result of a machine learning algorithm applied to certain training data. Depending on the task, the model can be chosen or adapted, as there are a large number of models available.

The databases used were the public ones collected by CONAGUA through the National Water Quality Measurement Network of 2019 [7]. For the training and validation of the model, the K-fold cross validation technique was implemented. In this work was used k = 3 since the database consists of 1711 measurements and allows us to use a large balanced number of data for training and testing. 1198 measurements were used for training and 513 for testing. R studio was the software used to implement the techniques. The parameters selected to classify water quality and their basic statistics in each group are shown in Table 1.

Table 1. Basic statistics of the parameters used to classify water quality.

Fold	Stage	Parameters (Units)											
		BOD5 (mg/L)		COD (mg/L)		TSS (mg/L)		FC (NMP/100 mL)		E_COLI (NMP/100 mL)		DO (%)	
		Mean	SD	Mean	SD	Mean	SD	Mean	SD	Mean	SD	Mean	SD
1	Train	20	33	63	75	58	90	7294	6591	2026	1819	68	31
	Test	20	35	62	73	61	94	7233	6597	1899	1814	67	33
2	Train	21	34	63	75	60	91	7306	6575	2027	1814	68	31
	Test	20	32	63	74	56	89	7244	6631	1980	1832	68	32
3	Train	20	33	62	73	58	90	7282	6611	2018	1827	68	32
	Test	21	34	65	78	60	92	7301	6547	2001	1800	69	31

The classification of water quality provided by the database is by a traffic light, green color is equivalent to not contaminated represented by a number 0 and red color is equivalent to contaminated represented by a number 1.

To classify the water quality data, the logistic regression model was used, where a binary classification was performed by using a logistic function based on the establishment of a threshold. For this case, two classes were established uncontaminated water and contaminated water.

The performance of the model was evaluated from the area under the curve (AUC) metric, by generating a ROC curve it can be determined how well the contaminated and uncontaminated water is distinguished. Sensitivity identifies water that is contaminated and was detected as contaminated and specificity identifies water that is not contaminated and was detected as non-contaminated.

4   Results

The results of implementing each stage of the UCD for the desktop application for water quality prediction and monitoring system are shown, and finally the preliminary performance of the water quality classification model.

4.1   Specification Context of Use

The survey was conducted with 38 people who perform chemical analysis in laboratories and their responses were analyzed. The age range was 20 to 60 with a native language of Spanish in 100% and a non-native language of English in 92.2% of the respondents. The participation rate was 47.4% for women and 52.6% for men. 78.9% have a bachelor's degree and 15.8% have a master's degree. The devices used when performing chemical analysis included specialized equipment (81.6%) and desktop computers (76.3%). The specialized equipment used in the laboratory, 50% have a screen on the equipment for feedback and 42.1% have a program for the desktop computer. 44.7% have an internet in the laboratory and 86.8% have a Windows operating system. This is shown in Fig. 3.

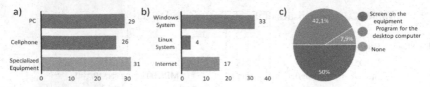

Fig. 3. a) Equipment used in the laboratory, b) Desktop computer characteristics, c) Feedback from specialized equipment.

In order to know the context of use, participants were asked what protective equipment they use in the laboratory obtaining 97.4% for gloves and gowns, 76.3% use glasses and 50% use masks. Figure 4 shows the responses. Finally, a common profile of the users was generated using the personas technique obtaining the result shown in Fig. 5 [17, 18].

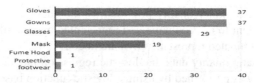

Fig. 4. Protective equipment in the laboratory.

Fig. 5. Common profile of users implementing the "personas" technique.

4.2 Specification of Requirements

Figure 6 shows user requirements included the tasks that take the most time when they are performing an analysis in the laboratory, with 73.7% for sample collection, 52.6% for equipment calibration and 18.4% for storage of values in a document.

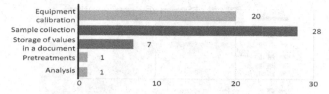

Fig. 6. Time-consuming tasks when performing chemical analysis in the laboratory.

The most important features and tools that users would incorporate in the system were: storage of measurements with 84.2%, 73.7% that it has internet connectivity to view data anywhere, 78.9% to view measurements in graphs or tables and 68.4% that it has an estimate of other water quality parameters. This is shown in Fig. 7.

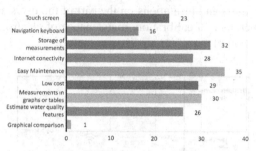

Fig. 7. User requirements.

4.3   Design Solution Production

Based on the analysis of the responses, a prototype of the complete system was designed. The system is shown in Fig. 8. The prototype of the complete system consists of electronic monitoring devices in the study area, a web server and a computer in the laboratory. This is a first step of the possible design and implementation of the complete system. The monitoring will be continuous and remote using low-cost and accurate sensors. It will be limited to an internet connection, web server capacity and basic PC or smart phone features.

The water quality parameters that can be measured by the sensors are varied, depending on the physical, chemical or biological determination method [8]. Based on some of the parameters considered by CONAGUA, pH, TSS, DO, turbidity, total dissolved solids, temperature, electrical conductivity can be measured by sensors [9]. The measurement of these parameters will allow to predict the level of water contamination. However, more parameters can be added as long as they can be measured in the study area.

The atmega328p microcontroller can be used as the main board to control the sensors and communicate via WI-FI module (ESP8266) with a web server to send and collect the parameter values. This will facilitate the visualization of parameters and water quality at any location. In addition, a charging and power module using a solar panel and batteries

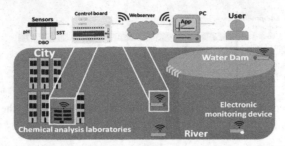

Fig. 8. Prototype of the complete system.

is proposed to enable energy self-sufficiency. The proposed design of the monitoring device is shown in Fig. 9. This design can be improved and adapted, since it is a first design and there are needs and limitations on the part of the users and the parameters. For example, the experience in calibration, maintenance of electronic devices and the methods of determination of the water quality parameters.

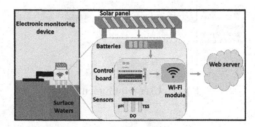

Fig. 9. Prototype of the electronic monitoring device.

For the design of the desktop application, 4 horizontal prototypes were made, taking recommendations from the design team and improving each one in the next prototype [23]. In the first design, the main operating features of the application were added, such as observing the parameter response. However, the design did not accomplish with the common elements and colors of an application.

For the second design it was included a more general environment for computer users. For the third design, more acceptable colors and pre-established areas were added to facilitate user navigation. In the fourth design all the functions of the prototype were added and the position of navigation icons between screens of the application such as restart and exit were modified. Figure 10 shows the 4 templates of the main screen that have been made.

The final prototype demonstrated a wide range of features, but was limited in certain functions. Figure 11 shows the user registration and login area which helps to identify the measurements that users will make. The desktop application shows the value of the water parameters to be monitored in the study area and a traffic light representing the ranges allowed by standards. A task bar for equipment calibration, a help tool and a save option are also present. In addition, there is an area for selecting and visualizing the values of the parameters over time with a graph and a table of values. Figure 12

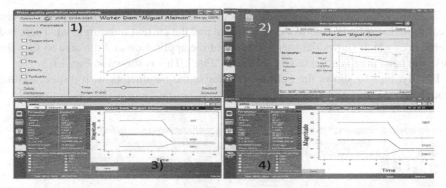

Fig. 10. 1) First prototype, 2) Second prototype, 3) Third prototype, 4) Fourth prototype.

shows the battery level of the monitoring device, an area showing the time and date of the measurement, a section for restarting the measurement and logging out the user.

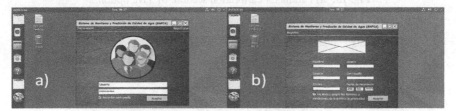

Fig. 11. a) Login, b) User Registration.

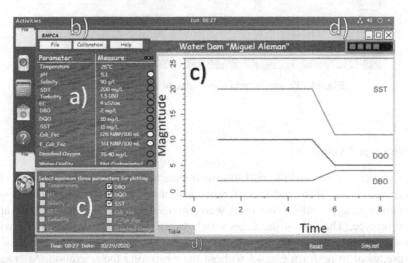

Fig. 12. a) Parameter measurement and range traffic light, b) Task bar, c) Parameter selection and time graph, d) Battery level, time, date and section for measurement restart and user sign out.

The calibration tab displays a reminder message and shows the parameters that can be calibrated, displaying the working standard and the current measurement. There is a "Help" area which shows the user's manual of the application and the area to save the work, the latter area is accessed by selecting "File". This is shown in Fig. 13.

Finally, Fig. 14 shows the option to visualize the parameters with respect to time through a graph area and a table of values.

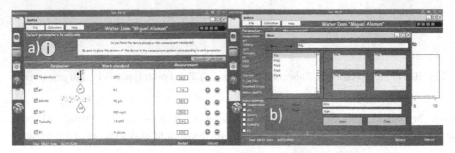

Fig. 13. a) Parameter calibration section. b) Save option.

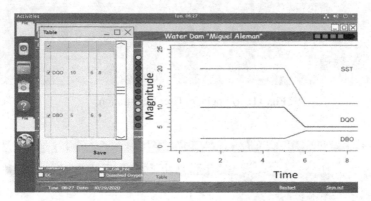

Fig. 14. Parameter graph and table of parameter values.

4.4 Prototype Evaluation

A video conference was held to perform the remote test separately for each user. Photographs were taken of the video conference and of the user's computer screen while manipulating the application. Four users were provided with a.pdf file to enter the application prototype. The age of the users was between 22 and 26 years old and with a bachelor's degree level of education. The objective of the application was explained and they were asked to perform 6 tasks without demonstrating the operation. Afterwards, the operation was demonstrated and they performed the 6 tasks again. This is shown in Fig. 15. For each task, the time it took them to complete was recorded as shown in Table 2.

Fig. 15. Remote user evaluation of design prototypes.

Table 2. Time in seconds it took users to complete tasks.

User	Register	Log in	Calibration	Parameter graph	Table	Save project
1	27	13	30	8	5	17
2	11	7	16	8	9	12
3	10	5	15	10	11	8
4	7	6	15	7	7	9

From Table 2, the task that took them the longest to complete was calibration and the task that took the least time was logging into the desktop application.

The questions formulated to the users had the objective of knowing their opinion about the functioning and improvements of the application. The questions were: Q1: What is your experience in laboratories? Q2: What is your age? Q3: Do you think the navigation was easy? Q4: What was more complicated to understand? Q5: The tasks are done quickly? Q6: What aspect and tool did you like? Q7: What would you add to the application? The answers are shown in the Table 3.

From the feedback of the users it was possible to identify the benefits of the application, being friendly and easy to navigate.

4.5 Evaluation of Machine Learning Algorithms

The performance of the logistic regression algorithm for the classification of water quality into contaminated and uncontaminated is shown in the training, testing and validation. Metrics using $k = 3$, area under the curve (AUC), sensitivity and specificity are shown in Table 4.

Table 3. User feedback on the desktop application prototype.

User	Q1	Q2	Q3	Q4	Q5	Q6	Q7
1	School lab	24	Yes	Calibration	Yes	Parameter graph	Out of range alert
2	Physical analysis lab	23	Yes	Calibration	Yes	Register	Measurement Control
3	Organic synthesis lab	25	Yes	Calibration	Yes	Traffic light representing the ranges	Change Table
4	Hospital lab	22	Yes	Calibration	Yes	Parameter graph	Modify work pattern

Table 4. Logistic regression algorithm performance.

Metric	Train		Test	
	Mean	SD	Mean	SD
Sensitivity	0.99	0.003	0.98	0.004
Specificity	0.99	0.006	0.99	1.58
AUC	0.99	0.003	0.98	0.003

5 Conclusions

After implementing the User-Centered Design methodology, a prototype of a desktop application for monitoring and predicting water quality was generated. The survey of 38 users specialized in the chemical area showed requirements and needs that were addressed in the desktop application. This prototype desktop application showed an alternative and first contact with the design of the complete system for water quality monitoring and prediction. Evaluation tests showed that the design of the prototype solved the main user requirements. In addition, it was possible to find more requirements, deficiencies and tool proposals from the comments provided by the users. The performance of the prediction algorithm showed us that the use of machine learning techniques and algorithms is a viable option since more parameters could be added for the prediction of water quality or to give an estimate of a specific parameter. With the design and implementation of the complete water quality monitoring and prediction system, a tool and alternative that supports the development and maintenance of cities will be obtained in the future.

References

1. Arreguin-Cortes, F.I., Cervantes-Jaimes, C.E.: Water security and sustainability in Mexico. In: Raynal-Villasenor, J. (ed.) Water Resources of Mexico. WWR, vol. 6, pp. 177–195. Springer, Cham (2020). https://doi.org/10.1007/978-3-030-40686-8_10

2. UNU-INWEH: Water Security & the Global Water Agenda. The UN-Water analytical brief, United Nat., vol. 53, no. 9. United Nations University, Canada (2013)
3. Global Water Partnership: Towards Water Security: A Framework for Action Foreword, Stockholm, Sweden (2000)
4. Peña, H.: Recursos Naturales e infraestructura. Desafíos de la seguridad hídrica en América Latina y el Caribe. Naciones Unidas (2016). https://repositorio.cepal.org/bitstream/handle/11362/40074/S1600566_es.pdf?sequence=1&isAllowed=y. Accessed 22 Oct 2020
5. Raynal-Gutierrez, M.E.: Water use and consumption: industrial and domestic. In: Raynal-Villasenor, J.A. (ed.) Water Resources of Mexico. WWR, vol. 6, pp. 103–116. Springer, Cham (2020). https://doi.org/10.1007/978-3-030-40686-8_6
6. Fonseca-Ortiz, C.R., Mastachi-Loza, C.A., Díaz-Delgado, C., Esteller-Alberich, M.V.: The water–energy–food nexus in. In: Raynal-Villasenor, J.A. (ed.) Water Resources of Mexico. WWR, vol. 6, pp. 65–82. Springer, Cham (2020). https://doi.org/10.1007/978-3-030-40686-8_4
7. CONAGUA: Calidad del agua en México (2020). https://www.gob.mx/conagua/articulos/calidad-del-agua. Accessed 22 Oct 2020
8. Guo, Y., Liu, C., Ye, R., Duan, Q.: Advances on water quality detection by UV-Vis spectroscopy. Appl. Sci. 10(19) (2020). https://doi.org/10.3390/app10196874
9. Park, J., Kim, K.T., Lee, W.H.: Recent advances in information and communications technology (ICT) and sensor technology for monitoring water quality. Water 12(2) (2020). https://doi.org/10.3390/w12020510
10. Carminati, M., et al.: A self-powered wireless water quality sensing network enabling smart monitoring of biological and chemical stability in supply systems. Sensors (Switzerland) 20(4) (2020). https://doi.org/10.3390/s20041125
11. Chowdury, M.S.U., et al.: IoT based real-time river water quality monitoring system. Procedia Comput. Sci. 155, 161–168 (2019). https://doi.org/10.1016/j.procs.2019.08.025
12. Rosero-Montalvo, P.D., López-Batista, V.F., Riascos, J.A., Peluffo-Ordóñez, D.H.: Intelligent WSN system for water quality analysis using machine learning algorithms: a case study (Tahuando river from Ecuador). Remote Sens. 12(12) (2020). https://doi.org/10.3390/rs1212 1988
13. Ahmed, U., Mumtaz, R., Anwar, H., Shah, A.A., Irfan, R., García-Nieto, J.: Efficient water quality prediction using supervised machine learning. Water (Switzerland) 11(11) (2019). https://doi.org/10.3390/w11112210
14. Maguire, M., Kirakowski, J., Vereker, N.: RESPECT: User Centered Requirements Handbook. Figshare (2019). https://hdl.handle.net/2134/2651
15. Ergonomics of human-systems interaction–Part 210: Human centered design for interactive systems, traduced from (ISO 9241-210) (2019)
16. Google. https://forms.gle/Mzx1QVrqv7pmWDE7A. Accessed 24 Oct 2020
17. Holden, R.J., et al.: Patient decision-making personas: an application of a patient-centered cognitive task analysis (P-CTA). Appl. Ergon. 87, 103107 (2020). https://doi.org/10.1016/j.apergo.2020.103107
18. Nielsen, L.: Personas - User Focused Design in Personas. Springer, London (2013). https://doi.org/10.1007/978-1-4471-4084-9
19. Pencil Project. https://pencil.evolus.vn/. Accessed 24 Oct 2020
20. Rubin, J., Chisnell, D.: Handbook of Usability Testing, 2nd edn., vol. 17, no. 2. Wiley Publishing, Inc., Indianapolis (2008)
21. Dumas, J., Redish, J.: A Practical Guide to Usability Testing, 1st edn. Intellect Books, Portland (1999)
22. Flach, P.: Machine Learning the Art and Science of Algorithms that Make Sense of Data, 1st edn. Cambridge University Press (2012). https://doi.org/10.1017/CBO9780511973000
23. Nielsen, J.: Usability Engineering, 1st edn. Morgan Kaufmann Publishers (1994)

Digital Ecosystem for Children's Rehabilitation with Psychomotor Deficit

María Libertad Aguilar Carlos[(✉)] ⓘ, Jaime Muñoz Arteaga ⓘ,
José Eder Guzmán Mendoza ⓘ, and César Eduardo Velázquez Amador ⓘ

Universidad Autónoma de Aguascalientes, Av. Universidad #940, Ciudad Universitaria, C.P.
20131 Aguascalientes, Ags, México
{jaime.munoz,eder.guzman,eduardo.velazquez}@edu.uaa.mx

Abstract. Introduction. In this paper we review the change that the psychomotor deficit's children rehabilitation system has had to further adapt due to the COVID-19 pandemic, explaining the importance of early care with the support of computer technologies. Because of the health emergency, many patients with a motor disability couldn't assist to the places that provided therapy services of various kinds, joined to the fact that therapists also had to avoid crowds in their rehabilitation centers and thus not spread the virus in this vulnerable population. **Methodology.** The approach used is a mixed approach, with children of 0 to 5 years old diagnosed with psychomotor deficit due to a development disorder which are coursing initial education as the objects of study. The instruments used have been observation with action research. **Results.** A solution is shown creating a digital ecosystem model that inserts Scrum agile methodology for the children's rehabilitation process, that allows interaction between all the actors in the process, such as children, parents or guardians, therapists, doctors, and specialists. Some related works are mentioned that offer a broader perspective of the scope that this technological approach has been generating. The proposed solution is tested in a study case at the APPAC Association. **Discussion-Conclusion.** The proposed model needs a lot of iterations to consider his value and get more detailed information about user experience and the perceived benefits at psychomotor deficit. It discloses important results with technologies' use to work in the future.

Keywords: Digital ecosystem · Scrum agile methodology · Initial education · Psychomotor deficit · Children's rehabilitation

1 Introduction

The use of virtual meeting platforms accessed from technological means such as desktop or laptop computers, mobile phones and tablets, has begun to be used with great popularity as software that allows communication in real time, especially in the field of distance education and rehabilitation for children with disabilities; This has allowed us to carry out a way of working called teleworking, mostly known worldwide as "telehealth", caused primarily as a result of the COVID-19 pandemic, but above all, it has established a new dynamic, both work and of social relations, achieving that educational

P. H. Ruiz et al. (Eds.): HCI-COLLAB 2021, CCIS 1478, pp. 58–72, 2021.
https://doi.org/10.1007/978-3-030-92325-9_5

institutions, business companies and people in general adapt more and more to the use of these technologies. Precisely like the Management Model of a Project for the Insertion of Educational Technology in a Multiple Attention Center [1], which used playful educational applications on devices such as tablets or desktop computers and jointly using m-Learning as a complement in the educational program for children with multiple disabilities in order to support the development of reading and writing skills, software engineering must also create spaces that allow rehabilitation, education, communication, and inclusion of children with disabilities, among which are some psychomotor deficits. It is worth mentioning that especially in European countries, robotic devices are being developed with the help of knowledge in software engineering and technologies that aim to help the rehabilitation of children with this deficit. Most of the children with psychomotor deficits who have access and the opportunity to receive care with rehabilitation therapies in various institutions, especially governmental institutions, civil associations, foundations or in a particular way in private centers, but there was contrasting pattern to the normal way to obtain this type of care a few months after COVID-19 was declared a global pandemic.

This work is made up by seven sections as follows: This first section with an Introduction where is briefly given the research panorama and theoretical framework; Sect. 2 about Problem Outline, explaining the origin of the main problematic, detailing the difficulties detected in the context of investigation; the Methodology in Sect. 3, that explains the study structure, the Sect. 4 defining a Digital Ecosystem Model as a proposed solution with its phases, a Case Study in Sect. 5 developing a scenario where the Digital Ecosystem Model is applied; then a Discussion at Sect. 6, expressing opinion regarding the use of the proposed model; and finally Sect. 7 with Conclusion section, describing what is deduced with the use of the model and possible future work.

1.1 Digital Ecosystem and Scrum Agile Methodology

A digital ecosystem is found in the field of software ecosystems, defined as the interaction of a set of main actors in a common technological platform [2] that gives results in software solutions and services, pointing out as a distributed adapted open sociotechnical system with properties of self-organization, scalability, and sustainability [3]. An agile methodology serves to develop software iteratively and with continuous feedback [4]. The Scrum methodology is based on process management, it assumes the existence of a project, which almost always exists in object-oriented software development [5], is faster and more efficient with regular communication. Each iteration is called a "sprint", the objective of which is to dynamically provide feasible deliverables in the process. In each sprint, the delivery of a work product stands out that adds value to the project and to the users. The outstanding characteristics of the Agile Scrum methodology are empirical feedback, team self-management and the construction of properly tested increments with short iterations.

1.2   Initial Education Services and Blended Rehabilitation

Initial Education is the educational service that is provided to boys and girls from zero to six years of age, to enhance their integral and harmonious development in an environment of formative, educational and affective experiences, which allows them to acquire skills, habits, values, autonomy, and creativity. This service is also applied to children with disabilities in Multiple Care Centers but must be complemented with appropriate therapies for each child's psychomotor deficit, while in combined interventions, where online treatment and contact with specialized care attention [6] in a physic way with professionals is mixed [7] and coordinated.

1.3   Psychomotor Déficit and Development

Monitoring of psychomotor development is considered an extremely important task in the health supervision of infants and preschoolers [8], since the diagnosis of a psychomotor deficit is largely due to neurological damage, observed mainly after the prenatal period, postnatal and infantile. The timely detection of disorders of psychomotor development offers the possibility of intervening early, correcting most of the alterations and attenuating others. The psychomotor deficit (PD) is the clinical manifestation of pathologies of the Central Nervous System (CNS), either due to genetic alterations and/or environmental factors, which affect the psychomotor development of the child in the first 24 to 36 months of life, what defines the developmental progress in a child in motor, language, manipulation and social areas [9]. Characteristics of a child with a psychomotor deficit may include muscle weakness, abnormal muscle tone, decreased range of motion of the joints, and decreased balance and coordination [10]. Brain or neuronal plasticity refers to the adaptive capacity of the central nervous system (CNS) to reduce the effects of injuries, through changes that modify the structure and function, both in the internal and external environment [11], with which effective rehabilitation procedures are every day. It is a neural reorganization capacity that occurs to try to compensate or restore lost function. It begins in the areas around the lesion and later spreads to other secondary areas belonging to the same hemisphere or analogous areas of the contralateral hemisphere. Rehabilitation therapy-type experiences modify neural circuits, since they are plastic, and in most cases the efficacy and the number of synaptic connections change [12].

1.4   Usable Services with Lean User Experience

Both rehabilitation therapies and initial education are necessary services in the support process of the psychomotor deficit's rehabilitation. Services are a series of interactions between customers and the service system through many different touchpoints during the customer journey [13]. And as such, they are accompanied by the user experience. To measure this, it can be supported by Lean User Experience, or simply Lean UX, which is a design practice centered around validating hypotheses, where instead of thinking of a product as a series of features to be built, Lean UX looks at a product as a set of hypotheses to be validated [14]. Lean UX stands on three important foundations: *user experience design, Agile Software Development,* and *Lean Startup* method. The goal is validating a proposed business solution-a hypotheses using customer feedback [15]. Usability is all about how easy it is to get the offering when using the service [13].

2 Problem Outline

Since 2020, COVID-19 has significantly interrupted rehabilitation treatments such as physical, occupational, language or sensory therapy to children with psychomotor deficits. The main problem is that the processes of brain plasticity of children with psychomotor deficit does not achieve its functions because of the lack of stimuli that the frequency of therapies provides, since with above mentioned, therapies received has been zero or less, affecting stages of development that is required for their recovery and adaptation to daily life and of the highest quality possible. Although this problem directly affects children, parents are undoubtedly also the harmed in several ways, so focusing on parents, the following specific problematics have been detected:

a) Lack of knowledge of elements from contemporary approaches, tools and activities for therapies that could help their children in brain restoration and motor learning [16].

b) Partial or total restriction assisting to institutions where their children used to receive rehabilitation treatments, since many health care services for children with disabilities were canceled [17] because of the pandemic time, which is uncertain to now when it will finish.

c) Lack of support from the government, since access to rehabilitation interventions for patients including those with psychomotor deficits was reduced, as well as elimination of group therapies [18], causing the closure of Rehabilitation Centers such as Integral Development of the Family (DIF for its acronym in Spanish), Center for Rehabilitation and Child Development (CREDI for its acronym in Spanish), Center for Rehabilitation in Special Education (CREE for its acronym in Spanish), and partially closed the Center for Child Rehabilitation Teletón (CRIT for its acronym in Spanish), among others in Mexico, to provide sufficient therapies.

d) The resources offered by the new model of Special and Inclusive Education at distance of the Public Education Secretary (SEP) in Mexico by television do not transmit a personalized way like an individualized program for appropriate therapies at each specific child, and the web page of the institution just have written manuals documents of suggested activities or videos with interviews, but not classes guided by therapists to observe positions and maneuver the kids according to every need [19].

e) Technological limits and barriers in the patients, clinician, organizational and system levels that do not allow implement an effective adoption of telehealth for mild psychomotor deficit children [17].

In summary, the brain plasticity of children with psychomotor deficit does not fulfill the functions of which it is enabled, so children should not be treated with therapies every day, in addition to the earlier the age of attention and rehabilitation, the greater the impact on the benefit to lead a quality of life as satisfactory as possible.

3 Methodology

In this research-action study with a mixed descriptive and exploratory approach, children in an age range of 0 to 5 years from a civil association of an educational and rehabilitation nature, that are conditioned with a diagnosis of psychomotor deficit condition. Speech and physical therapists who attend to children with psychomotor deficits derived mainly from a diagnosis of cerebral palsy participate. Observation and inquiries to the therapists were carried out to obtain information about the rehabilitation service in order to know the user experience, and also, the instrument developed by Doman (2005) [20] was used, in which the degree of psychomotor deficit of children is measured before starting to use the ecosystem model. This instrument is divided into six areas, which refer to six primary reflexes that each child has at birth, which will gradually become competencies, and these in turn are used in essential life skills. As a child advances in a competition to develop final ability, progress manifests itself in 7 stages of brain growth, beginning with the Early Brainstem and Spinal Cord stage, which is when all six primitive reflexes are present. As a comparison, in a healthy child, as these reflexes progress with rehabilitation and repetition experiences, thanks to plasticity in the brain, it is possible to reach the seventh stage at the average age of 72 months, which would mean achieve a Sophisticated Crust. The procedure that has been followed is to be guided by the ecosystem model during several predetermined iterations in a defined period of time of six months, and then a new measurement is carried out with the same instrument to collect the information, capture it and make the analysis with the comparison of the results obtained.

4   Blended Rehabilitation Digital Ecosystem Model

The earlier the age of educational care and rehabilitation of conditioned children with psychomotor deficits, the greater the impact on the benefit of leading a quality of life that is as satisfactory as possible. Thanks to information and communication technologies, in these circumstances specifically, virtual meeting platforms serve as content management systems to communicate with the main actors: therapists, parents/guardians, children, managers and specialists. It is proposed as a solution the development of a digital ecosystem that includes interaction with personalized programs on practices, exercises and activities designated by specialized therapists for children attending the initial level, which supports in suggesting procedures on how to use technologies to carry out distance therapies, and that, together with the human factor, makes it possible to study and evaluate the implications that the design of a digital ecosystem has on the psychomotor development of initial education, becoming a tool that provides a combined and complete online rehabilitation. Figure 1 shows the design of the digital ecosystem model, based on the agile Scrum methodology [4] creating a combined rehabilitation environment [7], that is, with a mix of both face-to-face and virtual services, to support children from the initial education stage with some psychomotor deficit. This type of combined work already exists in some Children's Rehabilitation Centers (CRIT) in Mexico, called tele-rehabilitation [21].

By having computers and using Zoom's virtual meeting platform, they schedule with some parents of children with psychomotor deficits being beneficiaries of their services and guiding online therapies from their workplace to their homes, following the program rehabilitation according to the goals and progress of the child. From the houses where they receive this type of therapy, parents must also have devices such as computers or their cell phones, in addition to the Zoom platform installed and the

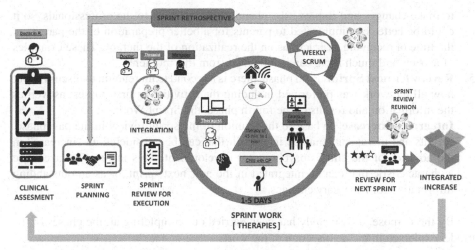

Fig. 1. Digital Ecosystem for Blended Rehabilitation Model for Children Development Centers inspired by [4].

WhatsApp platform to receive the access links to each therapy in Zoom. That is why the three pillars considered in this study that make up the model of the proposed solution are: *Digital ecosystem*, which allows working in a hybrid combination both in person for certain cases, and virtually offering data, resources and information concerning the rehabilitation of each particular child with psychomotor deficit, although it is aimed at parents or main caregivers of the families of children in the initial education stage, the ecosystem can be adapted to children of any age who require this service; the *Human part* made up of parents or caregivers, children in initial education with psychomotor deficits requesting therapy services for their development, therapists, doctors and specialists who monitor the progress in the development of infants, as well as managers who support ecosystem stewardship; and the *Technology* made up of both the physical resources that will favor communication between the parties, and the knowledge of digital skills.

The model is made up for six phases that create a re-feeding cycle:

1. **Clinical Assessment**. First phase the team of doctors and rehabilitation specialists examine the child and place him at his detected levels of the developmental areas according to the Glenn Doman instrument [20].
2. **Sprint Planning.** Second phase the team of doctors, rehabilitation specialists communicate with therapists and manager to plan the sprint, wich will consist of a week of various therapies that will support the progress of the child to reach the levels in the corresponding areas of development according to their age. The prescription of the amount and frequency of therapies is carried out at this stage.
3. **Sprint Review for Execution.** Third phase,the managers inform parents about the prescription of therapies for their children and always remind them days in advance of their work schedule so that the family prepares on the specified days and times.
4. **Sprint Work.** Fourth phase, the most important stage in the model, this is where therapists, children and parents come into play, this part give us crucial information

to make changes and improve the planning, the training to the professionals, so it could be better communicated to parents for a better preparation of the parents at the time of receiving instructions on the realization of the therapy. These examples of aspects and much more can be obtained from this moment.

5. **Review for next Sprint.** Fifth phase, there is a second team reunion to discuss about how all the work was performed including the activities in first phases; as well as the information and results of the fourth phase, the Sprint Work.

6. **Integrated Increase.** In base to the reunion of the sprint review in the past phase, parents and therapists coincide in a result that can be considered an "increase" in the advance of the child's psychomotor development. This increase is taken like a characteristic that can be integrated in the new next sprint, or as an outstanding information for necessary changes.

By the purpose, a case study has been carried out completing all the phases of the model explained in the next section of the work.

5 Case Study

The model explained on the previous section in Fig. 2 is applied with a case study research method at the Pro Paralytic Association (APPAC for the acronym in Spanish) a Civil Association of the city of Zacatecas that works to improve the quality of life of children with cerebral palsy [22] who in turn have psychomotor deficits due to certain disorders in development, among other diagnoses such as encephalopathies, intellectual disability, autism, among others. Two iterations are shown applying the model.

5.1 Case 1. Iteration 1

Alexander is a 3-year-old chronic boy, with different neurological ages in manual, language and tactile areas, demonstrating competencies in visual and auditory areas according to his chronic age. His diagnosis is that of a developmental disorder with symptoms of athetosic infantile cerebral palsy. The combined rehabilitation digital ecosystem model is applied in the Asociación Pro Paralítico Cerebral A.C. (APPAC) of the city of Zacatecas, Mexico as described below.

5.1.1 Clinical Assessment

The first stage consists of an assessment carried out by specialists in neuropediatrics and rehabilitation medicine, who rely on previous studies and clinical analyzes to specifically diagnose the degree of psychomotor deficit, carrying out a questionnaire to parents or guardians and previously requesting specific studies to review them, and also carrying out movement and posture tests to measure gross and fine motor skills, positioning case 1 on a scale within each area of development. Figure 2 shows the Development Profile of this case based on the instrument developed by Glenn Doman [20], according to the qualification and assessment of the specialists. This instrument is divided into six areas, which at birth refer to six primordial reflexes that gradually become competencies, and these in turn become essential life skills. As a child advances through his age in a competition to develop the final ability, progress manifests in 7 stages, beginning in the first stage of development with the early brainstem and spinal cord presenting all six primitive reflexes, and that as they grow with the rehabilitation and repetition experiences that your brain has, thanks to brain plasticity, you can reach the seventh stage in the average age of 72 months, your brain reaching a sophisticated cortex.

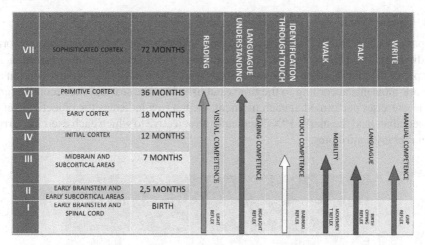

Fig. 2. Iteration 1. Development Profile for initial assessment. Inspired by [20].

The figure shows case 1 with visual and auditory skills according to their age, while the skills of touch, mobility, language and manual are in various stages not according to their age, diagnosing a mild psychomotor deficit.

5.1.2 Sprint Planning

Based on the previous assessment of psychomotor development, together with his diagnosis, the specialists and managers of the institution meet to define the necessary therapy program for case 1. They have decided to prescribe several therapies for his rehabilitation in the areas with deficit. Table 1 shows the therapies, days and times that have been prescribed.

Table 1. Therapy schedule.

Therapy	Days	Schedule	Times per week
Physic	2–6 Aug	9:00 am	5
Occupational	2, 4 y 6 Aug	11:00 am	3
Language	2,3,5 Aug	12:00 pm	3

5.1.3 Sprint Review for Execution

The project managers make a review at least two days before the therapy session to confirm the online assistance of the parents or guardians, the advice in case of ignorance regarding the use of the technologies and send links to the virtual family reunion via social network. Parents are notified of the days and times that they have been scheduled to connect to the Zoom platform to carry out online therapy.

5.1.4 Sprint Work

The parents connect daily to physical therapy, and to the other therapies on the corresponding days by entering the link previously sent by the managers of the institution. An example of the first iteration of physical therapy is shown in Fig. 3. The left column are the work moments according to the time established for the session, the second column are the exercises performed at each moment, the top row indicates the objectives set by the specialists, and the marked "Xs" indicate the objective to which each exercise carried out in therapy contributes.

Physic Therapy 9:00 am Case 1	Objective /Excercise	Head Control	Spasticity Absence	Four Points	Sitting	Turns	Drag
9:05	Calisthenics		X				
9:15	Bobath Movilizations		X	X	X		
9:25	Parachute	X	X				X
9:30	Opening hands		X	X	X	X	X
9:35	Got up sitting	X	X		X		X
9:45	Crawling	X	X	X	X	X	X

Fig. 3. Iteration 1. Physical therapy exercises

5.1.5 Review for Next Sprint

The sprint has provided the necessary information to learn more about needs in the ecosystem, relevant changes and more efficient application dynamics. After this first week, specialists and managers discuss the details of the sprint doing a retrospective, to improve aspects that have been obstacles, as well as check the progress observed in iteration 1, among any other matter of interest to the project stakeholders. creating feedback for each team member. This meeting defines what is called an "increment," which is a significant achievement achieved during this sprint.

5.1.6 Integrated Increase

In this first iteration, the increment has been the most accurate evaluation of the movements that the patient of case 1 manages to perform. This information is passed as information for the return to the first stage of the next iteration.

5.2 Case 1. Iteration 2

5.2.1 Clinical Assesment

For this second iteration, the evaluation of the pediatric neurologist is not necessary. This will be a review for progress assessment by a rehabilitation physician and therapists. Reports on the first iteration are gathered with information from the first sprint and the increment. The development profile instrument is filled out again as Fig. 4 shows, which has continued at the same levels, since it has only been the first week of work.

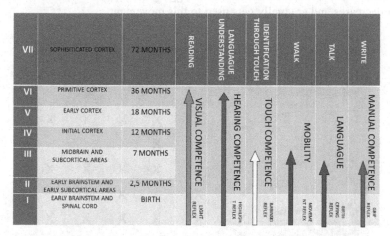

Fig. 4. Iteration 2. Development Profile. Inspired by [20].

5.2.2 Sprint Planning

Based on the documentation collected from the first sprint and the increase for this iteration, specialists and managers meet in person or online and discuss the implementation of the second sprint and other topics of interest for this case. They decide to continue with the same number of physical, occupational, and speech therapy sessions per week.

5.2.3 Sprint Review for Execution

Project managers do a review at least two days before the therapy session for the next sprint and confirm attendance online from parents or guardians. They send links to the virtual meeting to the family via social network to inform them that the days and hours remain the same.

5.2.4 Sprint Work

The actors are connected via the links sent by the managers of the institution. An example of second iteration of physical therapy is shown in Fig. 5.

5.2.5 Review for Next Sprint

The sprint of second iteration has given information that case 1 does not control his anxiety in exercises for dragging, showing high degree of discomfort, which prevented the parents from exercising in the correct way while receiving the indications from the therapist. In addition, there were lapses of internet disconnection from the APPAC, so indications were received in a short form and time was lost to follow-up therapy.

5.2.6 Integrated Increase

The increase detected has been to alternate dragging exercises when anxiety is shown, so that it decreases and gradually gets used to this movement.

Physic Therapy 9:00 am Case 1	Objective/ Excercise	Head Control	Spasticity Absence	Four Points	Sitting	Turns	Drag
9:05	Calisthenics		X	X	X	X	X
9:15	Bobath Movilizations		X	X	X		
9:25	Bridges			X	X	X	X
9:30	Got up sitting	X	X	X			
9:35	Sitting to upside down	X	X	X	X	X	X
9:45	Rehab Ball	X	X	X	X	X	X

Fig. 5. Case 1. Physical therapy exercises in iteration 2.

6 Discussion

The application of various disciplines and methodologies for the study has shown certain impressions. By combining software engineering, agile Scrum methodology, interaction design for the digital ecosystem model, and Lean UX, with the use of virtual meeting platforms and connectivity tools, several aspects highlighted a lot of things to consider. Naming the perceived obstacles, first, presents a considerable challenge in involving all stakeholders in carrying out all the stages within a methodology unknown to them, especially in compliance with it, although it has facilitated a very meticulous communication at many moments of the process, which allows looking for the appropriate ways to use the tools, the times for every rehabilitation service, planning, etc. Scrum methodology in the process of the digital ecosystem model is faster and efficient, there is regular communication with full releases that allows actors and interested parties to participate in the application of the model. There are reviews for each release done in look-back meetings and each sprint highlights the delivery of a work product that adds value to the project and users. That's why it could adapt to the rehabilitation process of psychomotor deficit's children because it is very similar to the process taken by therapists and specialists, but this one gives them more valuable information not only about the therapy service itself, also about the attention, the user experience, or the service design.

On the other hand, the optimization with the operation of the technologies is not always good, it goes through dilemmas such as failures with the internet connection or fall of the web platforms. And there was also lack of commitment by the parts, parents or guardians mostly, but also sometimes the specialists.

A frame of reference that details an important change in the health dynamic of rehabilitation services for children with psychomotor deficits is shown in Fig. 6, where it seems a scenario before the COVID pandemic and a scenario after, within a new roles and resources has been set because of the health situation.

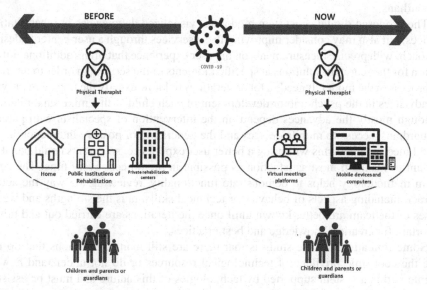

Fig. 6. Frame of reference for the disability's children's care such as psychomotor deficits before and after COVID-19. Based on [23].

The digital ecosystem model for a blended rehabilitation of psychomotor deficit of initial education's children has collaborated with the following attributes:

- It allows to communicate to actors such as parents, children, therapists, managers, doctors and other specialists in the process of therapy services for children with psychomotor deficits.

- Assists parents or guardians to manage comprehensive care with therapies for their children.
- Covers the role of guidance in rehabilitation issues and important issues in diagnosing conditioned children with psychomotor deficits.
- It makes it possible to carry out distance therapies using virtual meeting platforms and interactive computer systems to achieve a mirror or synchronous effect for parents to follow the instructions.
- Provides agendas to mix periodic evaluations and face-to-face therapies, being a type of combined rehabilitation.

7   Conclusion

The relevant data that the study has given is that it can be adapted to the parent's needs with children who have psychomotor deficits in many ways, offering communication viability regardless of the distance or the health circumstances of the world, also facilitating access to information that previously took longer to obtain, is undoubtedly useful for the treatment of patients who need rehabilitation at all early ages and as training for parents or guardians.

The proposed digital ecosystem model has visualized deficiencies in rehabilitation services, but also may consider improving these services through a user-centered design approach, with precise measurements on the user experience that offers additional information for the search in solutions at specific moments of the service, in order to improve the process in the model. It needs a lot of iterations to know exactly the impact of providing advances in the psychomotor development of each child with a mixt rehabilitation. Although mostly the advances depend on the intervention of specialists with parents or guardians, access to mobile devices and the generation of positive interaction in the virtual meeting platforms will bring a better user experience, so parents could be taken account to maintain most satisfaction as possible in the process every time. The agile scrum methodology helps to demonstrate functionality, reviewing the way the actors interact, including aspects of behavior or technical skills, plus the strengths and weaknesses of the team are better known until once the iterations are carried out and this is important for creating knowledge and best practices.

Some limitations on the study is that there are still many institutions that do not have the economic privilege of technological resources or do not understand how to operate within a system supported by technologies of this nature and must be assisted with instruction and teaching of basic issues.

The management of a digital ecosystem about disability situations such as psychomotor deficit is extremely helpful for various aspects of rehabilitation, inclusion and feasibility. The instruments that allow this exploration to be carried out from a more technological perspective should have the purpose of creating a closer commitment between parents or guardians with specialists and therapists that leads to a result of a more personalized accompaniment. In this sense, technologies such as robotics, artificial intelligence, augmented or virtual reality are other clear examples of disciplines that will evolve independently in this matter to serve as complements to the broad field of psychomotor deficit disability. A digital ecosystem must be designed in accordance with the environment where it will develop, creating relationships of inclusion, cooperation and equality.

All this can be enriched with digital skills, the securing of internet contracts and formal virtual meeting platforms, optimizing the space that ensures a connection that allows good audio and video, exploring ideas and perspectives of the stakeholders involved who will have important things for contribute in order to achieve better virtual relations, a good development in a digital ecosystem and the contribution to the psychomotor development of children and their family environment, as well as that of knowledge.

The technologies came to favor health processes in the care and rehabilitation of infants, remaining as practical tools in the face of the new normal with a not yet controlled or completely stopped pandemic. And although technologies are offering us autonomy and deeper digital skills, issues must be prioritized to find problems, understand them, and propose realistic solutions with the support of technological resources.

References

1. Aguilar Carlos, M.L.: Modelo de Gestión de Proyectos con Inserción de Tecnología Educativa en un Centro de Atención Múltiple. In: Aguascalientes, 2018. Informatic and Computational Sciences, Máster's thesis. Universidad Autónoma de Aguascalientes (2018)
2. Christensen, H., Hansen, K., Kyng, M., Manikas, K.: Analysis and design of software ecosystem architectures – towards the 4S telemedicine ecosystem. Inf. Softw. Technol. **56**(11), 1476–1492 (2014). https://doi.org/10.1016/j.infsof.2014.05.002
3. Briscoe, G., De Wilde, P.: Computing of applied digital ecosystems. In: Proceedings of the International Conference on Management of Emergent Digital EcoSystems - MEDES '09, France, p. 28 (2009). https://doi.org/10.1145/1643823.1643830
4. Cui, Y., et al.: Analysis of service-oriented architecture and scrum software development approach for IIoT. Sci. Program. **2021**, 1–14 (2021). https://doi.org/10.1155/2021/6611407
5. Năftănăilă, I.: Critical analysis of the scrum project management methodology. Ann. Univ. Oradea Econ. Sci. Ser. **17**(4), 435–441 (2008). Research Article
6. C.N. de P. de S. para la A. Infantil Cuidado y Desarrollo Integral: Educación Inicial, Secretaría de Educación Pública: gob.mx. http://www.gob.mx/consejonacionalcai/acciones-y-programas/educacion-inicial-secretaria-de-educacion-publica. Accessed 14 2021
7. van Vugt, V.A., de Kruif, A.J., van der Wouden, J.C., van der Horst, H.E., Maarsingh, O.R.: Experiences of patients and physiotherapists with blended internet-based vestibular rehabilitation: a qualitative interview study. BJGP Open, **4**(5) (2020). https://doi.org/10.3399/bjgpopen20X101092
8. Instituto Mexicano del Seguro Social (IMSS): Detección del Trastorno Específico del Desarrollo Psicomotor en niños de 0 a 3 años. CENETEC (Centro Nacional de Excelencia Tecnológica en Salud), México, D.F., Clinical Practical Guide (2014)
9. Martín Fernández-Mayoralas, D., Fernández-Jaén, A., Fernández Perrone, A.L., Calleja-Pérez, B., Muñoz-Jareño, N.: Detección y manejo del retraso psicomotor en la infancia. https://www.pediatriaintegral.es/publicacion-2015-10/deteccion-y-manejo-del-retraso-psicomotor-en-la-infancia/
10. Michaud, L.J.: Prescribing therapy services for children with motor disabilities. Pediatrics **113**(6), 1836–1838 (2004). https://doi.org/10.1542/peds.113.6.1836
11. Noriego, B.E.M.: Procesos de plasticidad cerebral en pacientes con daño adquirido, Thesis work, Sevilla, p. 40 (2016)

12. Berardi, N., Sale, A.: Ambiente, plasticidad y desarrollo cerebral. Los efectos del entorno en la construcción del individuo. In: Emse Edapp, S.L. (ed.) Editorial. España, 143 p. (2019)
13. Stickdorn, M., Schneider, J., et al.: This is Service Design Thinking. Basics-Tools-Cases. The Netherlands, 1st Ed. 367 p. BIS Publishers, Amsterdam (2011)
14. Klein, L.: UX for Lean Startups. Faster, Smarter User Experience. Research and Design. In: Ries, E. (ed.) 1st Edn. 206 p. O'Reilly, Sebastopol (2013)
15. Gothelf, J., Seiden, J.: Lean UX. Designing Great Products with Agile Teams. 2nd Edn. 181 p. O'Reilly, Sebastopol (2016)
16. Sakzewski, L., Ziviani, J., Boyd Roslin, N.: Delivering evidence-based upper limb rehabilitation for children with cerebral palsy: barriers and enablers identified by three pediatric teams. Phys. Occup. Therapy Pediatr. 34(4), 368–383 (2014)
17. Camden, C., Silva, M.: Pediatric teleheath: opportunities created by the COVID-19 and suggestions to sustain its use to support families of children with disabilities. Phys. Occup. Ther. Pediatr. 41(1), 1–17 (2021). https://doi.org/10.1080/01942638.2020.1825032.ResearhJourn alArticle
18. Laxe, S., et al.: Rehabilitation in the time of COVID-19. Rehabilitación, Editorial SERMEF, 54(3), 149–153 (2020). https://www.ncbi.nlm.nih.gov/pmc/articles/PMC7151338/pdf/main.pdf
19. SEP, Secretaría de Educación Pública; Modelo de atención y cuidado inclusivo para niñas y niños con discapacidad, Aprende en casa. Discapacidad Motora (2020)
20. Doman, G.: What to Do about Your Brain-Injured Child: Or Your Brain-Damaged, Mentally Retarded, Mentally Deficient, Cerebral-Palsied, Epileptic, Autistic, Developmentally Delayed, Down's Child, Editorial Square One Publishers 30th anniversary, p. 318 (2005)
21. Teletón, F.: Teletón (2020). https://teleton.org/tele-rehabilitacion/. Sitio Web
22. APAC Asociación Pro Paralítico Cerebral, APAC 2021- https://apac.mx/. Sitio Web
23. Rao, P.T.: A paradigm shift in the delivery of physical therapy services for children with disabilities in the time of COVID-19 pandemic. Phys. Ther. Rehabil. J. Phys. Ther. 101, 1–3 (2021)

Evaluating of Mobile User Interface: A Design Lenses Approach

Karina Sousa de Paula Santos$^{(\boxtimes)}$ (iD) and Ismar Frango Silveira (iD)

Universidade Presbiteriana Mackenzie, São Paulo, SP, Brazil
{karina.santos,ismar.silveira}@mackenzie.br

Abstract. In the last few years, mobile devices have become the main type of device used to access the Internet in several countries. The software normally used, the personal computer, is gradually being replaced by applications on mobile devices. These applications could be considered as compact versions of software (even though they usually present added features), designed to minimize what is required from the user, and to work quickly and easily. For desktop-oriented software, evaluation processes are designed with the purpose of verifying if the applications are easy to use. However, in the context of mobile devices, there is a dearth of methods for the same purpose. For these reasons, the present work focuses on proposing an evaluation process focused on interfaces for mobile devices. In this way, interviews were performed to understand how evaluation processes are considered within the routines of professionals who deal with mobile devices. The proposed process has a set of associated evaluation lenses. To facilitate access to the process, an application was developed, and it is presented at the end of this paper. This work concludes that there are discussions about processes that help in the evaluation and improvement of interfaces, but they are still deficient, or their executions deprioritized. Accessibility is generally not considered primarily for financial reasons. Therefore, it is necessary to develop more research like this one, which seek to propose new methods that are flexible and useful in practical market contexts.

Keywords: Evaluation · Mobile devices · Design lenses · Mobile apps

1 Introduction

Emerging countries are undergoing a digital transformation, where smartphones are becoming the main device for accessing the internet. Between the years 2013 and 2015, the percentage of adults who reported using a smartphone grew from 45% to 54%. The main responsible for the increase are Malaysia, China and Brazil [1]. In 2018 in Brazil, 98.1% of Brazilians reported using smartphones to access the Internet [2].

For mobile devices (tablets, smartphones or wearable devices) there are so-called applications, or apps, which are not only small versions of common software, but they could have some specific features, like geo-localization and a wide range of sharing methods. Specificities of the devices imply limitations imposed on the development of

© Springer Nature Switzerland AG 2021
P. H. Ruiz et al. (Eds.): HCI-COLLAB 2021, CCIS 1478, pp. 73–83, 2021.
https://doi.org/10.1007/978-3-030-92325-9_6

these applications, requiring that the apps be developed to work quickly and easily, without requiring much from the user. Small physical sizes, limited memory and several methods of data entry are some important aspects to be considered during the mobile development process [3].

In this context, it is important to create applications with easy-to-learn interfaces, effective in use and providing a pleasant user experience [4]. In order to verify that the general interfaces fulfill these objectives, processes that aim to validate these criteria are proposed, usually with sets of heuristics that help the specialist to identify problems. However, traditional assessment methods do not consider the specificities of mobile devices [5].

Given this context, the current work proposes an interface evaluation process for mobile devices that considers the specificities of these devices. This paper was divided in four parts and organized as follows: Item 2 discusses about the related works; Item 3 discusses about methods used in other items; Next section describes the result of the interviews and the phenomenological analysis of the data collected in the interviews; Item 5 presents and discusses about the proposed process, based on the results of the previous item; The paper finishes by presenting some conclusions about the results of this research and some directions for further work.

2   Related Works

Regarding the applicability of heuristics in the context of mobile interfaces, some studies that describe specific sets for this context were studied and they will be discussed in the next paragraphs.

A heuristic evaluation framework was proposed by [6] to analyze applications for mobile learning devices, based on the collection and analysis of articles with this theme in order to identify the best practices described in the literature. In order to show feasibility, the framework was applied in practice, with evaluations of mobile learning applications being executed. As a result, the authors find that the framework is efficient in guiding specialists during the evaluation.

In [7], the authors tried to identify problems related to the usability of games on mobile devices. As a result, they propose a set of new heuristics with an emphasis on this context, with the purpose of improving the usability of games for mobile devices. To develop the set of heuristics, the authors collected reports from users about the experience of playing a car racing game and from those categories they were created and generalized in the form of heuristics. For validation, the tested game was redesigned, based on the proposed heuristics, and the same sample as the first stage of the research was presented. It was concluded that the redesign of the game according to the heuristics represented a significant impact on the design.

In [8], the authors executed a systematic review in order to identify heuristics and usability metrics used in the literature and industry, and thus proposes a set of usability heuristics aimed at mobile applications. The result presents a set of thirteen heuristics that consider the tasks performed by the user, the context in which they are performed and the cognitive load as important attributes of usability. One of the suggested future works is the evaluation of applications that target people with disabilities, in order to obtain data to extend the model considering the range of social and cultural situations that mobile applications can be inserted into.

3 Methods

The research steps were as follows: Data collection; Analysis of the collected data; Synthesis of the findings; and Development of the proposal based on the knowledge acquired.

The data collection consisted of a semi-structured interview with professionals familiar with the development of applications for mobile devices, in order to understand how the evaluation of interfaces is handled by different contexts and professionals. The semi-structured format was chosen because it allows the insertion of relevant questions depending on the context, exploring the experience of the specialists interviewed in a specific way [9].

The analysis of the data collected in the interviews occurred following a phenomenological approach, in order to understand the phenomena reported in the experience of each professional [10].

The conclusion of the phenomenological analysis process goes through the stage of synthesis of the findings, the objective is to integrate all the insights into units of knowledge useful to the research and consistent with the reports of the phenomenon. This step guided the decisions taken to idealize the proposal for the interface evaluation process with an emphasis on mobile devices.

4 Interviews

The interviews aimed to collect data on how the interface evaluation is handled by different contexts and professionals. The questions were designed with the aim of acquiring answers that suggested methods and evaluation processes used in the context of the interviewed professionals. And in this way, the common characteristics of these methods were observed, how they are applied and what moment are used in practice. A convenience sample was used to select the people to be interviewed. This ensured that the interviewees were familiar with the research cut, and potentially could provide relevant data to achieve the intended objectives. Because of this, the group of interviewees was made up of professionals who deal with mobile devices, dealing with designers and developers, at different levels, from the beginner to the specialist. This diversity seeks to represent the different levels of contact that these professionals may have with development processes, including their practices and addictions. There is no intention to make the sample proportional.

In total, ten interviews were carried out, respecting the phenomenological rule of conducting interviews until the moment it is perceived that the reports are repeated; or until it is understood that there are enough reports to understand the essence of the phenomenon [10].

The interviews were conducted via videoconferencing tool, namely Zoom[1]. Each interview lasted approximately forty-five minutes, following the script described in

---

[1] Zoom – Video Conferencing Tool - https://zoom.us/.

Table 1. The data were recorded in text format, literally transcribing what the interviewee reported. The records were made without characterizing the interviewee, removing names of people, companies or institutions. The Notion[2] was used to enable the recording, storage and further analysis of these data. In total, four developers, four designers and two educators were interviewed.

Table 1. Semi-structured interview script.

Question	Objective
How do you describe your roles where you work?	Understand how the assessment processes fit into the professional's reality
In your context, how are the discussions about the quality of the product interface?	Open space to discuss quality and interface evaluation in the context of the interviewee
Are there processes in your professional context that seek to identify points of improvement in the interface?	Investigate the processes commonly performed within the scope of the labor market in order to evaluate and improve the interfaces
Do you see benefit in these processes?	Understand the points of benefit that the professional sees in these practices
Do you recognize efforts to implement accessibility functions in the projects you've worked on?	Understand whether accessibility is considered during the evaluation process as a relevant criterion

4.1 Phenomenological Analysis

With the conclusion of the interviews, the phenomenological analysis of the data began. This process aims to identify the essential nucleus of the phenomenon, for that it is necessary first to detach from previous beliefs to understand the desired phenomenon [11].

The rigor of the data documentation is relevant to the process, for this reason it was decided to transcribe the statements simultaneously during the interviews so that unwanted interpretations would not occur during the collection. This transcription process also accelerated the analysis stage, since the data was already available for reading and reviewing immediately after the interviews.

The phenomenological analysis followed the steps according to [12]. The first stage comprised the initial reading, with the objective of creating familiarity and understanding the interviewee's language, but with no intention of reaching conclusions. Subsequently was performed a new reading, with the objective of identifying units of meaning. This stage identified ninety-one units of meaning relevant to the understanding of the phenomenon, which were first highlighted and later organized in a table to facilitate the manipulation of the data in the subsequent phases.

---

[2] Notion – Text Editor - www.notion.so.

The third step is a time to look at the units previously identified to group them into categories. These categories group similar knowledge that together helps to understand specific aspects of the phenomenon. From the units of meaning highlighted in the previous step, eight categories were developed. The categories created were: Accessibility, Processes, Programmers, Designers, Educators, Quality, Investment and Evaluation.

The categories of Programmers, Designers and Educators comprises reports inherent to work positions, featuring units of meanings that describe the role of these professionals in the evaluation processes. The Accessibility category comprises descriptions that help to understand aspects related to how accessibility is treated during development processes. Processes is the category that comprises the described rites performed by professionals in order to evaluate and apply improvements to the interface. Evaluation and Quality comprise the units of meaning that comprise reports that speak respectively of evaluation and interface quality directly. The Investment category groups reports that describe how financial resources impact the interface design and accessibility efforts.

The last moment is focused on synthesizing the findings, producing descriptions that express the understood concepts related to the investigated phenomenon. Transcription of the reports to the common language of the researchers was performed, eliminating information that is not relevant to the focus of the investigation.

So finally, it was possible to carry out the synthesis by grouping the common aspects among the reports. The main conclusions of the phenomenological analysis include:

1. Most of the reported processes are flexible, without pre-defined rules and documentation standardization.
2. Usability testing with real users is often reported as the central testing process. But at least, reports say that these tests are procrastinated because they do not fit into the work routines.
3. Teachers seek to demonstrate the relevance of evaluating and criticizing the interface, regardless of which process is used.
4. Complex and lengthy text are ignored.
5. Collaborative work between designers contributes to a critical view of the project.
6. There is an expectation that the designer is the professional responsible for considering the accessibility aspects of the interface design.
7. Developers also participate in discussions to criticize and improve the interface. Usually, these processes are based on previous opinions or experiences.
8. Developers participate in the ideation stage in order to assess the technical feasibility of the solution.
9. Products are constantly remade without quality analysis.
10. Criticism without parameters can generate a feeling of dissatisfaction.

The reports also exposed the context that small companies hardly invest in accessibility. Programmers often participate in discussions to adjust functionality and consequently interfaces, but the focus of these professionals is to determine which technologies will be used and what is possible to develop within the stipulated period.

5 Proposed Process

The conclusions reached with the Phenomenology Analysis guided the decisions on the stages of the proposed process. We seek a process that is consistent with the reality of professionals who deal with the development of an interface for mobile devices.

Thus, the objective became to propose a process with characteristics of flexibility, applicability and usefulness. The process needs to be flexible to adapt to the different realities and functions of professionals who deal with the development of applications for mobile devices, including programmers, designers and educators.

Applicability refers to the ability to be applied by professionals of different levels of seniority, being useful for new professionals who are adapting the routines and concepts involved in the interface evaluation processes. It was also intended to generate useful material for consultation and use in the teaching process. Efforts have been made to make the usefulness of the process easily understood, including guidance on documentation and tasks that need to be performed to achieve the objectives of the evaluation.

5.1 Heuristics

To focus the process on mobile devices and to consider the specific characteristics of these devices, it was decided to use the set of heuristics proposed by [13]. From a systematic mapping with a focus on identifying and categorizing heuristics used in interface evaluation for mobile devices, a set of 65 heuristics divided into 4 categories was developed. The heuristics were divided into Accessibility, Aesthetics, Usability and User Experience, in order to cover all the concepts related to the interface design for these devices [13].

As also addressed by [13] it is possible to identify a pattern in the way the heuristics are made available in the analyzed studies. Formats such as lists, trees or tables are commonly used. In extensive sets of heuristics, these structures do not facilitate the understanding by beginners and tend to make the process more complex, since the query of data is not simplified [13].

Thus, in order to organize the heuristics proposed by [13] in a structure that facilitates the understanding and makes the process flexible, it was decided to use the Design Lenses structure. Design Lenses is a concept used in the design of user experience, but which first appeared within the scope of Game Design [14]. The lenses appear in order to guide the designer's eye. Each lens refers to a perspective, and there is a diverse range of lenses to address the breadth of interactive game design [15].

According to [15], lenses make it possible to perceive problems from several different perspectives. This concept is relevant in the context of the evaluation of interfaces for mobile devices, where we are faced with a complexity of interconnected concepts, due the relevant number of heuristics and the division into categories.

In this way 65 cards were diagrammed, forming a deck with four suits that represent the categories. Each card combined a heuristic with a set of questions, forming the lens [14]. Figure 1 shows the anatomy of the diagrammed lenses, each category was given a color to facilitate visual distinction, a code to identify each card and an area to relate cards with complementary concepts were added.

Fig. 1. Lenses diagrammed in Cards formats. Each card has a heuristic and a set of questions to guide the professional during the evaluation. In the upper right corner, there is the code for each card. In the third card, titled Simplicity, it is possible to see the codes of the related cards in the lower right corner.

5.2 Process

To visually represent the process and facilitate the understanding of its activities, steps and documents involved, Business Process Diagram (BPD) was chosen. BPD's goal is to make visual representations of processes viable, so that analysts, developers, entrepreneurs, and others involved in the development of technologies can understand easily. For this, it uses a set of graphic elements and flowchart logic [16].

Figure 2 represents the BPD of the proposed process and shows the three flows planned as a proposal for using the lenses in an evaluation process. Each flow was designed to demonstrate the versatility that the process has, but there is no intention to limit the possibilities.

However, it is always necessary to start the process by reviewing concepts related to the objective of the project, reviewing information known to the target audience and defining the objectives of the evaluation. This decision was made based on the conclusions obtained in the phenomenological analysis since the absence of formal rites for the evaluation processes performed for the professionals was identified as a standard. In order to demonstrate the relevance of carrying out the evaluation process, the elaboration of an action plan based on the information collected during the evaluation is scored as a final activity.

As a main flow, a complete evaluation should be carried out, going through each lens of each category. This flow was focused on longer and more time-consuming processes, which can occur sporadically, but have the potential to provide a large amount of information to the team about which improvements in the interface are necessary.

There are two possible alternatives flows, the first is to use all the cards of only one category. It is advisable to apply this approach when the professional is already aware that the interface is deficient in one of the categories. In this way the process will help the professional to identify arguments, structure the existing problems and define an action plan.

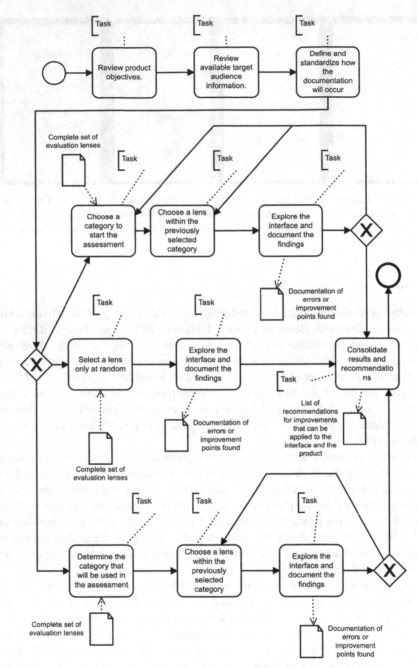

Fig. 2. Visual representation of the proposed process.

The second alternative flow option is to randomly draw one of the lenses and evaluate only using it. It is a shorter flow, which will not provide a large amount of information, but can assist in the incorporation of a culture of evaluations.

The lenses alone can be used as a review and study material, and can be applied within the academic scope, to introduce the concepts to students in a playful way.

5.3 Distribution

The phenomenological analysis also showed that it is common for professionals to report that they do not have knowledge about interface evaluation methodologies, while reporting that they consider that these methodologies can be useful in their work routines. Reports also criticize the way in which these processes commonly do not reach professionals easily, either due to factors related to language, lack of disclosure or absence of easily accessible content. Because of these reports, it was decided to take a first step towards making the results of this research easily available.

Fig. 3. Application developed to facilitate access to the proposed process and to the lenses. The first and second images are the home screen, where you can filter by categories or search for any word in the letter. The third screen is still under construction, it should contain complete explanations of the proposal and references.

Because of that a mobile application was developed, containing all lenses, separated by categories and with an explanation of how to use them. It is also possible to search by title, category or information contained in the body of the letter. In Fig. 3, it is possible to observe screens of the developed application. The application is available[3] for smartphones from the Apple ecosystem, on the App Store[4].

---

[3] Evaluation lenses – Developed application - https://apps.apple.com/br/app/evaluation-lenses/id1566382345?l.

[4] App Store - Digital mobile application distribution service developed and operated by Apple inc. - https://www.apple.com/br/app-store/.

6   Conclusions

In summary, discussions about processes that help in the evaluation and improvement of interfaces exist, but it is still deficient. There are gaps in the knowledge of professionals about the existing methods, especially in the case of beginners. There is also procrastination in relation to the execution of the methods, for reasons that involve project deadlines and priorities.

Accessibility is a question that is not normally considered, even in contexts that have formal evaluation rites. The justification that accessibility is neglected for financial reasons was recurrent.

These elements motivate the development of more research like this, which seeks to propose new methods that are flexible and useful in the practical contexts of the market. But going further is necessary, investing in dissemination so that the research is accessible by more professionals and can generate real impacts on the quality of interfaces for mobile devices.

Future work will be necessary to validate the ideas contained in this research, especially the aspects related to the proposed process. The next steps involve a series of tests and validations, seeking to identify whether the proposed process is useful, flexible and to prove its applicability.

References

1. Poushter, J.: Smartphone ownership and internet usage continues to climb in emerging economies. Pew Res. Center. **22**(1), 1–44 (2016). https://www.diapoimansi.gr/PDF/pew_res earch%201.pdf
2. Tokarnia, M.: Celular é o principal meio de acesso à internet no país. Agência Brasil, Rio de Janeiro, 2020-04, 29 Apr 2020. https://agenciabrasil.ebc.com.br/economia/noticia/2020-04/celular-e-o-principal-meio-de-acesso-internet-no-pais
3. Nacheva, R.: Standardization issues of mobile usability, pp. 149–157 (2020). https://www.learntechlib.org/p/216463/
4. Rogers, Y., Sharp, H., Preece, J.: Design de interação, Bookman Editora, ISBN 8582600062 (2013)
5. Inostroza, R., et al.: Usability heuristics for touchscreen-based mobile devices. In: 2012 Ninth International Conference on Information Technology-New Generations, pp. 662–667. IEEE (2012). https://doi.org/10.1109/ITNG.2012.134
6. Kumar, B.A., Goundar, M.S., Chand, S.S.: A framework for heuristic evaluation of mobile learning applications. Educ. Inf. Technol. **25**(4), 3189–3204 (2020). https://doi.org/10.1007/s10639-020-10112-8
7. Robson, R.S., Sabahat, N.: Heuristic based approach for usability evaluation of mobile games. In: 2020 International Conference on Computing, Electronics & Communications Engineering (iCCECE), 17 Aug 2020, pp. 156–161. IEEE (2020). https://doi.org/10.1109/iCCECE 49321.2020.9231175
8. Da Costa, R.P., Canedo, E.D., De Sousa, R.T., Albuquerque, R.D., Villalba, L.J.: Set of usability heuristics for quality assessment of mobile applications on smartphones. IEEE Access **11**(7), 116145–116161 (2019). https://doi.org/10.1109/ACCESS.2019.2910778
9. Longhurst, R.: Semi-structured interviews and focus groups. Key Methods Geogr. **3**(2), 143–156 (2003). ISBN: 9781446298602

10. Paulo, R.M.: A compreensão geométrica da criança: um estudo fenomenológico, Doctoral dissertation, Instituto de Geociências e Ciências Exatas da Universidade Estadual Paulista. http://mariabicudo.com.br/resources/TESES_e_DISSERTAÇÕES/Rosa%20Monteiro%20Paulo_M.pdf

11. Graças, E.M.: Pesquisa qualitativa e a perspectiva fenomenológica: fundamentos que norteiam sua trajetória. REME rev. min. enferm, pp. 28–33 (2000). https://pesquisa.bvsalud.org/portal/resource/fr/lil-733573

12. Bastos, C.C.: Pesquisa qualitativa de base fenomenológica e a análise da estrutura do fenômeno situado: algumas contribuições. Revista Pesquisa Qualitativa. 5(9), 442–451 (2017). ISSN: 2525-8222

13. Santos, K., Silveira, I.: Interface analysis criteria for mobile devices: a systematic mapping. Jornadas Iberoamericanas de IHC (2021, to be published)

14. Deterding, S.: Skill atoms as design lenses for user-centered gameful design. In: Workshop Papers CHI2013 (2013). http://gamification-research.org/wp-content/uploads/2013/03/Deterding.pdf

15. Schell, J.: The Art of Game Design: A Book of Lenses. CRC Press, Boco Raton (2008). ISBN: 0615218288

16. White, S.A.: Introduction to BPMN. IBM Cooperation (2004). http://yoann.nogues.free.fr/IMG/pdf/07-04_WP_Intro_to_BPMN_-_White-2.pdf

Face Recognition Efficiency Enhancements Using Tensorflow and WebAssembly: A Practical Approach

Ricardo Martín Manso$^{(\boxtimes)}$ ⓘ and Pablo Escrivá Gallardo ⓘ

Universidad Carlos III de Madrid, Madrid, Spain
`ricardma@inf.uc3m.es, 100348802@alumnos.uc3m.es`

Abstract. In this research paper we have studied the use of WebAssembly technology applied to the problem of facial recognition in real world Human-Computer Interaction (HCI) applications. Multiple parameters determining the system were tested using a large image data set. Experiments have shown how, with careful choice of system parameters, very high levels of accuracy can be achieved for large populations, even using only a few pre-stored images per person. In addition, a web application was developed to compare the efficiency of facial recognition using different backends of Tensorflow.js in the browser. The results show that WebAssembly technology is perfectly operational for use in this area and provides user experience improvements in terms of efficiency and stability. In the coming months, WebAssembly is expected to incorporate two relevant developments: Single Instruction Multiple Data (SIMD) and Multithreading (MT). Our experiments show that by enabling these features WebAssembly can provide a very suitable technical solution for in-browser face recognition.

Keywords: Webassembly · Wasm · Face recognition · Tensorflow

1 Introduction

Facial recognition provides a simple and convenient way for users to interact with computer applications, but there are still technological and social barriers to overcome in the real world. Elderly people are the group that can benefit the most from the extensive use of affordable, accurate and privacy-centered biometric solutions [1]. This population often faces many problems when using banking, health, or government agencies services. Authentication processes are, in many cases, overwhelming barriers and generators of stress for all users, particularly for those who have a more limited capacity for technological adaptation and thus need a better designed Human-Computer Interaction (HCI).

The different players that participate in the digital revolution, in one way or another, government agencies, institutions, companies, software engineers, are legally and ethically obliged to develop accessible solutions that ensure that no one is excluded from the effective use of digital services. Having access to free, efficient, and inherently respectful architecture with the user's privacy, can be an effective way to achieve this goal.

© Springer Nature Switzerland AG 2021
P. H. Ruiz et al. (Eds.): HCI-COLLAB 2021, CCIS 1478, pp. 84–97, 2021.
https://doi.org/10.1007/978-3-030-92325-9_7

The advances made in the last decade in computer vision algorithms, combined with the emergence of machine learning in this field, have facilitated the development of affordable facial recognition solutions [2]. At the software level, open-source libraries such as Tensorflow [3] and OpenCV [3] have greatly simplified the development of these types of applications through simple programming interfaces. For instance, Tensorflowallows the user to create, train and utilize neural models in various languages such as C or Python, while OpenCV contains a multitude of predefined computer vision algorithms. However, powerful servers available 24 h a day are needed to scale up these types of applications to a large number of users. Moreover, utilization of all this calculation capacity involves acquisition of equipment, maintenance, and energy consumption expenses. Thus, facial recognition application developers have traditionally delegated these processes to services such as Amazon Rekognition [5] or Google Cloud Vision [5] to reduce the initial capital investment, paying only for the actual number of users.

Nonetheless, this strategy carries significant risks and disadvantages. On the one hand, applications are becoming more and more expensive as the user base increases. Each call to Microsoft or Amazon services has a cost [7]. It is important to take into consideration that sensitive images that are used to carry out facial recognition, are sent through the internet to third parties.

Local processing through the web browser on the user's own device, t available in modern web applications, is becoming a more popular alternative to cloud computing for applications based on facial recognition [9], as it is currently possible to use the JavaScript and WebAssembly backends of powerful libraries, such as Opencv.js or Tensorflow.js. One of the many advantages of this approach is that it allows these applications to be scaled up to as many users as necessary, since most of the computational effort is carried out in the client's browser. In addition, by not depending on external services, user information never leaves their device and, therefore, the risk to their privacy is reduced. Thus, combining the *precision* provided by these libraries with the ease of scaling up, the extensive use of these solutions is at hand, even for companies and users with limited resources.

In this research paper, we have studied the use of WebAssembly technology applied to the problem of facial recognition in the client's browser.

2 Background

2.1 Tensorflow and Tensorflow.js

Tensorflow is an open-source platform, developed by Google, which consists of a series of tools and libraries for the development of projects using machine learning. It was developed in 2015 and its name refers to Tensors, multidimensional data arrays that form the basic unit of information when performing operations with neural networks [2].

It is mainly used with C and Python languages and is oriented to be executed on servers given the complexity of the operations and algorithms of neural models.

In 2018, the Google Brain team developed a Tensorflow implementation, Tensorflow.js (hereinafter, Tfjs). Tfjs allows the training, deployment and use of neural networks directly in the web browser, using the Tensorflow programming interface in languages from web environments like JavaScript, Node.js or recently WebAssembly [10].

In this way, applications that depend on neural models can be distributed more quickly and easily through the web and be executed by the users themselves. In addition, it not only provides flexibility for developers, but it also allows the use of neural models on any type of hardware, as long as they support current web browsers.

Tfjs is distributed in a modular way to be able to take advantage of different web technologies and simply choose which one to use depending on the characteristics of the device. Some of the backends that Tfjs includes are:

- CPU: It is the basic implementation of Tfjs, written in JavaScript.
- WEBGL: Uses the OpenGL standard to speed up the execution of algorithms by accessing the device's GPU.
- WASM: Use WebAssembly to speed up the process.
- NODE: Version for servers based on Node.js.

2.2 WebAssembly

WebAssembly [11], also known by its acronym WASM, is an open standard of instructions in the web browser that makes possible to reach execution speeds of neural models very close to the native applications written in C [12]. It was developed in 2015 and can be considered the "evolution" of the asm.js library, a subset of the JavaScript language that allows compiling C code for the web. It was not designed to replace JavaScript, but rather to complement it. With WASM it is possible to compile C or C++ code into an assembly-like language by using a compiler such as Emscripten. Projects like Google Earth or Figma use WebAssembly to offer an experience similar to desktop applications on the web.

The WebAssembly development process evolves based on proposals through their official Github repository. In this sense, each feature goes through a total of four phases, the last one being the standardization of the proposal by web browsers [13].

One of the most important proposals for WebAssembly is the adoption of the Single Instruction Multiple Data (SIMD) specification. It is a set of processor instructions that allows operations to be carried out on a multitude of data simultaneously using vectors and, thus, speed up the execution of algorithms [14]. The SIMD adoption proposal is in standardization phase of the WebAssembly development process. Although, it is not yet widely available in web browsers, it can be enabled experimentally. Google Chrome, for example, allows it through the use of flags in "chrome: // flags".

Another of the current WebAssembly proposals is the incorporation of multithreads (MT), through JavaScript webworkers [15], to be able to execute algorithms in parallel. This proposal is in the second phase, still a few months from its deployment.

2.3 OpenCV as an Alternative to Tensorflow

For the execution of this research project, the use of OpenCV has been considered as an alternative. It is a library developed by Intel in 1999 and oriented to Computer Vision, similar to Tensorflow and designed to be used with C and C++. It also has a version for

JavaScript and WASM: OpenCV.js. Both Tensoflow.js and OpenCV.js are open source software projects.

One of the main differences between the two is that Tensorflow has a more general approach, compared to OpenCV that specializes only in both new and traditional Computer Vision algorithms.

For this study, Tensorflow was finally chosen because of the degree of flexibility it provides, allowing us to experiment with almost any neural network model set up for facial recognition and incorporate any advance that occurs in the field almost immediately. Although the use of neural models is more complex, it offers more efficient and accurate results.

2.4 Neural Networks for Facial Recognition

In the last decade, convolutional neural network technology has become the *de facto* standard in image recognition with neural networks [20, 21]. To study how Tensorflow.js behaves in its different implementations, multiple neural networks were used throughout the experimentation process for the detection of faces in images and the extraction of vectors of facial coordinates.

The neural network used to identify a person's facial features is based on a ResNet34 architecture [16]. The choice of this model instead of more modern alternatives, is due to the engineering compromise between the *precision* of the network and his computational needs [22, 23]. For the choice of the network model, the main consideration was *precision*, limiting the search to models that can offer at least 1 FPS (in hardware low cost), do not require special features and can currently be implemented in WASM. Thus, Resnet50, MobileNet V3(small), SqueezNet and RestNet34 were considered. Finally, we have chosen Resnet34 because, in our experiments, it has been the most accurate, sufficiently fast, compatible and available in Wasm.

3 Experimental Design

The experiments have been grouped into the following categories: Experiment A, designed to precisely determine the values that the free parameters of the system should take, and Experiment B, designed to determine the relative efficiency of each implementation of Tfjs.

3.1 Facial Recognition Process

Throughout this study, we performed facial recognition as follows:

1. The face is detected in the foreground of each image, thus obtaining the coordinates of the rectangle that contains it.
2. Then, the system calculates the standard landmarks for each face.
3. Next, the descriptor vector for each face is calculated. Said vector, for the neural network models used here, is made up of 128 floating-point numbers, with values in the range [0.0, 1.0].

4. Once steps 1, 2 and 3 have been carried out, the image descriptor vector is compared with the vectors previously stored in a structure referred to as *model*, in these experiments. This data structure allows subjects to be associated with an arbitrary number of face descriptors. The comparison is implemented by calculating the Euclidean distance between the vectors containing the descriptors. The result of the comparison will be a number in the range [0.0, 1.0]. A value of 0.0 means the two faces are totally similar and 1.0 that there is no similarity at all.

An image is classified as belonging to person i if the distance between the image descriptors vector and the descriptors of any of the images included in the model, belonging to person i, has the lowest value of all the comparisons and, furthermore, is lower than the given threshold. If no comparison offers a distance less than the established threshold, the recognition result will be "unclassified". The threshold from which one face is considered sufficiently similar to another is a system parameter and allows adaptation to different possible applications. In some, where maximum *precision* is required, a low threshold will be used. In others, where false positives do not have a great impact, a higher threshold may be used.

3.2 Experiment A1

This experiment was designed to assess the Euclidean distance between descriptors of similar faces and between faces belonging to different subjects, in order to determine or guide the decision on the value to be used as a threshold in a real application.

For this, a database of 1,000 subjects was created, with 150 different faces for each subject. In total 150,000 images. The images have been obtained thanks to the datasets provided by the Visual Geometry Group, Department of Engineering Science, University of Oxford for research purposes [17].

The images corresponding to each subject are shown in different poses, angles, haircuts, lighting, and have often been taken with different devices.

The experimental process was assembled using a Node.js application, programmed using the same configuration and neural network models as those used in the live application.

The pretrained neural network models are based on those published by Vincent Mühler, in his software repository face-api [18].

The procedure used followed these steps:

1. The face in the foreground of each photo has been detected using "faceapi.nets.tinyFaceDetector" (Tiny Yolo V2 modified by face-api's author).
2. Next, the landmarks of each face have been calculated using "faceapi.nets.faceLandmark68TinyNet".
3. Then, the vector of descriptors for each face has been calculated, using a ResNet-34 type implementation, pretrained by GitHub user Davisking [18].
4. Once steps 1, 2 and 3 have been carried out, for all the images, each vector was compared to all the others.
5. Histograms were calculated for the distances obtained for both pairs of images of the same person, as well as for comparisons between images of different people.

6. Finally, the *precision*, TruePositive/(TruePositive + FalsePositive), and the rate of *rejection*, FalseNegative/(TruePositive + FalseNegative), was calculated.

3.3 Experiment A2

In a real application, (*i.e.,* a company or institution that wants to make use of the system), the data model will store *NF* faces of each person to be recognized for each of the *NP* people that make up the population of interest. For example, if a company wants to make an application that applies this technique available to its clients, it must model (*i.e.,* obtain the descriptors of a certain number of images of each client) to later be able to identify the client from a given image. Furthermore, the system must be able to reject images belonging to people who are not client. We denoted the total of clients of the company, in this experiment, as *population*. Experiment A2 was assembled to study this issue.

To perform Experiment A2, the global image dataset (explained in Sect. 3.2) was divided into random groups of people. The experiment was repeated 100 times, and each time dividing the people into different groups. Thus, P50 is a population of 50 different people, P250 corresponds to populations of 250 people and P1000 to populations of 1,000 people. Once the people were divided into populations, a small number of images of each person was randomly chosen to form part of the *model*. Models with 5, 10, 25 and 50 faces per subject were considered. Next, the rest of each person's images were traversed, and an attempt was made to classify using the general procedure explained in Sect. 3.1. The experiment was repeated using different threshold values.

With the data obtained, it was possible to compare the *precision* against the size of the target population and the number of images used to generate the *model*. Also, it was possible to study the effect of the threshold parameter on both ratios.

3.4 Experiment B: FaceApp

Experiment B was designed to determine the relative efficiency of the different backends of Tfjs. For this, a web application (FaceApp) that uses Tfjs and allows us to easily switch between CPU, WebGL, WASM and server backends was developed.

Using this application on different devices, detailed in Sect. 3.4.2, made it possible to obtain different usage metrics to compare the processing times for each backend. The average times of the first processed frame and the rest are given separately. This is done because there are technologies (*i.e.,* WebGL) that are very fast in general, but on some devices take time to process the first frame (initialization penalty), which is a problem for certain types of applications.

3.4.1 FaceApp Application

The application uses the React user interface development library and will be deployed to the clients through the Github Pages service. The server version was developed in a Node.js environment, hosted in an instance of Heroku service, and uses technology WebSockets to establish a real time communication with the user. FaceApp implements a responsive web design, so it can be used on both desktop and mobile devices.

The operation of the FaceApp application is very simple: when the user accesses the URL, the JavaScript code of Tfjs is downloaded alongside the binaries that make up the facial recognition neural networks. Then, React initializes the Tfjs library with the backend selected by the user.

First, the user will have to be registered by providing one or more images of their face with their name or unique identifier. Then, the application will generate an array of images descriptors vectors used to recognize the user. It will be saved in the local storage of the user's browser in JSON format as a dictionary with the name or ID as the key and the array as the value. In this way, it is possible to register multiple users on the same device.

Finally, the application will ask the user for permission to access their device's webcam through the WebRTC interface. After obtaining the user's permission, a stream of images will be generated from the camera, which are processed frame by frame by the different neural networks that make up the facial recognition system. The coordinates of the faces identified in each image will be extracted and the Euclidean distance will be calculated with the arrays previously saved in the browser, establishing a threshold, maximum distance for recognition, of 0.6.

An HTML canvas will be generated in each frame that includes: the original frame, a box marking the location of the face in the image, the name of the user that has been recognized and a percentage of confidence.

3.4.2 Selected Devices

A series of devices that represent the general public were chosen, ranging from desktops, laptops, mobiles and tablets and are described in Table 1.

Table 1. Description of the hardware of the devices selected.

Device	CPU	GPU	RAM
MacBook Pro 13	2,9 GHz Intel Core i5	Intel Iris Graphics 550 1536 MB	8 GB 2133 MHz
ASUS Laptop	Intel Core i5	HD Graphics 766 MHz	8 GB DDR3 1066 MHz
PC	3,9 GHz AMD Ryzen 3	GTX 970 4 GB GDDR5 7 GHz	
Intel NUC	3 GHz Intel Core i3 8109U	Iris Plus Graphics 655	16 GB DDR4-2400
iMac 2010	2.8 GHz Core i5	ATI Radeon HD5750 1024 MB	10 GB DDR3 1333 MHz
iPad Air 2	1.5GHz A8X 64-bit ARM	PowerVR GXA6850 450 MHz	2 GB LPDDR3

3.4.3 Procedure

To measure the efficiency of the different backends of Tfjs in each of the selected devices, it is necessary to obtain the processing times of the frames by using the FaceApp application.

First, FaceApp will show the time it takes for neural networks to load and process the first frame. Afterwards, it will calculate the average time of the rest of the frames of the stream and obtain an arithmetic average of all of them. Once the times stabilize, the mean in milliseconds will be recorded.

Finally, the process will be repeated a total of 10 times for each device and backend.

4 Results and Analysis

4.1 Results for Experiments A

Figure 1 shows the results of the comparison of the 150,000 images with each other. The Euclidean distances obtained when comparing the descriptors of images belonging to the same face are grouped mainly in the range of 0.3 to 0.6, with a maximum at 0.45. In the case of images belonging to different people, almost all the distances exceed the value of 0.6. In this case, the maximum is 0.85.

This distribution of distances implies that, the system is efficient in separating images of the same or different faces, simply using the value of 0.5 as the detection threshold.

The *precision* is high in all scenarios using a threshold of 0.5, as shown in Fig. 2, As the size of the population increases, the *precision* decreases slightly, although it remains in all cases above 95%. In small populations, the *precision* obtained is close to 100%.

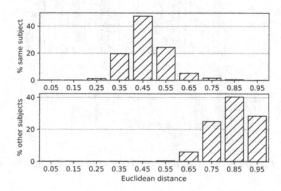

Fig. 1. Histograms of Euclidean distances for same subjects and different subjects.

On the other hand, the proportion of unrecognized images, called *rejection rate*, is lower than 10%. This ratio decreases when we use more faces in our model.

Therefore, by storing 5 faces of each person to be recognized by the *model*, we will be able to obtain a high *precision* in the recognition without having to make use of the space and the extra calculation capacity that would involve the consideration of a greater number of images per person. On the other hand, a rate of *rejection* of 10% is usually

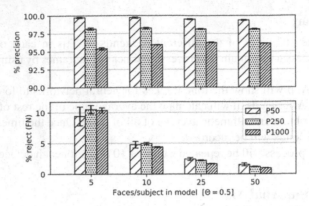

Fig. 2. *Precision* and ratio rejection by number of faces per subjects.

acceptable since it discards 10% of the video frames, but it does not confuse one person with another.

Figure 3 shows the *precision* and *rejection* rates obtained, in populations of 50, 250 and 1,000 people, with different threshold values and for different models with 5, 10, 25 and 50 faces. The results show that the *precision* decreases as the *threshold* increases, especially in large populations. The *rejection* rate decreases even faster as the threshold increases. Models with 10 faces obtain *precision* similar to those with 5 faces, and a lower *rejection* rate.

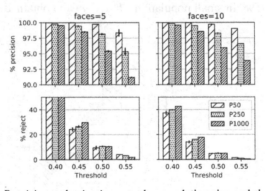

Fig. 3. *Precision* and *rejection rates* by population size and *threshold*.

4.2 Experiment B Results: Processing Time Per Frame (FaceApp Tool)

Tables 2 and 3 show the processing times for the first and all frames, respectively.

It is important to note that there are devices that are better suited (*i.e.*, better graphics cards) for the use of WebGL. WebGL is the technology that shows the highest mean and standard deviations in the processing time for the first frame (Table 2), which indicates that it is much more sensitive than others to the configuration of each device. These fluctuations in the processing time of the first frame by WebGL mean that the user will not have a consistent experience with the application and that the initial delay cannot be easily predicted. Plain JavaScript (CPU) is nearly 6 times more stable than WebGL, while WASM + SIMD + MT reduces variability by several orders of magnitude compared to CPU.

Table 2. Time and standard deviation for every 10 processing iterations of the first frame.

Device	CPU	WebGL	Server	WASM	Wasm + SIMD
MacBook Pro	1574 ± 24	7637 ± 37	476 ± 70	959 ± 206	1169 ± 53
PC	1295 ± 32	4117 ± 26	401 ± 93	562 ± 29	616 ± 14
iMac 2010	1963 ± 12	5093 ± 60	902 ± 203	548 ± 14	548 ± 14
Asus Laptop	2452 ± 45	4130 ± 61	N/A	1126 ± 57	1800 ± 00
iPhone X	923 ± 73	678 ± 10	653 ± 97	2965 ± 825	N/A
iPad Air 2	2039 ± 19	2423 ± 28	531 ± 164	7378 ± 1057	N/A
Intel NUC	1667 ± 34	569 ± 33	N/A	557 ± 35	N/A
AVERAGE	**1667 ± 45**	**4117 ± 264**	**531 ± 97**	**959 ± 57**	**892 ± 14**

Table 3. Processing time per frame.

Device	CPU	WebGL	Server	WASM	WASM + SIMD
MacBook Pro	1624 ± 51	104 ± 1	238 ± 36	208 ± 2	90 ± 2
PC	1535 ± 45	93 ± 3	217 ± 12	174 ± 3	93 ± 0.8
iMac 2010	2016 ± 58	92 ± 2	524 ± 64	128 ± 1	128 ± 1
Asus Laptop	2367 ± 170	250 ± 7	N/A	290 ± 65	297 ± 9
iPhone X	662 ± 72	95 ± 1	108 ± 2	202 ± 13	N/A
iPad Air 2	1411 ± 141	217 ± 11	403 ± 145	606 ± 89	N/A
Intel NUC	1668 ± 32	79 ± 16	N/A	177 ± 16	N/A
AVERAGE	**1624 ± 58**	**95 ± 3**	**238 ± 36**	**202 ± 13**	**110 ± 1.47**

Figure 4 shows that, on average, the first frame takes just over 4 s when using WebGL. With plain JavaScript (CPU) the processing time of the first frame is 1600 ms. WASM, on the other hand, takes only 960 ms in its basic implementation, reducing even more (300 ms) if the SIMD and MT functionalities are activated. Regarding the server backend (Node.js), the first frame only takes 530 ms on average, since it does not require a previous initialization (the server is always ready to process the images).

For the remaining frames, JavaScript (CPU) is far from the result with times greater than 1500 ms per frame while the rest do not exceed 250 ms in any case. All other local processing backends are more efficient than server processing. WebGL takes half the time to process each frame on average, compared to the basic WebAssembly backend. However, if we compare it to WASM with its experimental features enabled, we see a 10% improvement over WebGL.

The standard deviation of the mean of ms for each processed frame shows that the backend obtains the most variable times is JavaScript (CPU), with almost 60 ms of average difference between frames. Again, we see that the backends in the client (with the exception of CPU) are more stable than in the case of the server, which suffers the normal interferences of a communication through the Internet with WebSockets (added to the variability of the processing in the server). Although the stability of WASM is low compared to WebGL (slightly more than 4 times higher), if we activate SIMD the stability increases greatly until reaching single-digit figures (ms) with around 50% improvement over WebGL. In this case, the MT option in WASM does not improve the stability of the process but instead adds a few tenths of variability compared to using only SIMD. However, even in this case, WebGL times improved by 40%.

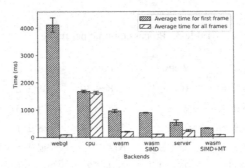

Fig. 4. Time to process first and all frames.

Figure 5 shows the analysis of the results grouped by device (only those that support SIMD and MT). The JavaScript times (CPU) in all cases are much higher than the rest (truncated in the graph to improve readability).

WebGL offers better results than WASM, in its default configuration. WASM, will outperform the rest when all its experimental features are enabled, with the exception of the iMac, where WebGL slightly improves the times.

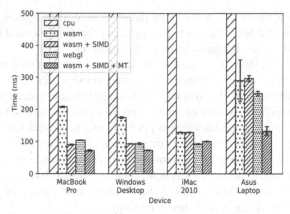

Fig. 5. Processing time for each of the devices. CPU times are truncated.

5 Conclusion

We conclude that, depending on the size of our population and the minimum acceptable rate of *precision* and *rejection*, we can design applications based on models with a small number of images per person, usually between 5 to 10 images, that correctly detect people. The 95% of the images will recognize a person properly and the remaining 5% will be classified almost entirely as unrecognized. The number of false recognitions may be kept relatively low by selecting the appropriate parameters.

In Experiment A, the system parameters, detection threshold and number of images per person were set. In Experiment B, different backends of Tensorflow.js in the browser, JavaScript (CPU), WebGL and WASM were compared. WASM was tested for three different configurations, default, SIMD enabled and SIMD and MT enabled. In addition, the recognition in the user's browser was compared to sending the images to a server. The remote recognition was carried out in a similar way, but with the computational resources of the server.

Of all the client backends, the most advantageous would be WebGL and WASM. WebGL has the advantage that it is widely available today and offers a very competitive *frames per second* (FPS) rate. However, depending on the graphic capabilities of each device, it presents a wide variability of recognition times. Consequently, it can create problems of user experience and of real compatibility with some less powerful devices. In addition to this, in applications where the processing time of the first frame is relevant, it generates a delay that is probably too high.

WASM, on the other hand, has proven to be a very promising technology. In its default configuration it does not yet reach the WebGL performance, it does not stray too far from it, with the added advantage of its lower variability between frames. In the first frame time, it proves to be available in less time than WebGL (5x speed-up). Moreover, WASM can also be ran on devices with very low graphics power since the graphics card is not used.

Regarding the experimental features of WASM: SIMD and SIMD and MT, they are clearly the winners in all the sections. When these features become widely available, and everything suggests that it will be in a few months, the WASM option with SIMD and MT enabled will probably be the best technological option to implement face recognition locally and provide better Human-Computer Interactions.

The results of this study indicate that the local recognition using only the browser resources approach is very competitive with respect to the server option. If we combine the technical possibility with the advantages offered by this solution, simple scaling up to many users and improved privacy by not sending face images outside the user's device, we can conclude that this architecture is perfectly usable in real applications and, in many cases, it is an advantageous design over the use of remote service-based solutions.

As future work, it would be convenient to extend the study to the use of other neural models potentially useful in this field, such as: SqueezeNet, EfficientNets, ShuffleNets and MobileNet v3. Also, obtaining feedback from real users could bring another important perspective to the use of this technology.

References

1. Sanchez, V., Pfeiffer, C., Skeie, N.-O.: A review of smart house analysis methods for assisting older people living alone. J. Sens. Actuator Netw. **6**(3), 11 (2017)
2. Haas, A., et al.: Bringing the web up to speed with WebAssembly. In: Proceedings of the 38th ACM SIGPLAN Conference on Programming Language Design and Implementation (2017). https://doi.org/10.1145/3062341.3062363
3. TensorFlow: Tensorflow.org. https://www.tensorflow.org/. Accessed 28 Apr 2021
4. OpenCV – OpenCV: Opencv.org, 09 Feb 2021. https://opencv.org/. Accessed 28 Apr 2021
5. Amazon Rekognition: Amazon.com. https://aws.amazon.com/es/rekognition/. Accessed 28 Apr 2021
6. Vision AI: Google.com. https://cloud.google.com/vision/. Accessed: 28 Apr 2021
7. Youssef, A.E.: Exploring cloud computing services and applications, Psu.edu. https://citeserx.ist.psu.edu/viewdoc/download?doi=10.1.1.649.485&rep=rep1&type=pdf. Accessed 28 Apr 2021
8. Zhou, M., Zhang, R., Xie, W., Qian, W., Zhou, A.: Security and privacy in cloud computing: a survey. In: 2010 Sixth International Conference on Semantics, Knowledge and Grids, pp. 105–112 (2010). https://doi.org/10.1109/SKG.2010.19
9. Taheri, S., Vedienbaum, A., Nicolau, A., Hu, N., Haghighat, M.R.: OpenCV.js: computer vision processing for the open web platform. In: Proceedings of the 9th ACM Multimedia Systems Conference (2018). https://doi.org/10.1145/3204949.3208126
10. Gerard, C.: TensorFlow.js. In: Practical Machine Learning in JavaScript, pp. 25–43. Apress, Berkeley (2021)
11. WebAssembly: Webassembly.org. https://webassembly.org/. Accessed 28 Apr 2021
12. Herrera, D., Chen, H., Lavoie, E., Hendren, L.: Numerical computing on the web: benchmarking for the future. In: Proceedings of the 14th ACM SIGPLAN International Symposium on Dynamic Languages (2018). https://doi.org/10.1145/3276945.3276968
13. WebAssembly proposals. https://github.com/WebAssembly/proposals. Accessed 28 Apr 2021
14. Jibaja, I., et al.: Vector parallelism in JavaScript: language and compiler support for SIMD. In: 2015 International Conference on Parallel Architecture and Compilation (PACT), pp. 407–418 (2015). https://doi.org/10.1109/PACT.2015.33
15. Green, I.: Web Workers: Multithreaded Programs in JavaScript. O'Reilly Media, Sebastopol (2012)

16. He, K., Zhang, X., Ren, S., Sun, J.: Deep residual learning for image recognition. In: 2016 IEEE Conference on Computer Vision and Pattern Recognition (CVPR), pp. 770–778 (2016)
17. Cao, Q., Shen, L., Xie, W., Parkhi, O.M., Zisserman, A.: VGGFace2: a dataset for recognising faces across pose and age. In: 2018 13th IEEE International Conference on Automatic Face & Gesture Recognition (FG 2018), pp. 67–74 (2018). https://doi.org/10.1109/FG.2018.00020
18. Mühler, V.: face-api.js. https://github.com/justadudewhohacks/face-api.js. Accessed 30 Apr 2021
19. King, D.E.: dlib-models. https://github.com/davisking/dlib-models. Accessed 30 Apr 2021
20. Serkan, K., et al.: 1D convolutional neural networks and applications: a survey. Mech. Syst. Signal Process. **151**, 107398 (2021). https://doi.org/10.1016/j.ymssp.2020.107398
21. Waseem, R., Zenghui, W.: Deep convolutional neural networks for image classification: a comprehensive review. Neural Comput. **29**(9), 2352–2449 (2017). https://doi.org/10.1162/neco_a_00990
22. Simone, B., et al.: Benchmark analysis of representative deep neural network architectures. https://doi.org/10.1109/ACCESS.2018.2877890
23. Learn Artificial Intelligence: Course, Deep Reinforcement Learning Free; CV, Self Attention. Best deep CNN architectures and their principles: from AlexNet to EfficientNet

Gamified Model to Support Shopping in Closed Spaces Aimed at Blind People: A Systematic Literature Review

Valentina Solano[1]([✉])[iD], Carlos Sánchez[1][iD], César Collazos[1][iD], Manuel Bolaños[1][iD], and Valéria Farinazzo[2][iD]

[1] Universidad del Cauca, Popayán, Colombia
{smvalentina,scarlos,ccollazos,mbolanos}@unicauca.edu.co
[2] Universidad Presbiteriana, Mackenzie, Brasil

Abstract. Visual impairment is defined as the condition that directly affects the perception of images in whole or in part, in the world there are approximately 1.3 billion people who have some type of visual impairment. Currently there are new technological developments or methodologies that support people with this disability to develop activities of daily life such as: physically moving in the environment, identifying colors, among others; The activity of interest for this paper is: the purchase of physical products in supermarkets for blind people. A systematic review of the literature was conducted to find out what has been done to enable blind people to shop independently in closed spaces. For the documentation search, we defined search strings with keywords related to the research, this allowed us to find a total of 1002 studies found in 5 databases. The results of this study show that it is possible to use less invasive technological developments to assist people during the different steps of the buying process in closed spaces and to identify that there is a tendency to use smartphone-based tool technologies.

Keywords: Shopping closed spaces · Blind people · Systematic review · Gamification

1 Introduction

In Colombia, building and implementing accessible spaces to include the needs of people with disabilities has always been a challenge for governmental entities. In particular, the visually impaired (VI) community presents difficulties in multiple sectors of society. During the world summit of local and regional leaders addressing these challenges was included in **the Agenda for Sustainable Development 2030** [1]. Adapting malls and supermarkets infrastructures to include people with disabilities is especially difficult, making tasks such as navigating and shopping for VI people, without external aids, almost impossible. Using a gamified model could help to create a system that allows VI people to shop autonomously while enjoying the process (user experience). The disabled people currently represent 15% [2] of the world population in which 1.3 billion people have some type of visual impairment. In Colombia, it is estimated that the population

P. H. Ruiz et al. (Eds.): HCI-COLLAB 2021, CCIS 1478, pp. 98–109, 2021.
https://doi.org/10.1007/978-3-030-92325-9_8

with some kind of disability is approximately 6.4% [3] of the residents. Included in this percentage is the VI community, which represents the 43.5% [3] of this population, this will be considered as the relevant market for this study. To interact with the environment, people rely on their senses (touch, sight, hearing, smell, and taste). This applies to the Shopping Process as well, so when people enter a supermarket is possible for them to get the products they need. However, for a visually impaired person, entering a supermarket is a challenging experience because they cannot interpret the cognitive signs, which usually are visual. This issue could be solved by changing the infrastructure of the supermarkets and transforming them into accessible places for VI people or by introducing innovative solutions that allow VI people to navigate and find products within the current framework [4]. Colombia is one of the countries that do not have accessible supermarkets for blind people. Therefore, the shopping process for the visually impaired is unpleasant due to the lack privacy and autonomy. This study aims to research what emerging technology-based tools have been implemented to support the shopping process in closed spaces for blind people around the world. This paper has 4 sections. Section 2 presents an overview of the shopping process in closed spaces for blind people. Section 3 describes the methodology used for the systematic review and the results obtained after the review. Finally, Sect. 4 concludes the study and defines the future work.

2   Background

2.1   The Shopping Process for Blind People

Adam Crosier and Alison Handford in their article "Customer Journey Mapping as an Advocacy Tool for Disabled People" [5] created a Customer Journey Map that described a case study involving between five to eight people diagnosed with different conditions of vision loss.

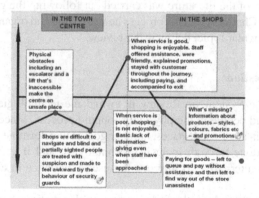

Fig. 1. Phase of interest of the costumer journey map [5]

For each person, a follow-up was carried out from their home to different points in the city such as supermarkets and warehouses. Based on these actions, the authors defined the phases of the Customer Journey Map and the emotions that the subjects were feeling throughout the process. For this study, the Customer Journey Map when the disabled person entered the supermarket was the main focus of interest (see Fig. 1).

Taking these findings into account, the Customer Journey Map confirms the critical points and situations where blind people have difficulties shopping in a store.

2.2 Gamification for the Blind People

Displayed equations or formulas are centered and set on a separate line (with an extra line or half-line space above and below). Gamification is a method to apply different elements of game playing to other activities with the purpose of engaging a product or service to a specific user. Nowadays, this is a technique widely used to create accessible technology. In the article "Interactive Gamification Learning Media Application for Blind Children Using Android Smartphone in Indonesia" [6], it is noticed that through gamification strategies, processes that sometimes are repetitive and tedious can be turned into something attractive improving user experience. In the article, the authors stated that: "Gamification creates entirely new engagement models, targeting new communities of people and motivating them to achieve goals they may not even know they have [7]. Gamification of learning as "the use of game elements, including action language, assessment, conflict/challenge, control, environment, game fiction, human interaction, immersion, and rules/goals, to facilitate learning and related outcomes" [8].". The results of the article showed that through gamification, children who were visually impaired were able to learn in a more enjoyable manner. Proving that gamification is often used on people with visual disabilities, making this a successful strategy to improve the way VI people learn to use new technology.

3   Research Method and Results

A systematic review of the literature was carried out following the guidelines proposed by Kitchenham and Charters [9]. This process helped to find and organize the information that exists on a particular topic, below is the review.

3.1   Research Questions

The objective of the Systematic Review is to find the technologies proposed by the academy to aid blind people in the physical shopping process. Since most of the supermarkets in Colombia are closed spaces, another goal is to determine whether navigation in these spaces is done through inclusive technologies; and if gamification has been implemented as an alternative to improve the user experience in emerging accessible blind technologies.

To answer these unknowns, the following research questions have been posed:

1. What are the technological developments that blind people can use to make purchases physically?
2. What technologies have been used to perform navigation in closed spaces for blind people?

3. Are there technological tools that allow blind people to participate in gamified environments?
4. what are the gamification benefits for visually impaired people?
5. there are gamified models or guides that help to visually impaired people to shopping process makes at closed spaces?

3.2 Search Strategies

The following databases were used to carry out the review, each search considered documents that have been published in the last 5 years (2015–2020) and the different filters that the databases allowed. Searches conducted in English:

- IEEE Xplore (http://ieeexplore.ieee.org)
- ACM Digital library (http://dl.acm.org)
- Ebsco (https://www.ebsco.com/)
- SCOPUS (https://www.scopus.com/home.uri)

Searches conducted in Spanish:

- Redalyc (http://redalyc.org)

Phrases such as: "indoor navigation blind", "blind assistive shopping", among others, were used to perform the search. However, the documents found were not specific enough. For example, in IEEE Xplore 1000 documents were obtained on the subject, which is why the databases' advanced search tools were used, as shown below:

- **IEEE Xplore:** The search was performed in Metadata and Full Text, adding the following keywords and logical operators.

    (((("assistive technology") OR ("indoor navigation shopping")) AND ("blind")))

    Where 149 documents were found.
- **ACM Digital library:** The search was performed with the command shown below only taking into consideration the title, the abstract and the keywords.

    [[All: "assistive technology"] OR [All: "indoor navigation shopping"]] AND [All: blind] AND [Publication Date: (01/01/2015 TO 12/31/2020)]

    Where 289 documents were found.
- **SCOPUS:** The search was performed by title, keywords and summary where 64 documents were found with the following search command:

    ((("assistive technology" AND "blind") OR ("indoor navigation shopping" AND "blind"))

- **EBSCO:** Initially, no documents were found taking into account only the title, abstract and keywords, for this reason we decided to perform the search on the entire document.

    (Assistive technology OR indoor navigation shopping) AND blind As a result, 342 documents were obtained.

- **Redalyc:** This database does not allow advanced searches with logical operators, so the Google tool is used with the following command:

  ("tecnología de asistencia" OR "navegación en espacios cerrados") AND ciegos site: redalyc.org filetype:pdf

  37 relevant documents were found.

Table 1. Data extraction string one.

Database	# Documents found	First step	Second Step	Reading complete
IEEE Xplore	149	35	10	8
ACM DL	284	15	9	2
Ebsco	342	10	5	2
Redalyc	37	9	5	–
Scopus	63	45	10	–
Total	875	114	39	12

Table 2. Data extraction string two.

Database	# Documents found	First step	Second step	Reading complete
IEEE Xplore	–	–	–	–
ACM DL	20	4	2	–
Ebsco	2	1	–	–
Redalyc	3	–	–	–
Scopus	102	27	16	4
Total	127	32	18	4

3.3 Inclusion and Exclusion Criteria

After the search was made, the following criteria was defined to reduce the number of documents to include in the bibliography.

- EC1: Documents not related to technologies for the possible development of the research work.
- EC2: Documents outside the 2015–2020-time range.
- EC3: Documents that have a title and an abstract related to the target population.

The selected documents were screened against the guidelines established below:

- IC1: Documents with models for mobilization in closed spaces for blind people.
- IC2: Documents that present technological support so that blind people can participate in the video game environment
- IC3: Documents that support the physical purchasing process of a blind person.
- IC4: Documents that mention gamification methods or techniques to visually impaired people.
- IC5: Documents that describe accessibility improvements to visually impaired people at closed spaces or supermarkets.

Due to the large number of documents found, the guidelines established by Keshav in his article "How to read a paper" [10] were applied. These determines a way to efficiently read an article through 3 steps, roughly defined below:

- First step: The abstract, titles and conclusions are read.
- Second step: The document is read more thoroughly taking into account the figures, graphs, and possible references.
- Step Three: The document is read in its entirety.

Based on this strategy, the documents of each database are delimited as illustrated in the Table 1 and Table 2.

This systematic review with the string number one was updated on July 30, 2020 and with a string number tow was update on October 9, 2020. A total of 1002 documents were obtained to which the defined inclusion and exclusion criteria were applied, obtaining a total of 18 articles. Additionally, a search on grey literature was performed on national thesis repositories. However, there were no other documents that met the desired criteria. Additionally, a search on grey literature was performed on national thesis repositories. However, there were no other documents that met the desired criteria. The chosen articles were sorted by title, authors, year of publication, place of publication, DOI, document ID, database, and keywords. To perform the data extraction an alphanumeric ID was assigned to each document starting with the letter D and followed by a number.

3.4 Data Analysis and Results

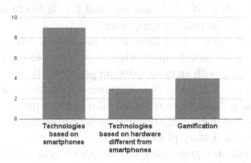

Fig. 2. Articles included on the review

The articles were reviewed and organized on groups (see Fig. 2). The sixteen articles be shown, presented different solutions to allow blind people to move in closed spaces, either by using a smartphone or an accessible hardware designed for this specific purpose.

- **Technologies based on smartphones:** Most of the articles found posed solutions developed as mobile applications [6]. As shown on a survey applied to 466 people with visual disabilities in the article "Exploring the use of smartphones and tablets among people with visual impairments: Are mainstream devices replacing the use of traditional visual aids?" [11], Smartphones have become the main accessibility tool for blind people. This leads to highlighting the importance of developing design parameters for inclusive mobile applications; to aid blind people on common daily tasks such as shopping.

The authors concluded that accessible technologies for visually impaired people are migrating to smartphone-based ones, this claim is supported by the results obtained in the survey:

- 87.4% of the respondents agreed that conventional devices such as smartphones are displacing traditional solutions.
- 69.6% of the respondents held that personal use of a smartphone is more important than a specialized device for daily activities.
- Among the respondents who were smartphone users most of them 89.8% had been using their smartphone for over 3 years, 7.5% with 1–2 years of experience, and 2.7% with less than one year from experience. I. Doush et al. in their article [12] developed an integrated system that helps blind people to localize objects within a range of 10 cm. The study is based on 2 pilot cases that helped them define a series of recommendations to improve navigation systems for the blind. Furthermore, they developed an application taking advantage of the WIFI, Bluetooth, and RFID modules of the smartphone device and designed an accessible interface for blind people.

Many other authors studied in this review focused more on navigating blind people to the entrance of establishments, omitting the process that takes place within the store. In [13, 14] S. Alghamdi and A. Meliones et al. respectively develop applications to know the relative position of the user in closed spaces, using technologies implemented in the store or supermarket such as WLAN, beacons, and Tactile Route Indicators integrated through an application in the user´s smartphone.

Some of the developments were limited to the characteristics of the space where the user intended to use the mobile application. In [15] people can move autonomously using an application along with an open software platform like Smart-Space Real-Time Location System (RTLS) Ubisense, but the places where the system is implemented cannot change regularly, the authors recommend its use for places such as hospitals or supermarkets. In [16] a probabilistic algorithm is defined so that blind people can move with an application in multi-story places.

[17] analyzes the requirements to develop navigation systems for blind people taking into account the challenges that emerge on existing ones, the different design parameters

Table 3. Technologies used on inclusive mobile applications

Name	ID	Year- Authors	Technologies used
ISAB	[12]	*2016- A. Doush (et al.)*	WIFI, Bluetooth, RFID
Shopping and Tourism as IOT app	[13]	*2019-S. Alghamdi*	WIFI, BLE, RFID
IBN	[14]	*2016-A.Meliones (et al.)*	WIFI, Tactile indicators
Ultra-Wideband INS	[15]	*2018- A.Alnafessah (et al.)*	RTLS Ubisense
Indoor Localization BN	[16]	*2018-M. Murata (et al.)*	BLE, RFID
Mobile Based INS	[17]	*2017-L. Arvai*	WIFI, Bluetooth, IMU

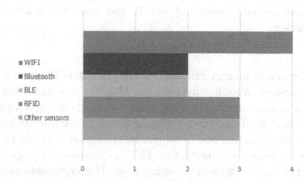

Fig. 3. Technologies used in inclusive mobile applications for the blind

created to overcome the challenges are explained in detail. They define a complete software structure divided into smaller modules that handle different phases of the navigation process.

In recent years, researchers have managed to integrate many available technologies into the development of mobile applications. The Table 3 summarizes the technologies used on inclusive mobile applications for blind people, found on the articles of this section.

As shown, the technologies used for the development of inclusive applications are mostly integrated into the hardware of current smartphones. WIFI is the most used technology on emerging inclusive mobile applications for the VI (see Fig. 3). This represents the tendency of developers to take advantage of the network infrastructure that already exists to guide blind people in closed spaces.

- **Technologies based on hardware different from smartphones:** The solutions proposed for hardware different to smartphones are mostly wearable devices so that VI people can navigate through spaces with their limbs free of any restrain. We found 3 fascinating prototypes that aim to help blind people perform tasks related to the shopping process.

In [18] The authors proposed a blind-sight navigator (BSN), which is a wearable device in the form of a backpack and a helmet. The device is integrated with PICS as microcontrollers to perform image recognition of the place where the user is moving. Also, there is a device that transmits vibratory signals to the user to alert them to possible obstacles in the way.

The second prototype [19] is a vest that blind people would wear to walk. The vest is integrated with a camera, an IMU, a laser sensor, and a headset to give commands to the user. The implemented logic modules allow navigation in closed spaces and the recognition of objects in space, is an integrated solution for closed environments with complex structures.

In the third prototype, [20] the main objective of the authors was to create a low-cost and opensource prototype to help blind people solve the primary task of navigation, orientation, and obstacle detection. The device consists of a bracelet made in 3D printing that integrates an ultrasound sensor and an IMU that are low-cost sensors and easy to acquire on the market.

Use Cases

The following documents present case studies using two mobile applications "MagNav and Ucap". [21] presents an application use case: MagNav, an accessible navigation app. It is a system that guides users employing auditory signals through a closed space, in this case, the test was performed in a shopping center in the United States. However, MagNav does not have the function for object identification. The other case found was also on a mobile application named UCap [22], a crowdsourcing application for the visually impaired persons on an android smartphone. The application uses the camera to allow customers to take pictures of the product they aim to identify; it should be noted that the application is exclusively responsible for identifying products.

Gamification. There was 1 article that show some research done regarding gamification strategies for blind people. However, not much information surfaced about gamification processes applied to blind people. The article [23] attempts to verify the accessibility of blind people to the gaming environment in mobile applications. They discovered that most games that offer accessibility do not allow interaction with other players, a feature that seeks to be improved by initiatives such as "Game2Senses"; which is an innovative project for blind people to participate in a multiplayer game using only the touchscreen and gyroscope of the device. The article [24] describe the making process of a mobile application for access to tourism services, the application is aimed at low vision users and users in blind condition. The gamification technique used for the implementation of this application, is based on rewards to user, these rewards or points are awarded for actions. A conclusion in this paper is that the results are very positives thanks to survey of 100 people that used this application successfully.

In the article [25], is evident that the gamification strategies can achieve that a tedious process can be turned into something attractive for the users, this paper mentioned: "Gamification creates completely new models of engagement, targeting new communities of people and motivating them to achieve goals they may not even know they have [7]". The paper results show that the use of gamification in learning environments allows increase the knowledge and understanding of the visual impaired children. In the same education area are the article [6], this presents the design and implementation of a tool to facilitate typing for elementary school students with visual impairment, in this work applied general gamification techniques which can adjust for the tool develop. The users indicated that the tool was advantage tool and value tool that it has a good performance but there are negative opinions and suggestions for improvement.

Considering the articles, it identified that gamification has generated different benefits in the learning of people with visually impaired and that it can be adjustments for made to the different techniques to be able to gamify processes that are of interest. Regarding accessibility, there was a significant number of documentations that referred to the accessibility of people with visually impaired to environments such as web or mobile applications, but there was no document that explicitly addressed the issue of accessibility in closed environments such as supermarkets.

4   Conclusions and Future Work

The Systematic Literature Review found that out of 1002 papers met the criteria of inclusion defined in this review, with this we can response the research questions:

1. We can see that in most developments they make use of smartphones, taking advantage of their portability and computing power to perform different tasks with the help of external sensors.
2. The solutions are largely based on Wifi, RFID, BLE, Bluetooth technology, among others. Some of these developments support the purchase process, but some of these are invasive for the user because they require a series of complementary sensors for operation.
3. The use of mobile devices or smartphones stands out, these being the appropriate ecosystem for the development of gamified environments.
4. Gamification allows users to increase their interest in activities that require concentration or a certain cognitive load. This is essential since most of the guides are not designed for visually impaired people, however some techniques can be used to obtain good results.
5. There aren't gamified models or gamified guides that help visually impaired people to make purchases in closed spaces such as supermarkets or stores.

There is a lot of research done regarding accessible technology for blind people. However, there was not much literature on an integral system to allow blind people to shop autonomously covering all the challenges that the process imposes. Most of the studies analyzed the navigation of closed unfamiliar spaces, rather than object recognition; and none of the studies found, proposed a gamified model for the shopping process, centering on the feelings, actions, steps, sensations of the user in each of the phases that this process has.

This search identifies that smartphone are slowly replacing traditional accessibility tools (see Fig. 3)., on the category "Technologies based on hardware different from smartphone", the great majority of the articles suggest a mobile application as a tool for transforming inadequate closed spaces into inclusive places for blind people.

Regarding hardware different from smartphones, the solutions are wearable devices that interact with the environment the way eyes do for sighted people. There were 3 promising prototypes found: a backpack with a helmet, a bracelet, and a vest.

All the solutions offered basic navigation functionalities such as obstacle avoidance and image recognition, but we believe that they are intrusive and uncomfortable solutions for the user. In terms of existing mobile applications "Mag-Nav" helps blind people navigate unknown closed spaces and "U-Cap" allows visually impaired people (low vision) to identify an object by taking a picture of it. Mobile games and applications mostly are not accessible for blind people however some recommendations on the subject were presented.

Future Work

Without a doubt, having no solution to aid the visually impaired shopping process has inconceivable effects both physically and emotionally on the person. As a result, there should be more research aimed at an integrated system that solves all the challenges that affect the visually impaired community. Based on the results obtained in this review and following the functional recommendations done in the analyzed documents, the development of a Gamified Model to Support Shopping in Closed Spaces Aimed at Blind People, based on ubiquitous system, will be the main objective of future research.

References

1. Durban2019: Ciudades inclusivas y accesibles (2019). https://www.uclg.org/sites/default/files/ciudades_inclusivas_y_accesibles_documento_de_politica.pdf. Accessed 01 Jan 2020
2. OMS, 10 datos sobre la discapacidad (2017). https://www.who.int/features/factfiles/disability/es/. Accessed 15 Jan 2020
3. Dane: Censo general (2005). https://www.dane.gov.co/files/censo2005/discapacidad.pdf. Accessed 23 Jan 2020
4. U. D. of Justice: Maintaining accessible features in retail establishments (2009). https://www.ada.gov/business/retailaccess.htm. Accessed 23 Jan 2020
5. Crosier, A., Handford, A.: Customer journey mapping as an advocacy tool for disabled people: a case study. Soc. Mark. Q. **18**(1), 67–76 (2012). https://doi.org/10.1177/1524500411435483
6. Sari, A.C., Fadillah, A.M., Jonathan, J., David Prabowo, M.R.: Interactive gamification learning media application for blind children using android smartphone in Indonesia. Procedia Comput. Sci. **157**, 589–595 (2019). The 4th International Conference on Computer Science and Computational Intelligence (ICCSCI 2019): Enabling Collaboration to Escalate Impact of Research Results for Society. http://www.sciencedirect.com/science/article/pii/S1877050919311767
7. Burke, B.: Gamify : How Gamification Motivates People to do Extraordinary Things. Bibliomotion Inc., Brookline (2014)
8. Landers, R., Armstrong, M., Collmus, A.: How to use game elements to enhance learning: applications of the theory of gamified learning. In: Ma, M., Oikonomou, A. (eds.) Serious Games and Edutainment Applications, pp. 457–483. Springer, Cham (2017). https://doi.org/10.1007/978-3-319-51645-5_21
9. Kitchenham, B., Charters, S.: Guidelines for performing systematic literature reviews in software engineering, vol. 2 (2007)
10. Keshav, S.: How to read a paper, vol. 1, (1997). David R. Cheriton School of Computer Science, University of Waterloo

11. Martiniello, N., Eisenbarth, W., Lehane, C., Johnson, A., Wittich, W.: Exploring the use of smartphones and tablets among people with visual impairments: are mainstream devices replacing the use of traditional visual aids? Assist. Technol. 1–12, (2019). pMID: 31697612. https://doi.org/10.1080/10400435.2019.1682084. Appendix: Springer-Author Discount

12. Doush, I.A., Alshatnawi, S., Al-Tamimi, A.-K., Alhasan, B., Hamasha, S.: ISAB: integrated indoor navigation system for the blind. Interacting with Computers, June 2016. https://doi.org/10.1093/iwc/iww016

13. Alghamdi, S.: Shopping and tourism for blind people using RFID as an application of IoT. In: 2019 2nd International Conference on Computer Applications & Information Security (ICCAIS). IEEE, May 2019. https://doi.org/10.1109/cais.2019.8769581

14. Meliones, A., Sampson, D.: Indoor blind navigator. In: Proceedings of the 10th International Conference on PErvasive Technologies Related to Assistive Environments. ACM, June 2017. https://doi.org/10.1145/3056540.3064959

15. Alnafessah, A., Al-Ammar, M., Al-Hadhrami, S., Al-Salman, A., Al-Khalifa, H.: Developing an ultra wideband indoor navigation system for visually impaired people. Int. J. Distrib. Sensor Netw. 12(7), 6152342 (2016). https://doi.org/10.1177/155014776152342

16. Murata, M., Ahmetovic, D., Sato, D., Takagi, H., Kitani, K.M., Asakawa, C.: Smartphone-based indoor localization for blind navigation across building complexes. In: 2018 IEEE International Conference on Pervasive Computing and Communications (PerCom). IEEE, March 2018. https://doi.org/10.1109/percom.2018.8444593

17. Arvai, L.: Mobile phone based indoor navigation system for blind and visually impaired people: VUK—visionless supporting framework. In: 2018 19th International Carpathian Control Conference (ICCC). IEEE, May 2018. https://doi.org/10.1109/carpathiancc.2018.8399660

18. Boudreault, A., Bouchard, B., Gaboury, S., Bouchard, J.: Blind sight navigator. In: Proceedings of the 9th ACM International Conference on PErvasive Technologies Related to Assistive Environments - PETRA '16. ACM Press (2016). https://doi.org/10.1145/2910674.2910709

19. Mekhalfi, M., Melgani, F., Zeggada, A., De Natale, F., Salem, Mohammed A.-M.., Khamis, A.: Recovering the sight to blind people in indoor environments with smart technologies. Expert Syst. Appl. 46, 129–138 (2016). https://doi.org/10.1016/j.eswa.2015.09.054

20. Petsiuk, P.: Low-cost open source ultrasound-sensing based navigational support for the visually impaired. Sensors 19(17), 3783 (2019). https://doi.org/10.3390/s19173783

21. Giudice, N.A., Whalen, W.E., Riehle, T.H., Anderson, S.M., Doore, S.A.: Evaluation of an accessible, real-time, and infrastructure-free indoor navigation system by users who are blind in the mall of America. J. Vis. Impairm. Blindness 113(2), 140–155 (2019). https://doi.org/10.1177/0145482x19840918

22. Hoonlor, A., Ayudhya, S.P.N., Harnmetta, S., Kitpanon, S., Khlaprasit, K.: UCap: a crowd-sourcing application for the visually impaired and blind persons on android smartphone. In: 2015 International Computer Science and Engineering Conference (ICSEC). IEEE, November 2015. https://doi.org/10.1109/icsec.2015.7401406

23. Smith, K., Abrams, S.: Gamification and accessibility. Int. J. Inf. Learn. Technol. 36(2), 104–123 (2019). https://doi.org/10.1108/IJILT-06-2018-0061

24. Moldoveanu, A., et al.: Sound of vision 3D virtual training environments-a gamification approach for visual to audio-haptic sensory substitution. Revue Roumaine des Sciences Techniques Serie Electrotechnique et Energetique, 63(1), 112–117 (2018). https://www.scopus.com/inward/record.uri?eid=2-s2.0-85045937724partnerID=40md5=a81de0bd608008c7599b886837122853

25. Ceccarini, C., Prandi, C.: Tourism for all: a mobile application to assist visually impaired users in enjoying tourist services. In: 2019 16th IEEE Annual Consumer Communications & Networking Conference (CCNC). IEEE, January 2019. https://doi.org/10.1109/ccnc.2019.8651848

Interface Analysis Criteria for Mobile Devices: A Systematic Mapping

Karina Sousa de Paula Santos(✉) ⓘ and Ismar Frango Silveira ⓘ

Universidade Presbiteriana Mackenzie, São Paulo, SP, Brazil
`{karina.santos,ismar.silveira}@mackenzie.br`

Abstract. The COVID-19 pandemic has accelerated the digitization process. Interface design and human-computer interaction become political tools in this context, which can guarantee quality in the experience of users of mobile devices, reducing these social distances. In this study a systematic mapping was executed to clarify the outlines of criteria that are commonly evaluated on mobile device interfaces in the light of the literature, trying to emphasize more specific aspects, investigating the heuristics, metrics, and recommendations described in each study. This mapping identified 65 heuristics, which were divided into four groups: Usability, User Experience, Accessibility, and Aesthetics. Further research is needed to investigate how to structure the heuristics in a way that facilitates understanding, consultation, and the evaluation processes.

Keywords: Evaluation · Interface · Mobile devices · Systematic mapping

1 Introduction

It is notable that the COVID-19 pandemic has accelerated the digitization process in different contexts of our society, including education. The emerging actions to maintain classes taking place in the remote context have evidenced social differences and impacted access to education for several children, specifically students in public schools. These children often do not have access to computers and depend on the use of smartphones from members of their household in order to attend classes [1].

Socially, we have a division between those who have the best equipment and those who do not. In this context, interface design and human-computer interaction become political tools, which can guarantee quality in the experience of users of mobile devices, reducing these social distances.

Investigating how the literature deals with the evaluation of interfaces for mobile devices is the first step to focus on this discussion. Thus, the execution of systematic mappings allows the researcher to have a broad view of an area of studies, giving the opportunity to categorize the findings. These reasons made relevant the execution of the mapping in a context where the objective was to explore the common methods described in the literature used to evaluate interfaces for devices, trying to obtain both: a macro view of the major areas covered and a micro view seeking to identify the heuristics used [2]. This mapping follows the well-defined structure of Systematic Reviews, with steps

© Springer Nature Switzerland AG 2021
P. H. Ruiz et al. (Eds.): HCI-COLLAB 2021, CCIS 1478, pp. 110–125, 2021.
https://doi.org/10.1007/978-3-030-92325-9_9

that aim to guarantee the reliability of the data obtained and in accordance with their procedures of [3]. In this approach, the mapping begins with the definition of a protocol specifying the research question being addressed and the methods that will be used to perform the mapping.

This study distinguishes from a systematic review because it focuses on extracting information from the analyzed studies, answering broader questions, and creating categories from the findings [4]. Following the guidelines, the protocol was defined in order to contribute to the impartiality of the research, contributing to the analysis of the data without influence of the researcher's bias and expectations [3].

2 Methods

The protocol of the Systematic Mapping includes the definition of the research questions and the strategy used to find the studies. Also, the definition of the research databases for performing the searches, search strings definition, the creation of the criteria for selecting studies, and the data extraction strategies are part of this protocol too. Finally, the synthesis of the extracted data is performed.

Following this structure of the protocol, the guiding questions are defined, which will assist the execution of the research and highlight its objectives:

- Q1: What are the main criteria evaluated in a mobile interface?
- Q2: What are the heuristics for mobile devices currently described in the literature?

Q1 aims to clarify the outlines of criteria that are commonly evaluated on mobile device interfaces in the light of the literature, using a macro view to identify the central themes of the studies. Q2 will emphasize in more specific aspects, investigating the heuristics, metrics and recommendations described in each study.

The selected databases were IEEE, Scopus, and the Web of Science. This definition was made considering the characteristics of the databases of addressing relevant content about Computing and Engineering, and related themes like development, mobile devices, evaluation, interaction, experience user, among others. The search string delimits and standardizes the words used in the selected databases to search for studies. It is another resource that assists in the impartiality of the research. The chosen words were: "evaluation" + "mobile" + "interface".

In order to make it possible to use the three words in this way, we used the filter resource contained in the databases of the selected databases. This feature allowed to filter first by the word "evaluation", starting from the filter results using "mobile" and finalizing the filter with the word "interface".

The publications of the selected works are distributed between the years 2007 and 2020. It is interesting to note that in 2007 the first iPhone was launched, which was responsible for popularizing smartphones and touch screens [5], which explains the time cut. The databases have search resources that help to sort the results according to the criteria chosen by the researcher. Thus, it was first decided to order the results according to the number of times cited. However, it was observed that this ordering brought results with content outside the expected scope, so it was necessary to adjust this criterion. Because of that, the collection of the studies occurred following the order of relevance, following the algorithm of each database.

After that, it was necessary to define the inclusion criteria for the texts, to enable the evaluation of the studies collected. For this research, four criteria were defined for the evaluation, containing two sub-criteria. To classify the articles collected into the criteria, a pre-analysis was executed. This pre-analysis consisted of reading the title and abstract, so it was possible to fit each analyzed study into one of the criteria:

- Selected: When reading the title and the abstract were sufficient to define their relevance within the scope of the research and the guiding questions of the systematic mapping. In this case, the article was immediately included in the systematic mapping.

  A study was included immediately when it was identified that the methods used considered the opinion of experts and included devices related to the scope of the research.

  Studies with Tests and studies with users that explained the heuristics and metrics were also selected.

- Excluded: When reading the title and the abstract was sufficient to define that the text dealt with themes outside the scope of the research and that they would not contribute to the direction of the research. In this case, the article was immediately excluded from the systematic mapping.

  The immediate exclusion occurred when an article presented a theme outside the scope of the research, mainly in relation to the devices treated. Articles with devices such as augmented reality glasses or personal computers were not considered because they have a type of interaction with characteristics distinct from mobile devices and their own particularities.

- Subsequent evaluation: When reading the title and abstract were not enough to define its immediate inclusion or immediate exclusion, the article fell into this criteria.

  This meant that a complete reading would be necessary to define the study criterion. After this reading, the article could assume one of the following sub-criteria:

  - Evaluated and selected: When the complete reading resulted in the inclusion of the article in the mapping.
  - Evaluated and excluded: When a complete reading resulted in the article being excluded from the mapping.

    The evaluation occurred mainly when an article mentioned using users in their evaluation tests, but it had the potential to cite heuristics, guidelines, and recommendations that could be relevant to complement the understanding of the theme and answer the mapping questions.

- Without access: When despite using the access provided by Universidade Presbiteriana Mackenzie, which facilitates access to various databases, it was not sufficient to access the article. Sometimes it occurred due to the absence of valid links, at other times there was a request for payments to allow access.

Following the defined protocol, the search and extraction of studies contained in the databases was initiated. This stage was carried out between the 25th of July 2020 and the

25th of September of the same year. The searches using the defined strings still identified results in the thousands, being necessary to define one more cut criteria in relation to the quantity, to make the research viable. In this way it was defined to collect a hundred articles from each of the three bases used. This definition resulted in the collection of 300 studies, which were reduced to 266 when removing duplicates. The Table 1 shows the statistics from this stage.

Table 1. Statistics from studies.

Database	S	AS	E	AE	N	Total
iEEE	2	2	67	27	0	98
Scopus	12	3	16	51	10	92
Web of Science	3	3	40	26	4	76
Total	25		241			266

Caption: S - selected; AS - evaluated and selected; E - excluded; AE - evaluated and excluded; N - no access found;

To organize the collected studies and facilitate subsequent queries, Airtable[1] was used, which consists of a database that has several filters, grouping, and selection resources. In total there were 10 columns (Title, Authors, Publication Year, Database, Language, Mapping classification, Method, Objectives, Results and Central theme) that aimed to standardize the data extracted from the studies to support the synthesis that would occur in the sequence.

The last column, entitled Central Theme, is a definition made after the end of the extraction of information. It then was tried to create groups of themes for the selected articles, grouping them through the central theme discussed in the study. In total, four categories were created: Accessibility, User Experience, Usability, and Aesthetics. To classify a study in the accessibility group, articles that focused on audiences that have specific limitations and where standard resolutions are not necessarily positive or don't facilitate usability through this audience were considered, including articles that have a focus on the elderly.

To include articles in the User Experience category, those that covered a more general theme than usability were considered, as considering emotional aspects in their evaluation for example. In order to classify in Usability or in Aesthetics, articles were considered that had these themes as their main themes and primarily evaluated these topics. The classification of studies in systematic mapping resulted in 17 articles selected immediately, classified as Selected, and 8 that were selected after a thorough evaluation of the text, which were classified as Evaluated and selected. In total, 25 articles were considered for the next stages of data extraction and synthesis. Table 2 shows these data. When defining the central theme of the articles, there were 12 articles with an emphasis on Usability, 8 with a focus on Accessibility, 3 with a central theme on user experience and only 2 with an emphasis on aesthetics.

---

[1] Airtable – https://airtable.com/.

Table 2. Statistics from selected studies.

Central theme	S	AS	Total	Articles
Usability	10	2	12	[6–17]
Accessibility	6	2	8	[18–25]
User experience	0	3	3	[26–28]
Aesthetics	1	1	2	[29, 30]
Total	17	8	25	

Caption: S - selected; AS - evaluated and selected;

2.1 Common Practices

The common practices in the studies selected for the mapping are diverse, especially those using Automated Assessments, Nielsen Heuristics, Checklists, Tests with controlled users in the laboratory and Systematic or literature reviews. Table 3 quantitatively compiles these highlighted methods.

Table 3. Methods identified in studies classified as selected and evaluated and selected in the mapping.

Method	Amount	Articles
Automated evaluation	4	[15, 16, 18, 29]
Checklists	6	[12, 19, 24, 26, 28, 30]
Nielsen's heuristics	9	[6–10, 12, 13, 16, 17]
Users tests	8	[8, 9, 14, 20, 21, 23, 25, 27]
Systematic review or review of the literature	4	[11, 17, 22, 27]

Note that the number of methods is greater than the number of articles selected for systematic mapping, this occurs for two main reasons: Firstly, because some articles [19, 27] address more than one method. The second reason is the fact that Nielsen's Heuristics appear among the checklists, and it was decided to point out whenever this set of heuristics appeared in the papers

There are also texts that seek to automate [15, 16, 18, 29] the way of evaluating interfaces, according to some previously established criteria. These are important because the criteria used for the automation of the evaluation show us the topics that are relevant, making evident aspects that are considered during the evaluation of interfaces for mobile devices. The results are delivered in a quantitative way, which can assist in the verification of measurable metrics. Automated assessments explore computer content that has the potential to be strong allies in assessments, such as genetic computing and Fuzzy Logic.

Nielsen's heuristic (NH) can be considered a subgroup of Checklists, but in this case, it was decided to create segregation because the NH gained notoriety and has a specific method of execution. However, if we look at these two categories as one, we will have the method with the largest sample in view of the studies analyzed. This can denote the relevance of these methods to the literature.

Some of the Checklists analyzed were focused on Mobile Learning [28]. An even more specific context than mobile devices. However, the heuristics and metrics were considered, because they were broad and had the potential to be used in other contexts.

The second category with a significant number of studies is that of User Tests [8, 9, 14, 20, 21, 23, 25, 27]. The common characteristic of the tests described are the execution in a controlled environment, such as laboratories and using auxiliary equipment for the evaluation, such as eye tracking. Systematic reviews or literature reviews analyzed [11, 17, 22, 27] contained a structure very similar to this research. In general, they focus on investigating the literature and adapting heuristics considering the specific characteristics of mobile devices.

2.2 The Heuristics, Guidelines and Recommendations

The studies were primarily selected for their potential to point out relevant heuristics, guidelines or recommendations in the context of evaluating interfaces for mobile devices. In order to extract these elements from the selected texts, a new stage of information extraction has been realized. At this moment the emphasis was to extract all the elements that would be considered as heuristics, regardless of how they appeared in the text.

In order to identify, list, and eliminate duplicates, it was decided to execute a Card Sorting (CS) method. This is a method used by Information Architects to create categories in an intuitive way for websites, systems, and applications, but in general, it comes down to creating a grouping of information in a simple way to be understood by those who will use these categories. It is a simple, inexpensive, and quick method to be performed, as it uses few materials and can be performed individually or in a group [31]. In addition, it is flexible, adapting to the needs of each application. The method was performed using the Miro[2], which made it possible to use the card format to list the heuristics.

Following the specifications of [31], the CS starts with the selection of the content, which in this case are the heuristics identified from the analysis of the texts selected for the Systematic Mapping. In total, 172 heuristics were listed. Crossing the quantity of heuristics with the Central Themes of the articles we come across 93 heuristics from the Usability theme, another 34 from the Accessibility theme, while 32 was from the User Experience theme and finally 13 from the Aesthetics theme, as shown in Table 4.

Previously we observed a greater number of studies with an emphasis on the theme of Usability, which is reflected in this stage of the research, where we also obtain a greater number of heuristics related to this theme. The numbers also are proportional, about 50% of the texts analyzed in the review have usability as their central theme, and about 54% of heuristics identified has the same central theme.

---

[2] Miro – https://miro.com/.

Table 4. Number of heuristics by central theme.

Central theme	Amount
Usability	93
Accessibility	34
User experience	32
Aesthetics	13
Total	172

Following the CS process, the next two steps are: select the participants and prepare the cards. One of the researchers participated in the role of participant, using her knowledge as a design expert and those recently obtained through this systematic mapping to group the heuristics.

The cards were separated by colors, just to identify them visually. The colors blue, yellow, green, and lilac represent respectively the themes of User Experience, Aesthetics, Usability, and Accessibility. The first stage consisted of the identification and grouping of the duplicates. For this, it was analyzed not only the title of the heuristic but also its description when available. This was a process that showed that the same heuristic can be seen from different perspectives and helped to carry out the next step, which was consisted of creating categories for similar groups of heuristics.

Thus, it was decided to use the same approach as before for the main themes. Separating the heuristics between Accessibility, User Experience, Aesthetics and Usability is a strategy that helps to segregate different groups of heuristics, with different objectives and that have the ability to guide the specialist to look at the interface not only through the heuristic, but also under the category context. Thus, we can have similar heuristics between categories, but with different objectives, guiding the observation of important details of the interface, whether related to aesthetics, accessibility, usability, or user experience.

Once the cards are organized and the categories have been created, the CS process is finally finished. New interactions can be realized, with new participants or with them, in order to refine the process and answer new questions. However, in this case it was decided to conclude this way. This process reduced the amount of heuristics from 172 to 65. It is important to note that the decrease in heuristics is also reflected between the categories, with the exception of the aesthetics theme, which ended the process with 2 more heuristics than at the beginning. In all, 19 heuristics of Usability, 16 of User Experience, 15 of Accessibility and 15 of Aesthetics were obtained, as shown in Table 5.

Table 5. Number of heuristics by category after the card sorting process.

Category	Amount
Usability	19
User experience	16
Accessibility	15
Aesthetics	15
Total	65

Usability heuristics comprise inherent aspects of the interaction. The fact that there is a strong reference to Nielsen's heuristics is noteworthy, due to their predominant presence in the studies analyzed, this characteristic only confirms the relevance of this set of heuristics in the literature. However, in the Usability Heuristics group, shown in Table 6, there are other aspects considered relevant to the success of products, which are not considered in Nielsen's heuristics, examples of which are the Completeness, Privacy and Navigation and Access to information heuristics.

Table 6. Usability heuristics group resulting from card sorting.

Id	Title	Description
US1	Completeness	Ability to look like a finished and complete product
US2	Privacy	Explain the reasons for requesting information and accessing data. Understand the features needed to protect user's data
US3	Complexity	Develop simple and objective interactions, which help the users to achieve their goals and do not distract them
US4	Suitability of the component for its functionality	There are components created for specific situations, know and use them the way they were designed to work
US5	Narratives to structure the content	Thinking of the content as a narrative means making it interesting, while useful
US6	Effectiveness	Refers to the way the product acts in relation to its intended purpose
US7	Easy to reverse actions	Provide visible and accessible ways to reverse, undo or cancel actions
US8	Navigation and access to information	Use known navigation patterns

(*continued*)

Table 6. (*continued*)

Id	Title	Description
US9	Helping users to recognize, diagnose and recover from errors	When errors occur, it is necessary to provide the user with the means to recognize and recover from them
US10	Understandability	Ability to be understood easily
US11	Efficiency	Degree to which the product is allowing tasks to be carried out in a quick, effective and economical way or is hampering performance
US12	Visibility of the system status	Ensure that the feedback from the application is coherent and consistent, for this the user must always be informed by the system in a reasonable time about what is happening
US13	Satisfaction with decision support	The user must receive support to make decisions, especially when they represent non-recoverable actions. The texts must be clear and informative, the user must feel helped and satisfied
US14	Error prevention	Designing by thinking what mistakes are possible and how to make them less frequent
US15	Suitability of the message for functionality and the user	Understand how to communicate to your audience
US16	User control and freedom	The system must make available functions that allow the user to control and personalize it
US17	Consistency and standards	Respect pre-established standards and repeat them throughout the interface
US18	Flexibility and efficiency of use	Opportunity to manage the application according to the user's own ability and understanding
US19	Match between system and real world	The logical model of the system must be compatible with the logical model of the user

For the context of the User Experience, the focus was on selecting heuristics that considered broader aspects than the Usability ones. The User Experience heuristics are described on Table 7. The accessibility heuristics described in Table 8 have a tone of recommendation, as they are described in the studies analyzed. It is observed that in this group it is necessary to consider the characteristics of the target audience carefully. Target audience characteristics define how to properly apply the recommendations described. Table 9 presents the heuristics with an emphasis on the topic of aesthetics.

Table 7. User experience heuristics group resulting from card sorting.

Id	Title	Description
UX01	Simplicity	The interface's design shouldn't be too complex because mobile device users often need to focus on more than one task
UX02	Pleasant and respectful interaction	Awakening good feelings in the user throughout the interaction
UX03	Measurable metrics	It is necessary to establish measurable metrics to help the team understand if the product has achieved its goals
UX04	Easy to learn	Operations can be learned by looking at the object
UX05	Easy to use	It is essential to create a user-friendly interface for a good and reliable user experience
UX06	Useful	The usefulness of the product must be easily understood
UX07	Affordable	It is important to take disabled users into account when designing and developing technology applications and systems
UX08	Preventing errors	There is always a chance of human error. Therefore, the interaction and the interface must be designed in order to avoid confusion and mental overload
UX09	Connectivity	That is the ability to access information quickly in a short amount of time. It also allows the application to be stopped, started and resumed with little or no effort. Consider mobile connectivity
UX10	Personalization	Experienced users strongly desire the feeling that they are in charge of the interface and that the interface responds to their actions

(continued)

Table 7. (*continued*)

Id	Title	Description
UX11	Desirable	A user's emotional response to a product is important. Feelings attracted by images and brands are important when asking for desire
UX12	Interactivity	This requirement allows users to use the application in any situation
UX13	Likely	It is essential to understand the various elements that influence users to trust and use any product. Designing reliable elements can help influence users to trust a product and believe what they are told
UX14	Naturalness	A common, natural interface makes the system intuitive, which reduces the learning curve significantly
UX15	Know your user	The interaction and interface must meet the needs and capabilities of end users
UX16	Continuity	A good interface is consistent in your interactions. Consistency will help users to form their perception and interpretation of the application

2.3   The Heuristics, Guidelines and Recommendations

A characteristic observed among the analyzed studies was the structure used to visually represent the heuristics and the sub-heuristics. At first the form of representation that stands out is the trees [17], since in most cases only lists are used. Another type of visualization commonly found is the tables [10, 15, 16, 29], which cluster larger amounts of content, and sometimes include descriptions. In the context of computing, trees are a widespread technique of information visualization, because these structures are used in the scope of programming [32]. However, they are structures with the capacity to become complex, according to the number of branches and depth. Information visualization techniques are diverse and each of these techniques has characteristics that are best suited to specific contexts. It is necessary to understand what type of technique is used to represent the right information, so it can be possible to support the data analysis in an effective way [32].

In this context, using the tree to represent the hierarchy between heuristics and sub-heuristics has the potential to make the display of data complex, due to the vertically extensive structure (depth), which does not facilitate the understanding of the information contained. Analyzing the tables contained in the selected studies, it is concluded that, in general, they are structures that can organize a larger amount of data. And compared to the sets of heuristics structured in a tree format, have the potential to be simpler, due the distribution of the spacing that opens the possibility of including descriptions and maintaining a linear reading of the data presented.

Table 8. Accessibility heuristics group resulting from card sorting.

Id	Title	Description
A01	Explicitly display the current mode	The mode change indicators must be persistent and large
A02	Consider specific difficulties for each audience	In order to make the product more usable in many circumstances it is important to ensure that people with different disabilities benefit from using it
A03	Testing	Testing accessibility features throughout development. To be effective in your accessibility, it is important to learn from your audience what best meets their needs
A04	Interaction	Emphasis on popular and simple patterns, this helps due to the familiarity with previously used systems
A05	Simplicity	Display headers, lists, tables and other structures in a simple way. Make your interface look simple and efficient. Use contextualized language
A06	Ease of use	All features that are available by touch must also be available by other means on the device
A07	Navigation	Simplified navigation helps to use accessibility features
A08	Appearance of texts	Make available ways to modify the size and aspects of the text, in order to make them more adapted to the user's reality. Always choose simple, unadorned fonts with an emphasis on legibility
A09	Colors	Use colors with the awareness that there are several conditions that change the way people see colors
A10	Prioritize the use of simple gestures	Although applications do not need to avoid using drag and pinch operations, the application must provide clear visual instructions and tips to show which gesture invokes which function
A11	Use larger targets	Larger and clear targets, and adequate spacing
A12	Understanding resources	Use text and image together to convey the message
A13	Ease of understanding	The information and components of the user interface must be presented in ways that can be perceived by the user
A14	Help	Implement help for complex features

Table 9. Aesthetics heuristics group resulting from card sorting.

Id	Title	Description
E01	Interface style	Follow the aesthetic movements and understand how to benefit and apply in a coherent way in the project
E02	Distribution	Equal arrangement of interactive objects between the four quadrants
E03	Composition	Use visual weight and balance to convey importance
E04	Density	The aesthetic and information set must not visually overload the interface
E05	Aesthetic and Minimalist Design	Reducing and simplifying the elements contained in an interface is not only an aesthetic strategy, but it is an approach that emphasizes information that is relevant and facilitates the understanding of the interface by users
E06	Colors	Choose colors that work well individually and in combinations. Considering systems with light and dark backgrounds
E07	Use of screen space	Customize your app's response to different screen sizes and orientations
E08	Organization	Alignment, grouping and spacing are key elements for the visual organization of the screens
E09	Text size	Consider different sizes for different fonts, always prioritizing readability and keeping in mind that text size is configurable
E10	Coherent use of multimedia	Different screens have the ability to render media differently. Understand the context and what is the best medium to use
E11	Homogeneity	Good homogeneity is achieved by an equal distribution of the elements among the four quadrants
E12	Attractiveness	The attractiveness of the design will make the user get involved, be satisfied and use the app frequently
E13	Ordering	Components must be positioned in such a way as to guide the user's eye through the interface in a logical and sequential order that refers to the user's needs
E14	Presentation	Everything presented needs to be legible and consistent with the usefulness of the product
E15	Text structure	The text must be structured in order to guide the reading, using the visual hierarchy created through differentiation of type, weight and appearance, to demonstrate the difference between titles, subtitles and textual body

3   Conclusions

The systematic review was proposed in view of the need to answer two central questions: What are the main criteria and What are the heuristics for the interface of mobile devices described by the literature? In this way, the grouping created to classify the articles in the review according to the central theme helped to highlight the main criteria that these texts addressed. It was also possible to list a considerable number of heuristics described by the literature and synthesize them in order to facilitate understanding and application. It is also observed that there is interest in the community to propose methods that are specific, for different contexts, within the scope of mobile computing. However, there is an inclination to focus only on Usability, where it was the central theme of at least half of the evaluated studies and frequently cited in other studies.

Nielsen's Heuristics are protagonists when the central theme is Usability. Especially when the focus is evaluations that place the specialist at the center of the process. It is possible to notice that relevant studies began to emerge within the context of mobile computing with the central theme of User Experience around the years 2015. This denotes that further research is needed considering the scope of User Experience for mobile applications. During the grouping of heuristics performed in the Card Sorting process, it was decided to maintain similar heuristics, but which have different objectives according to the category. This creates the opportunity to focus on the same aspect of the interface through many different perspectives but it is necessary to analyze how this decision could impact the evaluation process. The studies analyzed do not make it clear how heuristics are used in the evaluation processes and which instruments are used to support specialists during the evaluation process. In future works tests of the identified criteria and heuristics could be executed, seeking to verify the applicability of this set of heuristics on the proposed context of mobile applications. Further research is needed to investigate how to structure the heuristics in a way that facilitates understanding, consultation, and evaluation processes.

References

1. Iivari, N., Sharma, S., Ventä-Olkkonen, L.: Digital transformation of everyday life–How COVID-19 pandemic transformed the basic education of the young generation and why information management research should care? Int. J. Inf. Manag. 1(55), 102183 (2020). https://doi.org/10.1016/j.ijinfomgt.2020.102183
2. Petersen, K., Feldt, R., Mujtaba, S., Mattsson, M.: Systematic mapping studies in software engineering. In: 12th International Conference on Evaluation and Assessment in Software Engineering (EASE), 12 June 2008, pp. 1–10 (2008). https://www.scienceopen.com/hosted-document?doi=10.14236/ewic/EASE2008.8
3. Kitchenham, B.: Procedures for performing systematic reviews 33(2004), 1–26. Keele University, Keele (2004). ISSN:1353-7776
4. Dermeval, D., Coelho, J.A., Bittencourt, I.I.: Mapeamento sistemático e revisao sistemática da literatura em informática na educaçao. In: Jaques, P.A., Pimentel, M., Siqueira, Sean, Bittencourt, I.G. (eds.) Metodologia de Pesquisa em Informática na Educação: Abordagem Quantitativa de Pesquisa. SBC, Porto Alegre (2019). https://metodologia.ceie-br.org/wp-content/uploads/2019/11/livro2_cap3.pdf

5. Mickalowski, K., Mickelson, M., Keltgen, J.: Apple's iPhone launch: a case study in effective marketing. Bus. Rev. **9**(2), 283–288 (2008). https://5y1.org/download/0e13f6d318da371754 41054f0af0f177.pdf

6. Abubakar, H.I., Hashim, N.L., Hussain, A.: Usability evaluation model for mobile banking applications interface: model evaluation process using experts' panel. J. Telecommun. Electron. Comput. Eng. (JTEC). **8**(10), 53–57 (2016). e-ISSN: 2289-8131

7. Inal, Y.: Heuristic-based user interface evaluation of the mobile centralized doctor appointment system: a case study. Electron. Libr. (2019). ISSN: 0264-0473

8. Ivanc, D., Vasiu, R., Onita, M.: Usability evaluation of a lms mobile web interface. In: Skersys, T., Butleris, R., Butkiene, R. (eds.) ICIST 2012. CCIS, vol. 319, pp. 348–361. Springer, Heidelberg (2012). https://doi.org/10.1007/978-3-642-33308-8_29

9. Lumsden, J., MacLean, R.: A comparison of pseudo-paper and paper prototyping methods for mobile evaluations. In: Meersman, R., Tari, Z., Herrero, P. (eds.) OTM 2008. LNCS, vol. 5333, pp. 538–547. Springer, Heidelberg (2008). https://doi.org/10.1007/978-3-540-88875-8_77

10. Machado Neto, O., Pimentel, M.D.: Heuristics for the assessment of interfaces of mobile devices. In: Proceedings of the 19th Brazilian Symposium on Multimedia and the Web, pp. 93–96 (2013). https://doi.org/10.1145/2526188.2526237

11. Nayebi, F., Desharnais, J.M., Abran, A.: The state of the art of mobile application usability evaluation. In: 2012 25th IEEE Canadian Conference on Electrical and Computer Engineering (CCECE), pp. 1–4. IEEE (2012). https://doi.org/10.1109/CCECE.2012.6334930

12. Omar, K., Rapp, B., Gómez, J.M.: Heuristic evaluation checklist for mobile ERP user interfaces. In: 2016 7th International Conference on Information and Communication Systems (ICICS), pp. 180–185. IEEE (2016). https://doi.org/10.1109/IACS.2016.7476107

13. Orlandini, G., Castadelli, G., Presumido Braccialli, L.: Ergonomics and usability in sound dimension: evaluation of a haptic and acoustic interface application for mobile devices. In: Marcus, A. (ed.) DUXU 2014. LNCS, vol. 8518, pp. 193–202. Springer, Cham (2014). https://doi.org/10.1007/978-3-319-07626-3_18

14. Pathak, A., Kumazawa, I.: Usability evaluation of touch panel-based mobile device on user interface with multimodal feedback. In: IEEE-International Conference on Advances in Engineering, Science and Management (ICAESM-2012), pp. 703–708. IEEE (2012). e-ISBN: 978-81-909042-2-3

15. Soui, M., Chouchane, M., Gasmi, I., Mkaouer, M.W.: PLAIN: PLugin for predicting the usAbility of Mobile User INterface. In: VISIGRAPP (1: GRAPP), pp. 127–136 (2017). https://doi.org/10.5220/0006171201270136

16. Wang, S., Li, B., Zhu, Y.: Comprehensive evaluation of usability at the mobile end interface. In: IOP Conference Series: Materials Science and Engineering 2019 Jul 1, vol. 573, no. 1, p. 012037. IOP Publishing (2019). https://iopscience.iop.org/article/10.1088/1757-899X/573/1/012037/meta

17. Yáñez, G.R., Cascado, C.D., Sevillano, J.L.: Heuristic evaluation on mobile interfaces: a new checklist. Sci. World J. **1**, 2014 (2014). https://doi.org/10.1155/2014/434326

18. Arrue, M., Vigo, M., Abascal, J.: Automatic evaluation of mobile web accessibility. In: Stephanidis, C., Pieper, M. (eds.) UI4ALL 2006. LNCS, vol. 4397, pp. 244–260. Springer, Heidelberg (2007). https://doi.org/10.1007/978-3-540-71025-7_16

19. Carvalho, L.P., Ferreira, L.P., Freire, A.P.: Accessibility evaluation of rich internet applications interface components for mobile screen readers. In: Proceedings of the 31st Annual ACM Symposium on Applied Computing, pp. 181–186 (2016). https://doi.org/10.1145/2851613.2851680

20. De Barros, A.C., Leitão, R., Ribeiro, J.: Design and evaluation of a mobile user interface for older adults: navigation, interaction and visual design recommendations. Procedia Comput. Sci. **1**(27), 369–378 (2014). https://doi.org/10.1016/j.procs.2014.02.041

21. Kobayashi, M., Hiyama, A., Miura, T., Asakawa, C., Hirose, M., Ifukube, T.: Elderly user evaluation of mobile touchscreen interactions. In: Campos, P., Graham, N., Jorge, J., Nunes, N., Palanque, P., Winckler, M. (eds.) INTERACT 2011. LNCS, vol. 6946, pp. 83–99. Springer, Heidelberg (2011). https://doi.org/10.1007/978-3-642-23774-4_9
22. Nathan, S.S., Hussain, A., Hashim, N.L.: Usability evaluation of DEAF mobile application interface: a systematic review. J. Eng. Appl. Sci. 13(2), 291–297 (2018). ISSN 1816-949X
23. Rezae, M., Chen, N., McMeekin, D., Tan, T., Krishna, A., Lee, H.: The evaluation of a mobile user interface for people on the autism spectrum: an eye movement study. Int. J. Hum. Comput. Stud. 1(142), 102462 (2020). https://doi.org/10.1016/j.ijhcs.2020.102462
24. Ruzic L., Harrington C. N., Sanford J. A. Design and evaluation of mobile interfaces for an aging population. InProc. 10th Int. Conf. Adv. Comput.-Hum. Interact.(ACHI) 2017 Mar (pp. 305–309). Recovered from: https://www.thinkmind.org/download.php?articleid=achi_2017_15_10_28016
25. Smaradottir B., Håland J., Martinez S. Accessibility of Mobile Devices for Visually Impaired Users: An Evaluation of the Screen-Reader VoiceOver. Studies in health technology and informatics. 2017 Jan 1;245:1381-. Recovered from: https://europepmc.org/article/med/29295460
26. Muslim E., Lestari R. A., Hazmy A. I., Alvina S. User interface evaluation of mobile application krl access using user experience approach. In IOP Conference Series: Materials Science and Engineering 2019 Apr 1 (Vol. 508, No. 1, p. 012110). IOP Publishing. Recovered from: https://iopscience.iop.org/article/https://doi.org/10.1088/1757-899X/508/1/012110/meta
27. Veldsman A., van Greunen D. Comparative usability evaluation of a mobile health app. In2017 IST-Africa Week Conference (IST-Africa) 2017 May 30 (pp. 1–8). IEEE. doi: https://doi.org/10.23919/ISTAFRICA.2017.8102383
28. Zamri K. Y., Al Subhi N. N. 10 user interface elements for mobile learning application development. In2015 International Conference on Interactive Mobile Communication Technologies and Learning (IMCL) 2015 Nov 19 (pp. 44–50). IEEE. doi: https://doi.org/10.1109/IMCTL.2015.7359551
29. Ines, G., Makram, S., Mabrouka, C., Mourad, A.: Evaluation of mobile interfaces as an optimization problem. Procedia computer science. 1(112), 235–248 (2017). https://doi.org/10.1016/j.procs.2017.08.234
30. Miniukovich, A., De Angeli, A.: Visual impressions of mobile app interfaces. In: Proceedings of the 8th Nordic Conference on Human-Computer Interaction: Fun, Fast, Foundational 26 Oct 2014, pp. 31–40 (2014). ISBN: 978-1-4503-2542-4
31. Warfel, T., Maurer, D.: Card sorting: a definitive guide. Boxes and arrows (2004). http://www.iimagineservicedesign.com/wp-content/uploads/2015/07/Card-sorting-a-definitive-guide-%C2%AB-Boxes-and-Arrows.pdf
32. Vaz, F.R., Carvalho, C.L.: Visualização de informações. Universidade Federal de Goiás (2004). https://ww2.inf.ufg.br/sites/default/files/uploads/relatorios-tecnicos/RT-INF_003-04.pdf

Lepi-Board: An Infrastructure
for the Development of Digital Storytelling
Games by Blind-Users

Gabriel Cheban do Prado Mendes[(✉)] [iD], Luciano de Oliveira Neris[iD],
and Vânia Paula de Almeida Neris[iD]

Department of Computing, Federal University of Sao Carlos, São Carlos, Brazil
gabrielcpm@estudante.ufscar.br, {lneris,vania.neris}@ufscar.br

Abstract. The Digital games and the practice of modding are becoming even
more common and popular. However, the target public is still largely homogeneous
and does not include people with disabilities. This paper presents a computational
solution that involves using a digital game editor for blind end-users. This solution
is part of a larger project based on end-user development, which consists of a
storytelling desktop editor tool with graphic elements and a web version for cloud
storage. Design Science Research was adopted as the methodology employed for
this investigation. The research products obtained by this work include a haptic
board to design scenes, software to transform the physical scene into a digital scene
and a set of instructions. Although it was not possible to carry out an evaluation
with the public of interest because of the current health restrictions in Brazil, we
demonstrate how the infrastructure created allows the use of a haptic device to
create digital storytelling games with the minimum system requirements.

Keywords: Digital game · Storytelling · End-user development · Accessibility ·
Blind-user · Haptic · Board

1 Introduction

Games are increasingly becoming a feature of everyday life, and expanding their goals
and audiences, beyond simply being a hobby. There is a growing trend to provide players
(end users) with creative roles owing to the popularity of play-acting. The practice,
known as modding, enables users (modders) to modify or adapt a game to their interests
or sense of creativity. There are games ranging from media provided by studios to tools
designed for a specific purpose, which include some gameplay changes and encourage
modifications. Moreover, it is worth noting, the growing academic and industrial interests
in allowing end users to create their own digital games.

Game development by end users is supported by tools or software modules for
creating or modifying games. These kinds of tools are often intuitive as they do not
require the user to have prior knowledge of programming. However, accessibility issues,
in general, are not taken into account when creating these tools [1]. It is necessary to

© Springer Nature Switzerland AG 2021
P. H. Ruiz et al. (Eds.): HCI-COLLAB 2021, CCIS 1478, pp. 126–135, 2021.
https://doi.org/10.1007/978-3-030-92325-9_10

build new solutions for the inclusion of people with disabilities in the activities when creating digital games.

In light of this, our research group has established a framework named Lepi [1] to support the creation of games by people with different capacities and interaction skills in game development. The framework consists of software architecture, a collaboration model, and a visual editor for creating storytelling games. It was evaluated by people suffering from alcohol and drug addiction in a public healthcare service. Although the framework was designed to be inclusive, a solution has still not been found for blind people.

To fill this gap, this paper provides a solution that takes account of the tactile abilities of blind users and offers a haptic board to design game scenes. The infrastructure is also embedded with software to change a physical scene into a digital scene with a set of instructions. It should be noted that the game created can be enjoyed by both blind people (through audio description) and non-blind users (with the aid of audio/visual resources). This means a blind person can create a game for a non-blind person, as well as including all the other combinations of models with regard to creators/modders and players within this public.

When carrying out this project, the methodology of Design Science Research (DSR) was adopted; this supports the idea of attempting to solve a problem through the construction of an artifact. The steps for this project described by Hevner and Chatterjee [2] were followed: identification of the problem and motivation, definition of objectives, design and development, demonstration, evaluation and communication. These enabled the study of the state-of-the-art and the creation of artifacts to be carried out. In addition, in the methodological stage, a feasibility study was carried out, although only by users without visual impairments, because of the COVID-19 pandemic which restricted contact with external participants. The results suggest that the computational solution created, which explores both touch and hearing, allows end-users to create digital games that can be played by everyone.

This article is structured as follows: Sect. 2 provides a summary of works related to the use and programming of games by blind users. Section 3 outlines the methodology used for the planning of the Lepi-Board. Section 4 examines the proposed solution. Section 5 describes the feasibility study and in Sect. 6 the conclusion is summarized and some recommendations are made for future work.

2 Related Works

The use and programming of games by blind users are based on studies that demonstrate that there is a relationship between the sense of touch, especially with haptic peripherals for data entry, and hearing, mostly as an output in the form of an audible warning. Aspects of teamwork involving people with different skills are also explored, which encourage inclusion and joint action [3–5]. Another approach adopted is the writing of codes with the aid of screen readers. However, navigation and code writing that only depend on screen readers can become difficult for some blind users, especially because the navigation in complex code documents [5].

The use of Braille or audio feedback improves the user´s understanding of haptic devices and makes the creation environment more inclusive [6]. It is often not feasible to make a one-to-one transformation of graphic elements to audio for audio games, and it may be necessary to create a new auditory interface [7]. Commands can be used in a cyclic menu by means of text-to-speech features so that each command option can be read to the user in programming through an auditory interface [8].

We relied on some of these successful solutions to build a haptic platform and software systems which allow blind users to develop digital games. Moreover, our solution differs from others as it focuses on allowing the creation of a game that could be played by sighted and blind gamers.

3 A Methodological Approach

The DSR was the methodology employed for this study, and this is recommended when there is an opportunity to solve a problem through the construction of an artifact (such as an algorithmic solution, infrastructure, or new architecture). Thus, this methodology was chosen because the aim of this project is to solve human problems through the creation of artifacts. Hevner and Chatterjee [2] recommend carrying out the DSR in six stages:

- **Problem Identification and Motivation:** Definition of a specific research problem and an explanation of how it can find the value of a solution. This stage also includes obtaining knowledge of the state of the problem and assessing the importance of its solution;
- **Defining the Objectives for the Solution:** Inferring the objectives of a solution based on the previous stage and determining what is possible and feasible. Objectives can be quantitative (how much greater in terms of values) or qualitative (a description of how the use of the new artifact will assist in finding solutions to problems not yet addressed). This stage also includes knowing the status of current problems and solutions, if any, and their effectiveness;
- **Design and Development:** Creation of artifacts, determining the desired functionality and its architecture. This stage also includes finding out about the theory on which a solution will be based;
- **Demonstration:** Demonstrating how the artifact can solve instances of the problem, which may include experiments, simulations, or case studies, among other activities. This stage also includes finding out how to use the artifact to solve the problem;
- **Evaluation:** Observing and assessing how well the artifact assists in finding a solution to the problem. This involves comparing the objectives of a solution with the real results observed in the previous stage and this requires knowledge of metrics and analytical techniques. It might contain quantitative measures, such as the budget, system performance metrics, and response time. This stage also includes iterative decision-making and returns to the Design and Development stage to improve the effectiveness of the artifact or else goes to the last stage and leaves the improvements for future work;
- **Communication:** this involves the need to communicate, publish, or disseminate to other researchers and people of interest the problem addressed and its importance, as well as the artifact, its usefulness and what is new, the rigor of its design, and its effectiveness.

Section 4 examines the solution created by following the steps of the DSR.

4 Lepi-Board Infrastructure

We selected and studied some works related to the theme in the stages of the DSR "Identification of the Problem and Motivation" and "Definition of the Objectives for the Solution" [3–5]. It was noted that there was often a combination of models after the studies had been carried out: haptic input and auditory feedback (feedback). Following this, the objectives that the solution had to achieve were defined: 1. With the aid of a haptic board, users must be able to incorporate media features, originally graphic, for each scene in the creation phase; 2. By means of software that communicates with the board and that has a simple interaction with it, users should be able to create their own stories with connected scenes, character dialogues, and narration through audio recording and add scores about the options for choosing your story; and 3. The software must be able to create files compatible with the desktop version of the graphics editor.

The definition provided by Hevner and Chatterjee [2] formed the basis of the "Design and Development" of the artifacts, which states that a design research artifact can be any projected object in which a research feature is incorporated into the design. The development of the solution was divided into three parts: 1. a definition of the character traits and scenarios for their identification by the blind user; 2. creation of the haptic board encompassing the preparation of tactile sprites and the use of the board sensors; and, finally, 3. The construction of software that obtains data from the board and turns it into a game. In addition, there was a mapping of the stages of creation and use by the blind and those with sight. The task was undertaken in an iterative and incremental way, especially with regard to the software.

4.1 Characters and Scenarios

The description of the character traits and scenarios occurs in two phases: 1. on the label in Braille writing to identify A Subsection Sample the character sprites when the user is assembling the components of his story on the board and 2. on the basis of the auditory output (via software) for the description of a complete scene when checking/editing it and, at another time, when a user is playing.

Snyder's guidelines [9] for audio description were followed in the creation of the game and the graphic elements so that they could be identified and understood by blind users both in the software and in the haptic sprites:

- **Scenarios:** description of the space as a whole (a square, a room, an alley, etc.), together with more characteristic objects and elements;
- **Characters:** gender (only for the software, since the sprites have a silhouette for gender identification - see Fig. 1), age group, ethnicity, hairstyle, height, physical size, style of clothing style, and individual physical features such as beard and tattoos).

4.2 The Haptic Board

Corrugated polypropylene sheets (the same plastic material used for school folders) were used for the construction of both the haptic board (Lepi-Board) and the haptic sprites. This material is suitable for construction as it is not expensive and has, among other factors, chemical resistance, easy molding, moderate impact resistance, good thermal stability, resistance to flexion, and low moisture absorption [10].

Nine Radio Frequency Identification (RFID) devices were fixed to the board and connected to an Arduino module. This module is responsible for generating a single string containing the identification of the RFID module and the code of the identified RFID tags. This string is sent through the serial port to the processing software (Lepi-Builder) that obtains the data from the Lepi-Board that transforms it into a game. The labels have been attached to the haptic sprites and represent either a specific character or scenario.

Haptic sprites, that are objects that represent graphic elements, were also created. Tactile sprites can be of four types:

- **Character:** The object has the shape of a person's silhouette, one of four types of silhouette: a child (girl or boy) or adult (man or woman). In addition, each character sprite has its own label with a Braille description of its features;
- **Scenario:** The object has a square shape and also has a label with a braille description of its features;
- **Narrator:** The object has a rectangular shape, but does not need an additional description of its features;
- **Choices:** The object has a shape similar to a magnifying glass and, as in the previous item, does not need an additional Braille description.

In addition, nine sensors are attached to the board in such a way that each sensor can read a tactile sprite nearest it. A string with the tag id detected is sent to the software. The sensors were arranged as shown in Fig. 1. The leftmost position is reserved for fitting the sprite of the scenario type; the other positions are for fitting the other sprites. In the case of these character-type sprites, the sensor number will define the position (among the eight predefined ones) in which the character will be positioned in the visual game. As we know previously the possible positions for the character-type, we left these spaces available (without other objects) in the visual scenarios representations to avoid visual overlap. Finally, the narrator's sprites and choices have fixed positions in the visual game and can be placed in any position on the board.

Extensive use is made of RFID technology for the identification of the actors and the determination of their positions in the scenario. Given that the same actor can be positioned in different places and a scene can contain several actors, its exact location must be determined. In view of this, we sought a solution without an electrical connection between the actor and the board to simplify its construction and avoid glitches and, hence, an incorrect portrayal of the scenario. Thus, radio frequency identification proved to be suitable for the construction of the board since several readers can be spread across the board and the resolution (number of actors in the scenario) is easily scalable.

Fig. 1. Opened up haptic board with three haptic stencils for a man, woman and children.

4.3 The Haptic Board

Lepi-Builder was developed by means of the Python programming language and was based on the libraries designed for opening and creating folders and files, reading the serial port, using text-to-speech by means of the synthetic voice of the operating system itself, the use of the microphone, the manipulation of JSON files, the reproduction of audios and the issuing of audible warning signals (beeps).

A limited number of keys were used to increase the efficiency of the software systems for blind users. The keys were defined in terms of their daily use:

- **Keyboard arrows:** these are responsible for navigation within the software and they are mapped in such a way that the up and right arrows are equivalent and the same for the down and left arrows and the menus look like as a carousel;
- **"Enter" key:** this is used to open an option and to confirm actions;
- **"Esc" key:** this is used to cancel an action or exit;

- **Space bar:** this is used for actions that involve attempting again to rewrite the name of the project, renaming a character, reentering a value, redoing the search, and replay;
- **"Equal" key:** it is used to allow listening after a recording.

The following interaction options are available in Lepi-Builder:

- **Main menu:** presentation of the software, and telling the user how to interact with it;
- **Create a new act:** the user is asked to enter a name for the new story (game) to be created, after which the user (or the responsible professional) must select the number of score parameters to be used in the game and select them from a predefined list of parameters (each selected parameter is removed from the list to avoid being selected multiple times), in all the stages of this option, there is an opportunity for a confirmation;
- **Load an act:** the user is asked to enter the name of his story (the game), the program then checks whether this story exists and informs him if it was found; after this, there is a confirmation of the opening of that game;
- **Options:** list of options to be activated or deactivated, by default: Text-to-speech: Enabled, Record audios: Enabled, Enter dialogs: Deactivated, Insert videos (Pounds): Deactivated;
- **Help:** instructions for using the software and best practices that must be followed when creating a game;
- **Exit:** ends the program, and shows a confirmation message;
- **Add new scene:** this option is used to add the scenes of the story after creating or loading an act (game). In this function the serial port connected to Lepi-Board gets the string and transforms it into a JSON fragment; an interaction may be necessary for each inserted element:

  – Scenario: no additional interaction is required;
  – Narrator: a request is made to record an audio file via a microphone; after this, it is possible either to listen to it or re-record it if you wish;
  – Character: a name is requested for the character; the first time is included (the name is stored in a dictionary associated with its sprite), the possibility of adding speech for the character is offered by recording an audio file via a microphone; in this case, you cannot perform the recording (character without speech in this scene) or perform it, listen to it or re-record it, even if you wish to;
  – Choices: the statement (or the question asked) through the audio recording is requested so that there are options to choose from. Then the number of options is asked (currently, only 2 or 3 are considered to be valid) and the recording of the audio of each choice and the score of each parameter previously defined for each choice (the score values are defined as integers and fall within to the range $[-10, 10]$).

A stack is used in nested scenes of choice. First, you must end the sequence for the last scene of choice that has not yet been completed, to obtain permission to end the sequences of scenes of choices that are at higher levels. This will be a scene that follows all the final scenes of each sequence of choices if a new scene is added (i.e. after all the sequences of choices have been completed).

Although the main use for Lepi-Builder is to support blind users to finish the game creation process, and therefore we designed the interaction through audio output and inputs and keyboard selection, we also provided a visual user interface. Our intention was to facilitate the participation of a sighted user if needed or desired as in a collaborative section, for instance.

5 Feasibility Study

As stated above, we were unable to evaluate the solution with real users owing to the health restrictions in Brazil due to the coronavirus pandemic. Therefore, we performed the DSR phases "Demonstration" and "Evaluation" through a feasibility study. We performed four situations to demonstrate how to make use of the solution:

- **Blind user as creator:** Use of Lepi-Board and Lepi-Builder to create games. The interactions between the characters in the game were recorded in audio;
- **Blind user as a player:** Using Lepi-Desktop we ran the game. There were audio files associated with the texts and other graphic elements so that the blind user can follow the narrative of the game;
- **Sighted user as creator:** Use of Lepi-Desktop for creation. The creator or the collaborator was concerned with a) the details described (audio description) and b) the addition of the audios recorded for all the texts for the creation of a game - so that a blind user can play;
- **Sighted user as a player:** The way in which Lepi-Builder creates the game allows the user to wish sight to play without his experience being affected. The game was generated by transforming the haptic sprites into digital sprites in the game while preserving their positions and features.

The left side of Fig. 2 illustrates the use of the board to create the visual scene that is shown on Fig. 2 right side. At the bottom of the left side, it is illustrated Lepi-Builder visual interface. Besides the visual, all the instructions are available in audio format to guide the creator in adding the audio files.

In the feasibility study, we created a game with three characters that are in a park. The first step was to choose the scenario. A blind user could do that by selecting the tactile sprite with the Braille tag indicating a park and adding it to Lepi-Board. After that, the blind user could add the characters. In this case, we selected one man, one woman, and one girl. A blind user could select them using the tactile sprites by their format and know their characteristics such as skin and hair color, and clothes description by the Braille tags. The characters may be placed in the seven available different positions in Lepi-Board and this position will be the same in the visual scene. We also added sprites for the narrator, dialog, and for option (aiming to add a question and multiple-choice answer with points associated).

After using the Lepi-Board, we used the Lepi-Builder on a laptop. We tested all the audio options and used them without relying on the visual interface. While following the

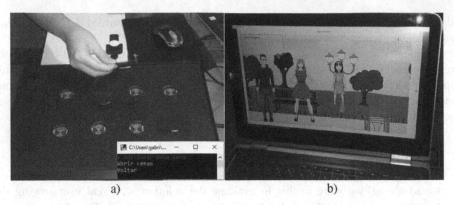

a)   b)

Fig. 2. a) Lepi-Board and Lepi-Builder in use. b) Visual scene available at Lepi-Desktop.

audio instructions, we could listen to the character's audio descriptions (the same that were in the Brailler tag in the tactile sprite), thus recognize them. Using Lepi-Builder, we recorded audio files and associated them with the sprites. For the narrator, we added an audio file describing that there was a family in a park and we optioned to present an audio description of the characters on our own at this same file. Then, we added an audio file in which the father tells the girl information about the park's history and then there was a multiple-choice question about the information provided. When we finished, we saved and the JSON file is available for Lepi-Desktop.

Using Lepi-Desktop, and now performing as a sighted user, we were able to open the game created and we saw the scene in Fig. 2 right side. Clicking on the microphone icon in the narrator balloon, we were able to listen to the first audio. As sighted users, we also were able to see the park and characters. We moved between scenes, listen to the fathers' explanation about the park's history, and saw the question with multiple answers about it. We selected the right answer, got 10 points, and finished the game.

As previously known, as sighted creators using Lepi-Desktop we were able to mod the game adding a new question about the parks' history. We added it in text and associated it with an audio file recorded using the recorded tool of the Windows operating system. After that, we were able to play this extended game without relying on the visual elements of the user interface simulating the use by a blind person as a player. After performing these actions, we can say the feasibility studied results suggest the solution proposed allows game creation and play in a more inclusive approach.

6   Conclusion and Future Work

The graphic editor that already existed in the project allows different users to interact in its two phases: creation and gameplay. This serves, first, as a game creation tool and, second as a means of forming, a bridge for people with different skills to create games.

The Lepi-Board solution created and outlined in this article makes it possible to include blind people in the creation of games. A striking feature is the fact that the solution allows the graphic elements, (which are important for the interaction of those who are able to see), to be incorporated automatically. In addition, a game created by a user who has vision, will be provided with an audio description of the scene (scenery and characters) and also audio in all its text boxes. These accessibility features can be designed by the author of the game or even added, a posteriori, by a collaborator.

Although it was not possible to carry out the evaluation stage with the public of interest, the feasibility study showed that it is possible to create a game, especially of a genre that has graphic elements, by including an alternative, haptic interface. Another interesting point worth highlighting is the simplicity of the software, which requires only three interactions to create a game, two of them by pressing the same key and one to name the story. Thus, the objective of assistive technology research in the creation and experience of playing can be attained, as well as the study and development of a haptic device for the creation of games with minimum software requirements. It is worth noting that the solution can also be used by other audiences such as children and people with low literacy.

In future work, we hope to be able to perform more lab tests and apply our research findings to real users and disseminate the construction of the board in do-it-yourself initiatives, computer education, and gaming communities.

References

1. Garcia, F.E., de Almeida Neris, V.P.: A framework for tailorable games: toward inclusive end-user development of inclusive games. Univ. Access Inf. Soc. (2020). https://doi.org/10.1007/s10209-020-00779-8
2. Hevner, A., Chatterjee, S.: Design Research in Information Systems: Theory and Practice. 1st edn. Springer, Heidelberg (2010). https://doi.org/10.1007/978-1-4419-5653-8. ISBN 1441956522
3. Thieme, A., et al.: Enabling collaboration in learning computer programming inclusive of children with vision impairments. In: Proceedings of the 2017 Conference on Designing Interactive Systems (DIS 2017), pp. 739–752. Association for Computing Machinery, New York (2017). ISBN 9781450349222
4. Branham, S.M., Kane, S.K.: Collaborative accessibility: how blind and sighted companions co-create accessible home spaces. In: Proceedings of the 33rd Annual ACM Conference on Human Factors in Computing Systems (CHI 2015), pp. 2373–2382. Association for Computing Machinery, New York (2015). ISBN 9781450331456
5. Kane, S.K., Koushik, V., Muehlbradt, A.: Bonk: accessible programming for accessible audio games. In: Proceedings of the 17th ACM Conference on Interaction Design and Children (IDC 2018), pp. 132–142. Association for Computing Machinery, New York (2018). ISBN 9781450351522
6. Westin, T., Engström, H., Brusk, J.: Towards sustainable inclusive game design processes. In: [S.l.: s.n.], pp. 390–396 (2020). ISBN 978-3-030-53293-2
7. Friberg, J., Gärdenfors, D.: Audio games: new perspectives on game audio. In: International Conference on Advances in Computer Entertainment Technology, pp. 148–154. ACM Press, Singapore (2004). ISBN 1-58113-882-2
8. Sánchez, J., Aguayo, F.: Blind learners programming through audio. In: CHI 2005 Conference on Human Factors in Computing Systems [S.l.: s.n.], pp. 1769–1772 (2005)
9. Snyder, J.: Audio description guidelines and best practices. Manual, p. 98 (2010)
10. Junior, J.C.M.: Análise das propriedades mecânicas do polipropileno EP448R injetado com adição do polipropileno reprocessado em percentuais menores que 50% em Peso. Dissertação de Mestrado, p. 93 (2017)

Modeling and Evaluating Personas with Software Explainability Requirements

Henrique Ramos(✉) ⓘ, Mateus Fonseca ⓘ, and Lesandro Ponciano ⓘ

Pontifical Catholic University of Minas Gerais, Belo Horizonte, Brazil

Abstract. This work focuses on the context of software explainability, which is the production of software capable of explaining to users the dynamics that govern its internal functioning. User models that include information about their requirements and their perceptions of explainability are fundamental when building software with such capability. This study investigates the process of creating personas that include information about users' explainability perceptions and needs. The proposed approach is based on data collection with questionnaires, modeling of empathy maps, grouping the maps, generating personas from them and evaluation employing the Persona Perception Scale method. In an empirical study, personas are created from 61 users' response data to a questionnaire. The generated personas are evaluated by 60 users and 38 designers considering attributes of the Persona Perception Scale method. The results include a set of 5 distinct personas that users rate as representative of them at an average level of 3.7 out of 5, and designers rate as having quality 3.5 out of 5. The median rate is 4 out of 5 in the majority of criteria judged by users and designers. Both the personas and their creation and evaluation approach are contributions of this study to the design of software that satisfies the explainability requirement.

Keywords: User modeling · Persona · Explainability requirement

1 Introduction

The relationship between people and interactive systems has been an object of study in the area of Human-Computer Interaction [1, 2]. This area is interested in designing and evaluating interactive systems, considering the user, the interface, the interaction and the context of use [1, 3, 4]. The requirements of usability, accessibility, and communicability are precursor challenges in the design process in this area, which seeks to maximize the quality of the experience of its users from the early stages of system design to phenomena associated with use.

Over the last years, as interactive systems come to play a decisive role in the lives of individual people and in their collective behavior, new challenges have emerged in terms of requirements, usually described as new restrictions on system construction and functioning dynamics. Depending on how it is designed, interactive systems may inadvertently influence the opinions, choices and actions of their users, reflecting on social, political and economic dynamics. For example, when a system recommends a

© Springer Nature Switzerland AG 2021
P. H. Ruiz et al. (Eds.): HCI-COLLAB 2021, CCIS 1478, pp. 136–149, 2021.
https://doi.org/10.1007/978-3-030-92325-9_11

decision to the user over another or when it prioritizes some content over others without providing an explanation. In this context, it is increasingly required that this type of system be able to explain for a user its computation steps and how its outputs are generated [5]. It has been treated as a non-functional requirement, called "explainability requirement" [6, 7].

Designing and implementing software so that it meets the explainability requirement is a major challenge. It is essential to understand to what extent people are concerned with explainability and to what extent they perceive the importance and feel the need for the system to be self-explainable. However, little is known about how users of interactive systems perceive this requirement. This work seeks to contribute to filling this gap by studying the process of modeling users including their perceptions, needs and concerns associated with the explainability requirement. In doing so, this study focuses on the technique of modeling users as personas, which are fictional characters created from real data to represent the target audience.

Our persona modeling approach integrates studies on the concept of explainability requirement [6], people's perception of the explainability requirement [7], creation of empathy maps and personas [8, 9], and evaluation of personas through the Persona Perception Scale [10]. It is a five-step process that can be summarized as follows: 1) questionnaires are applied to users to collect their perceptions and needs; 2) the responses obtained are used to create empathy maps including what the user says, feels, does and thinks about explainability; 3) similar empathy maps from different users are aggregated; 4) from the groups of empathy maps the personas are generated; 5) the personas are validated with the target public of users and designers. At the end of the fifth step, there is a set of personas that can be considered during the interface and interaction design so that the software may meet users' demands for explainability.

The proposed approach for persona creation and evaluation is investigated in this study in an empirical study with participation of 61 users in the first step (data collection), and 60 users and 38 designers in the fifth step (evaluation). The obtained results include a set of 5 distinct personas. Considering attributes of the Persona Perception Scale method [10], we found that personas are rated by the users as representative of them at an average level of 3.7 out of 5 and are rated by designers as having quality 3.5 out of 5. The median rate is 4 out of 5 in the majority of evaluation criteria. Both the personas and their creation and evaluation approach are contributions of this study for designers and researchers looking for strategies to guide the development of software with the explainability requirement.

The rest of this paper is organized as follows. We provide first a background of key concepts related to explainability and personas, and discuss relevant previous work (Sect. 2). Next, we discuss our approach to model and evaluate personas considering the explainability requirement (Sect. 3). After that, we detail the materials and methods of evaluation (Sect. 4). Then, we discuss the obtained results (Sect. 5). Finally, we discuss the conclusions of the study (Sect. 6).

2 Background and Related Work

This section presents the works related to the creation and use of user Empathy Map and Personas, as well as the advantages and disadvantages of its use. The section concludes with an analysis of the context of software explainability and recent advances in user modeling for that context.

As part of user modeling, this work uses *empathy maps*. Empathy Map is a user modeling technique that favors a better understanding of the user's context represented from 6 variables to be considered: what he says, does, sees, hears, feels and thinks. In addition to these, there are also areas of pain and need [11]. On the traditional Empathy Map, there are only the quadrants "thinks", "says", "feels" and "does", with the user represented in the middle. The first says about what the user thinks, but is not willing to vocalize. The "says" quadrant is what the user believes and that, if necessary, would speak without problems. Finally, the "feels" and "does" quadrants represent the user's feelings and attitudes, respectively. Empathy Map can be used to create personas [8].

A *persona* is a fictional character created to represent the target audience [12]. Its creation and use are relevant in User-Centered Design, a development approach in which the user must be understood during the entire process of conception, development and implementation of the product [13]. In this context, this model contains textual and graphic elements that incorporate the traits of target users. Personas help designers to have a more concrete view of who the users are [14], and make the product developers sympathize with the represented people [15].

Even though the use of personas in collaborative design environments is well established, little research has been done to quantify the benefits of using this technique [16]. Previous results indicated that the groups of students who used personas produced products with superior usability characteristics. In addition, it is attested that the use of personas provides a significant advantage during the research and conceptualization stages of the design process. The fact that this study presents the advantages that the use of personas can bring to the users' experience makes it appropriate to be evaluated in the current study. Seeking to overcome limitations related to time and resources for data collection for the generation of personas, Mahamuni et al. (2018) evaluate the effectiveness of using the tacit knowledge of stakeholders in this process [17]. The use of tacit knowledge was effective in an organizational context, especially when time is a limitation.

Although personas are widely used in many domains, its evaluation is difficult, mainly due to the lack of validated measuring instruments. With this, the authors prepare a survey to assess the perception of individuals about a persona [10]. This artifact consists of 8 evaluation criteria, which can be modified to meet only those relevant to the research, each containing a maximum of 4 statements on a Likert scale:

1. **Credibility:** How realistic is the persona;
2. **Consistency:** The information in the description is consistent;
3. **Completeness:** Captures essential information about the described users;
4. **Clarity:** Information is presented clearly;
5. **Likability:** How nice the persona seems to be;
6. **Empathy:** How much the respondent empathizes with the persona;
7. **Similarity:** How much the persona looks like the respondent;
8. **Willingness:** Measures the respondent's willingness to learn more about the persona.

Applying the Perception Persona Scale [10], studies use clustering to validate automatically generated personas [18]. Among the criteria used in their validation survey are: similarity, empathy and credibility. Based on the results, it was noticed that two of the four generated personas achieved good results in the validation criteria, demonstrating that the participants have similar interests and think like the personas.

A useful way to understand the needs of users of a product or system is through the use of personas. However, Ferreira et al. (2015) consider that the creation of personas requires creativity and its validation, in terms of representativeness, is very difficult [9]. To assist in the creation of these models, the authors suggest the use of an empathy map. In the study, the designers' perception of the ease of use and usefulness of the empathy map for the creation of personas is assessed. To conduct the research, 20 user experience (UX) students participated, creating personas through textual content and then based on an empathy map. In line with this study, the work confirms that most designers found the Empathy Map technique easy to use and useful for creating personas.

In this work, personas were created in the context of software explainability. The challenge of developing software capable of explaining its outputs becomes greater the more sophisticated the computation performed by the software. One of the areas in which explainability has been widely addressed is the area of artificial intelligence, generally defined as Explainable Artificial Intelligence (XAI) [5, 6]. An additional challenge in XAI is that the behavior of the software is not only dependent on its implementation, but also on the data used for training and learning the software. In the context of "deep learning" algorithms, there is a gap between the social meaning associated with users and the technical meaning associated with the implementation of the algorithms, which makes implementing the explanation even more challenging. Studies have shown that there are several gaps associated with the development of systems that adhere to the explainability requirement [5]. Studies on public participation systems have highlighted the importance of the explainability requirement being considered on system interaction with people [19].

In the context of user modeling contemplating information about the explainability requirement, a technique that has already been considered is profile [7]. Louzada et al. (2020) seek to identify similarities and differences between users of interactive systems in terms of the importance of the requirement of software explainability, using the profile technique based on clustering. The study found 6 profiles, each with their level of interest in explainability of an interactive system. The study discusses the importance of creating personas and motivates further studies in this direction. Thus, this paper helps to advance this literature on this aspect of user modeling by including information on demand for explainability.

3 An Approach for Modeling and Evaluating Personas Considering the Explainability Requirement

In this section, we present our approach for modeling and evaluating personas that include information about how users perceive the explainability requirement and their needs regarding such requirements. In general, this approach integrates studies on the concept of explainability requirement [6], people's perception of the explainability requirement

[7], creation of empathy maps and persona [8, 9], and evaluation of personas through the Persona Perception Scale [10]. The proposed approach for creating and evaluating personas has 5 steps as summarized below:

1. Questionnaires are applied to users in order to collect their perceptions and needs about explainability;
2. The obtained answers are used to automatically create the four dimensions of an empathy map for each user;
3. Users with similar empathy map are aggregated on only one group of empathy maps;
4. From the resulting groups of empathy maps, the personas are generated;
5. Personas are validated with the public of users and designers.

The questionnaire used in the **first step** to analyze perceptions and explanatory needs is based on the questionnaire proposed by Louzada et. al (2020). The questionnaire investigates needs and requirements on explainability (Table 1). Depending on each context of use, other demographic information may be included, such as age, gender and schooling. The public to which the questionnaire is applied has a wide effect on the personas that will be obtained. For example, if the public are mostly male, at the end of the process, the results tend to be more personas with this characteristic. In the **second step**, the questions in this questionnaire are mapped on the dimensions of the empathy map [9], as shown in Table 1. The answers to each of these questions are on the 5-point Likert scale, being coded in answers from 1 to 5. For the quadrants "feels", "thinks" and "says", the subtraction of the answer pair, for being contradictory issues. For the "does" quadrant, the average of the answer pair is calculated. In the four dimensions, if the result is greater than or equal to 2.5, it is classified as "positive", otherwise, as "negative". Thus, at the end of the second step, for each user, there are four dimensions and each of them has a value defined as positive or negative.

In the **third step**, the empathy maps are grouped. For example, if 4 users have "positive" value in all 4 dimensions of the empathy map, then these users are equal and can be represented by only 1. As a result of this process, there is at least 1 empathy map, if all users are equal, and at most 16 empathy maps, which is the case that there are the two combinations of values (positive and negative) in each of the four quadrants of the empathy maps, so $2^4 = 16$ possibilities.

In the **fourth step** the grouped empathy maps are transformed into personas. For this, there are two fundamental activities. The first activity is to identify the demographic characteristics of the participants. This is done for each group, in which the modal value of age, gender, education and other user characteristics of users in each group is obtained. The second activity is to interpret the quadrants of the group's empathy map to describe it as an element of the persona. This interpretation is done following Table 2.

In the **fifth step**, two questionnaires with questions from Persona Perception Scale [10] with answers in Likert scale, between 1 (I totally disagree) and 5 (I totally agree), are applied. The questionnaire available in Table 3 is applied to users to quantify their perception of representation, taking into account the criteria: similarity, empathy and sympathy. The questionnaire available in Table 4 is applied to designers to measure their perception of the quality of the artifact, taking into account its clarity, completeness and credibility.

Table 1. Questions used to derive the quadrants from the empathy maps. Items in the "think", "feel" and "say" quadrants are answered in a five-point Likert scale. In the quadrant "does" answers are options that refer to acting positively or negatively in relation to the software explanations.

Quadrant	First question	Second question
DOES	Suppose you are using software where you enter the address of the location you are at and the address of the location you want to go to and the software tells you which street path you must follow to get to the desired location. Select the option that most closely matches your behavior in this situation	Suppose you are using software that is a social network where you can follow people and be followed. Suppose also that the software recommends someone to you to follow. Select the option that most closely matches your behavior in this situation
THINKS	If a user is interested in knowing how software generates recommendations that it makes, so the software must provide such an explanation to that user	I follow a software generated recommendation if it is useful to me, regardless of whether or not it has an explanation associated with it
FEELS	I feel more confident in following a recommendation made by a software when it explains to me why it considers the recommendation suitable for me	I usually feel confused by recommendations that the software I use makes me when they are not explained
SAYS	Software should be required by law to provide explanations of how they generate the recommendations they present to users	I have no interest in knowing how the software I use generates recommendations for me

Table 2. Positive and negative interpretations per quadrant of the Empathy Map.

Quadrant	Positive rating	Negative rating
DOES	Tends to follow the recommendation provided by the software	Tends not to follow the recommendation, makes his decisions alone
THINKS	Tends to believe that systems should explain its recommendations	Tends not to care about software explanations of its recommendations
FEELS	Feels more comfortable following a well-explained recommendation	A well-explained recommendation does not change his decision to follow it
SAYS	Says that explanations must be provided to users who are interested	It says that explanations should not be obligatorily provided

Table 3. Questionnaire about user perception of personas representativeness from Persona Perception Scale. The items are answered in a five-point Likert scale.

Construct	Item
Similarity	This persona feels similar to myself
Similarity	The persona and I think alike
Similarity	The persona and I share similar interests
Similarity	I believe I would agree with this persona on most matters
Empathy	I feel like I understand this persona
Empathy	I feel strong ties to this persona
Empathy	I can imagine a day in the life of this persona
Likability	I find this persona likable
Likability	I could be friends with this persona
Likability	This persona is interesting
Likability	This persona feels like someone I could spend time with

Table 4. Questionnaire about designer perception of personas quality from Persona Perception Scale. The items are answered in a five-point Likert scale

Construct	Item
Credibility	Those personas seem like real people
Credibility	I have met people like those personas
Credibility	The picture of those personas looks authentic
Credibility	Those personas seem to have a personality
Completeness	Those personas profiles are detailed enough to make. decisions about the customers they describe
Completeness	Those personas profiles seem complete
Completeness	Those personas profiles provide enough information to understand the people they describe
Completeness	Those personas profiles are not missing vital information
Clarity	The information about the personas is well presented
Clarity	The text in the persona's profile is clear enough to read
Clarity	The information in the persona's profile is easy to understand
Clarity	Those personas are memorable

Both questionnaires applied have a set of personas. In the questionnaire on the perception of users shown in Table 3, the user must select which persona most represents her/him and then answer the questions, taking into account only the selected persona. In the questionnaire on the perception of designers, shown in Table 4, designers must evaluate each group of personas as a whole.

4 Materials and Methods of Evaluation

This work seeks to analyze the quality of personas in relation to the representation of users and their construction in the context of software explainability, taking into account their creation through the approach proposed in the previous section. The research carried out is a case study in which the proposed approach was followed from its first step to fifth step. It is a case study because the study is carried out with a specific audience, although the proposed method can be applied to other audiences. This section describes the materials and methods employed in such a case study.

All questionnaires applied in this study, whose questions are described in Sect. 3 are prepared in Google Forms. The questionnaire about perception and needs of explainability (first step) was applied to 61 people in 2020; they are mostly members of laboratories and technology development companies. The personas evaluation questionnaires (fifth step) were applied between April 13, 2021 and April 24, 2021. There were 38 participants who acted by answering the questionnaire as designers, being people who work in design interaction teams in software development companies in the city of Belo Horizonte, Minas Gerais state, in Brazil. There were 60 participants who responded to the questionnaire as users, being people with the same characteristics as the target audience consulted in the first step, in which the needs and perceptions of explainability were collected.

In the user perception questionnaire, the participant sees a set of personas and the questions are answered taking into account the persona with which the participant most identifies. In the questionnaire on the perception of designers, the set of personas is evaluated as a whole. Analysis is always done separately for users and designers.

The results reported in this study are the participant's level of agreement for the Persona Perception Scale items and the average agreement. Participant's level of agreement is quantified from 1 to 5. The higher the value, the more participants agree with the evaluated item. The average agreement is calculated by summing the level of agreement from all participants and dividing by the number of participants. The higher the average value, the more participants agree with the evaluated item.

The average agreement metric is calculated in two different scenarios: average agreement by construct and overall average agreement. In the average agreement per construct, the average agreement is grouped by the assessment construct defined in the Persona Perception Scale, thus, for each respondent, there is an assessment value per construct and the average obtained from the set of respondents is reported. In the overall average agreement, there is the general value for each participant and the reported average is the overall average value in this set of participants.

In all results reported in this study, the error bars are shown for a statistical error at a confidence level of 95%, being the calculations performed by using the R-statistics language.

5   Results

In this section, we detail the results of our case study in generating personas that include information about users' perceptions and needs of software explanations. In doing so, we first present the set of personas generated by using the approach described in Sect. 3. After that, we analyze the perceptions from users and from designers about representativeness and the quality of the personas. Finally, we discuss the results of the distribution of responses of participants per item of the Persona Perception Scale questionnaire. Figure 1 shows the five personas generated in the case study.

Fig. 1. Personas generated from the responses of 61 participants considering their needs and perceptions of software explainability, aggregated empathy maps, and demographic data.

As discussed earlier, personas are produced from the aggregation of the empathy maps created with the responses from the perception and need for explainability questionnaire. As shown in Fig. 2, considering the public of 61 respondents, the personas were originated as follows: Marcos Assis (34% of respondents), Renata Silva (23% of respondents), Mateus Umbelino (18% of respondents), Rodrigo Rodrigues (17% of respondents), and Felipe Rabelo (8% of respondents). Thus, in addition to modeling different types of users, there are personas that are more common in the target audience and others that are less common.

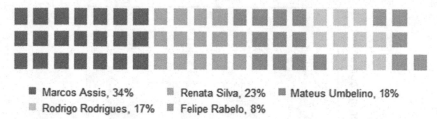

■ Marcos Assis, 34%   ■ Renata Silva, 23%   ■ Mateus Umbelino, 18%
■ Rodrigo Rodrigues, 17% ■ Felipe Rabelo, 8%

Fig. 2. Number of respondents whose empathy maps were aggregated and originated each of the personas.

Figure 3 shows results of the average agreement of users, per construct considered in the Persona Perception Scale. On the X-axis are the construct (Similarity, Empathy and Likability) and also the overall case, which includes all constructs together. The results show an overall rating of 3.7 on users' average agreement. There was more agreement on the Likability construct, indicating that the respondents like the personas.

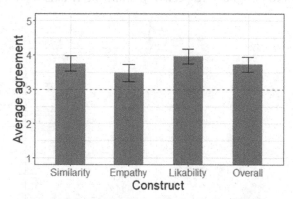

Fig. 3. Users' average level of agreement to the criteria of representativeness and quality. The dashed line is the level of agreement equivalent to "neither agree nor disagree" Each error bar represents the 95% confidence interval.

Figure 4 shows results of the average agreement of the designers, per construct considered in the Persona Perception Scale. On the X-axis are the construct (Credibility, Completeness and Clarity) and also the overall case, which includes all constructs together. The results show an overall rating of 3.5 on designers' average agreement. There was more agreement on the Clearness construct and less agreement in the Completeness, indicating that the designers perceive the personas as succinct and direct, but not complete. This is an expected result, as the personas seek to contemplate the explainability requirement but not cover information relevant to other domains that are not relevant in this domain.

Figure 5 and Fig. 6 show the agreement distribution of both designers and users regarding personas. In them, the Y axes are the questions of the questionnaire on the perception of representativeness, applied to users, and the questionnaire on the perception

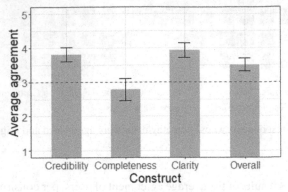

Fig. 4. Designers' average level of agreement to the criteria of representativeness and quality. The dashed line is the level of agreement equivalent to "neither agree nor disagree" each error bar represents the 95% confidence interval.

of quality, applied to designers, respectively, while the X axis represents the level of agreement.

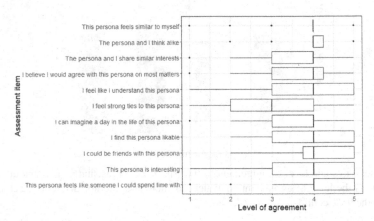

Fig. 5. Users' perception. Distribution of responses from users about the personas, considering items of the Persona Perception Scale method.

This result shows that most interquartile ranges are positioned between 3 and 5, this means that the assessment of at least 50% of the questionnaire items is greater than or equal to 3, that is, above the average of 2.5. In addition, the medians of both graphs also present evaluations above the average in most, except in Fig. 6, where the evaluation items that correspond to the completeness criterion mix medians between 2 and 4. Furthermore, the questionnaire outliers are, predominantly, of evaluations below 3, showing that these evaluations are minority.

Finally, the statements "This persona feels similar to myself" and "I have met people like this persona", belonging to the similarity and credibility criteria, respectively, had the values of median, 25th percentile and 75th percentile in 4, indicating that the majority

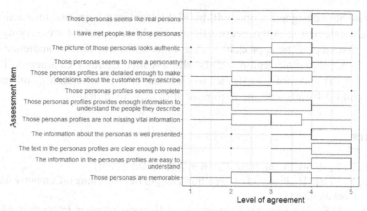

Fig. 6. Designers' perception. Distribution of responses from designers about the personas, considering items of the Persona Perception Scale method.

of the participants found similarities of the personas with themselves or with people close to them. In contrast, the statements "I feel strong ties to this persona" and "This persona is memorable", which belong to the criteria of empathy and clarity, respectively, have responses in a practically normal distribution, indicating total convergence between the central tendency measures.

6   Conclusion

In this work, we focused on the context of software explainability, which is the production of software capable of explaining to users the dynamics that govern its internal functioning. An approach of creating user models that include information about their requirements and their perceptions of explainability are fundamental when building software with such capability. So, our study investigated an approach of creating personas that include information about users' explainability perceptions. The proposed approach has five steps as follows: 1) questionnaires to collect users' perceptions and needs on the context of explainability; 2) the responses obtained are used to create empathy maps; 3) such maps are grouped by similarity; 4) from the groups the personas are generated; 5) the personas are validated with the public of users and designers.

In a case study, we employ the approach with the participation of 61 users. The obtained results include a set of 5 distinct personas representing mostly members of laboratories and technology development companies. A public of 60 users and 38 designers participate in the evaluation. The personas were rated by the users as representative of them at an average level of 3.7 out of 5 and are rated by designers as having quality 3.5 out of 5. The median rate is 4 out of 5 in most evaluation criteria, for both users and designers. We believe that both the personas and their creation and evaluation approach are relevant contributions for designers and researchers looking for strategies to guide the development of software that satisfies the explainability requirement.

Several future works can be conducted based on what is presented in the study. In particular, we plan to employ personas in the software development process, that is, to investigate how designed people will build different interfaces and interactions from them. We also intend to seek the creation of more inclusive personas, by carrying out data collection (first step of the approach) with a wider and more diverse audience in terms of gender, race, geographic region and also the so-called Extreme Characters. Thus, this study can support and motivate further work in the context of creating and using user models to build software with the requirement of explainability.

References

1. Nielsen, J.: Usability Engineering. Elsevier, Amsterdam (1994)
2. Rogers, Y., Sharp, H., Preece, J.: Interaction Design: Beyond Human-Computer Interaction. Wiley, Hoboken (2011)
3. De Souza, C.S.: The Semiotic Engineering of Human-Computer Interaction. MIT Press, Cambridge (2005)
4. Ponciano, L., Brasileiro, F., Andrade, N., Sampaio, L.: Considering human aspects on strategies for designing and managing distributed human computation. J. Internet Serv. Appl. 5(1), 1–15 (2014). https://doi.org/10.1186/s13174-014-0010-4
5. Nunes, I., Jannach, D.: A systematic review and taxonomy of explanations in decision support and recommender systems. User Model. User-Adap. Inter. 27(3–5), 393–444 (2017). https://doi.org/10.1007/s11257-017-9195-0
6. Köhl, M.A., Baum, K., Langer, M., Oster, D., Speith, T., Bohlender, D.: Explainability as a non-functional requirement. In: 2019 IEEE 27th International Requirements Engineering Conference (RE), pp. 363–368 (2019). https://doi.org/10.1109/RE.2019.00046
7. Louzada, H., Chaves, G., Ponciano, L.: Exploring user profiles based on their explainability requirements in interactive systems. In: Proceedings of the 19th Brazilian Symposium on Human Factors in Computing Systems. IHC 2020. ACM, New York (2020). https://doi.org/10.1145/3424953.3426545
8. Junior, P.T.A., Filgueiras, L.V.L.: User modeling with personas. In: Proceedings of the 2005 Latin American Conference on Human-Computer Interaction, CLIHC 2005, pp. 277–282. ACM, New York (2005). https://doi.org/10.1145/1111360.1111388
9. Ferreira, B., Silva, W., Oliveira Jr., E.A., Conte, T.: Designing personas with empathy map. In: Proceeding of the 27th International Conference on Software Engineering and Knowledge Engineering, pp. 501–505. KSI Research Inc. and Knowledge Systems Institute Graduate School, Pittsburgh (2015). https://doi.org/10.18293/SEKE2015-152
10. Salminen, J., Santos, J.M., Kwak, H., An, J., Jung, S.G., Jansen, B.J.: Persona perception scale: development and exploratory validation of an instrument for evaluating individuals' perceptions of personas. Int. J. Hum. Comput. Stud. 141, 102437 (2020). https://doi.org/10.1016/j.ijhcs.2020.102437
11. Gasca, J., Zaragozá, R.: Designpedia. 80 herramientas para construir tus ideas. LEO, LID Editorial Empresarial, S.L. (2014)
12. Lidwell, W., Holden, K., Butler, J.: Universal Principles of Design, vol. 1. Rockport, Gloucester (2010)
13. LaRoche, C.S., Traynor, B.: User-centered design (UCD) and technical communication: The inevitable marriage. In: 2010 IEEE International Professional Communication Conference, pp. 113–116 (2010). https://doi.org/10.1109/IPCC.2010.5529821
14. Pruitt, J., Adlin, T.: The Persona Lifecycle: Keeping People in Mind Throughout Product Design. Morgan Kaufmann Publishers Inc., San Francisco (2005)
15. Cooper, A., Saffo, P.: The Inmates Are Running the Asylum. Macmillan Publishing Co. Inc., USA (1999)

16. Long, F.: Real or imaginary; the effectiveness of using personas in product design. In: Proceedings of the Irish Ergonomics Society Annual Conference, Dublin, pp. 1–10, May 2009

17. Mahamuni, R., Khambete, P., Punekar, R.M., Lobo, S., Sharma, S., Hirom, U.: Concise personas based on tacit knowledge - how representative are they? In: Proceedings of the 9th Indian Conference on Human Computer Interaction, IndiaHCI 2018, pp. 53–62. ACM, New York (2018). https://doi.org/10.1145/3297121.3297126

18. Branco, K.d.S.C, Oliveira, R.A., Silva, F.L.D., de H. Rabelo, J., Marques, A.B.S.: Does this persona represent me? Investigating an approach for automatic generation of personas based on questionnaires and clustering. In: Proceedings of the 19th Brazilian Symposium on Human Factors in Computing Systems, IHC2020, ACM, New York (2020). https://doi.org/10.1145/3424953.3426648

19. Ponciano, L., Pereira, T.E.: Characterising volunteers' task execution patterns across projects on multi-project citizen science platforms. In: Proceedings of the 18th Brazilian Symposium on Human Factors in Computing Systems, IHC 2019. ACM, New York (2019). https://doi.org/10.1145/3357155.3358441

Project-Based Learning Focused on Professional Skills: An Approach Applied on Human-Computer Interaction and Software Requirements Under-Graduation Courses

Maurício Serrano$^{(\boxtimes)}$ ⓘ, Milene Serrano ⓘ, and André Barros de Sales ⓘ

University of Brasília, Gama, Brasilia, DF, Federal District 72.444-240, Brazil
{serrano,mileneserrano,andrebdes}@unb.br

Abstract. Human-Computer Interaction and Software Requirements are courses that demand special attention to concepts. Precisely, and because they are more theoretical, it becomes difficult to motivate undergraduate students to acquire professional skills that are desired in the market. The idea is to bring them closer to the new profile of the Software Engineer. In this profile, skills such as proactive behaviour, critical sense and harmony in collective work are expected. Based on this context, educational approaches that allow the development of these skills become necessary. This paper presents an experience report on the use of Project-based Learning in the Software Requirements and Human-Computer Interaction courses, during two terms. The application was conducted with Participatory Action Research, accompanied by data collection using questionnaires, and qualitative analysis of these data, from the perspective of undergraduate Software Engineering instructors and students from the University of Brasilia. The experience report described in this paper addresses the use of Project-based Learning in subjects, in which the topics taught are on a higher level of abstraction (in other words, more theoretical and conceptual). Theses particularities differ our contributions from other analyzed proposals, in which there is a more practical and applied profile. The obtained results are promising and indicate that Project-based Learning improves professional skills, allowing a review on the traditional-based learning methods commonly used in courses with similar profiles. As further work, we intend to adjust some perceived weaknesses, such as: dealing more adequately with social aspects.

Keywords: Project-based learning · Active learning · Teaching · Software engineering · Human-computer interaction · Software requirements education

1 Introduction

Masson et al. [1] state that the modern world imposes significant changes in different areas of knowledge. These transformations are linked to the technological development itself, which acts intensely and constantly in people's daily lives [2] and [3]. In the area of engineering knowledge, it is necessary to train more proactive engineers, who in

© Springer Nature Switzerland AG 2021
P. H. Ruiz et al. (Eds.): HCI-COLLAB 2021, CCIS 1478, pp. 150–163, 2021.
https://doi.org/10.1007/978-3-030-92325-9_12

addition to having good technical expertise, are aware of social, humanitarian and ethical aspects. Therefore, there is a need for a more collaborative and integrated professional in society.

According to Barbosa and Moura [4], among the desirable skills for these new professionals, the following are noted: ethical conduct, initiative, creativity, entrepreneurial attitude, flexibility, self-control, communication, oral and written expression, and others.

The ideal is to align the curricular frameworks to this reality, promoting curricula revisions in undergraduate courses. Resolution N° 5/2016 [5], which determines the new National Curricular Guidelines for undergraduate courses in the area of Computing of Brazil, including Software Engineering (SE), clearly defines that it is important to seek a professional with a generalist, humanistic and critical profile, allowing the comprehension and development of activities with expertise, as well as solving problems in various domains, such as in political, economic, social and environmental.

There are many challenges to be faced by instructors. Among the main ones, in Kenski et al. [6], the authors mention: (i) the sense of choice about which information is really relevant and deserves to be treated with more attention in the classroom, and (ii) the perception of how to deal with that information, turning it into knowledge, and relying on concrete, creative, flexible and exciting resources for the students. In search of greater alignment between Higher Education Institutions and market demands, as well as in addressing the challenges above mentioned, several authors suggest the use of Active Learning. Bender [7] and Minuzi et al. [8], for example, mention Project-based Learning.

In this methodology, students are encouraged to identify real-world problems; experiencing a selection process on which problems are most relevant, and pointing out possible solutions. All involved activities are carried out cooperatively through teamwork. The teacher reserves the role of observer, advisor, and not the only provider of knowledge.

The University of Brasilia, through an initiative called the 3rd Millennium Learning Program (A3M), has supported research, production of new knowledge, and development of innovative educational methodologies in the teaching and learning process.

This paper is organized as follows: Sect. 2 presents the main objectives of the research, centered on Active Learning Methodologies; Sect. 3 describes some relevant ongoing work and contributions, focused on theoretical framework, methodological procedures; and the results of the experience carried out in the courses; and in Sect. 4, concluding remarks are presented. The paper ends with bibliographic references.

2   Objectives of the Research

Given the difficult of implementing a more comprehensive approach, which would cause a break with the curricular framework adopted by the SE course, at the University of Brasilia, the first approach was selected for the Software Requirements and the Human-Computer Interaction courses, focused on Project-based Learning, in addition to some of the disruptive model strategies.

The main objective of this research is to apply this methodology, aiming to evaluate its behavior in undergraduate courses in the area of SE. Furthermore, this methodology was applied during two terms in the courses of Software Requirements and Human-Computer Interaction, in the SE undergraduate course. Based on the gained experience, the observations collected by Participatory Action Research are enlisted in this paper. Guided by a predominantly qualitative approach, impressions are presented from the perspective of undergraduate Software Engineering instructors and students.

3   Ongoing Work and Contributions

Following, in Sects. 3.1, 3.2 and 3.3, the theoretical framework; methodology's details and some obtained results are presented.

3.1   Theoretical Framework

The research is oriented by a theoretical framework, which is based on some theoretical references, such as: Educational Approaches and Active Learning with emphasis on Project-based Learning.

Educational Approaches. Some authors, regarding the review process of educational institutions, point out different educational approaches. Morán [9], for example, defends two approaches: a softer one, based on progressive changes, and a more comprehensive one, based on deeper changes.

The first approach can be more easily applied by institutions, as it maintains the concept of a curricular framework, and seeks, with the use of Active Learning, to prioritize student engagement.

In Active Learning, [7] and [8], interdisciplinary or multidisciplinary methods, such as Flipped Classroom [10] and Project-based Learning, are valued and seen as alternatives to promote less expository, more productive and participatory classes, capable of engaging students and improving the use of the teacher's time and knowledge. In this case, there is no break with the traditional curriculum model. Therefore, it is a softer approach, and it is possible to be implemented, progressively, into current undergraduate courses. It should be noted that these courses are already recognized by the Brazilian Ministry of Education and comply with rigid Curricular Pedagogical Projects.

The second approach supports a disruptive model, without courses, in which a remodeling of physical spaces and methodologies is necessary. In this case, the use of project-oriented methodologies, challenges, problems, games or other playful and tangible resources is recommended. The learning time of each student is considered, while encouraging them to interact collectively, with collaborative work in engaged teams. The role of the teacher becomes, primarily, that of an advisor. It is up to the advisor is responsible for guiding the student in learning transforming information - that is widely available in a globalized world - into knowledge. This role demands dealing with multidisciplinary content, as well as dealing with the interrelation between these and the technical area to be mastered within the scope of each profession (interdisciplinarity).

Active and Project-based Learning. Mills and Treagust [11] and Correia and Oliveira [12] provide reflections on the relevance of Project-based Learning and on the profile of

Engineering graduates. The action of designing something represents an intrinsic activity of Engineering. Therefore, the strategy of teaching design practices has been proposed in several Engineering programs for some years. This strategy has some aspects in common with Active Learning approaches, as highlighted by Neto and Soster [13]:

i.   Greater contact with real cases, giving the undergraduate student more experience as an acting professional.
ii. Encouragement of undergraduate student proactivity, developing management and leadership skills.
iii. Stimulating a search for solutions, including the aspects that will emerge.
iv. Motivating the creation of perceptions about confrontations and achievements.
v.   Greater approximation between theory and practice.

3.2 Methodology

Based on the classification regarding the research modalities described in Gil [14], the present work was guided by Participatory Action Research, of an exploratory nature, whose main goal is to provide an approximate overview of a given fact.

The approach of this research is, mainly, qualitative, being that "the qualitative research is not concerned with numerical representativeness, but with the deepening of the understanding of a social group, of an organization, etc." [15]. The social group that was analyzed consisted of undergraduate Software Engineering instructors and students from the University of Brasilia.

This paper is one of the results of the research project on the application of the Project-based Learning approach in some courses of the SE course of the University of Brasilia. Other results of this research project are presented in [16, 17] and [18].

Participatory Action Research is a scientific methodology well suited to allow the evolution of something under study in an iterative and incremental way. In this project, this methodology has allowed cyclical refinements in the Project-based Learning approach, based on data collected from undergraduate instructors and students through the application of questionnaires.

Study Setting. In its first version, the approach was guided by modules, with lectures, focused on theoretical contents; followed by lessons to clarify doubts and oral presentations (seminar model) (see Fig. 1). Each module had a focus on a relevant topic in Software Requirements (e.g. techniques for elicitation and prioritization of requirements).

The main topics related to Requirements Engineering are covered throughout the modules taught in the course of Software Requirements. Figure 2 illustrates part of the content taught, with the course organized in topics.

In each topic, there are one or more modules being taught. In summary, the topics are as follows:

1.   Introduction to provide an initial view of the discipline and the main concepts about Requirements Engineering, such as Universe Of Discourse, Stakeholders, Requirements Engineer Profile and other relevant contents. Duration: One module with 3 classes or 6 h of dedication.

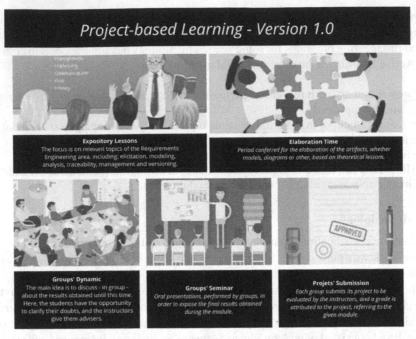

Fig. 1. Project-based learning - version 1.0

2. Pre-traceability in order to deal with software requirements' traceability. The idea is to allow the trace between the requirements baseline and Universe of Discourse (e.g. information sources and stakeholders). Informal and formal models are covered, including Argumentation Graph to trace the decisions made by the team. Duration: One module with 3 classes or 6 h of dedication.

3. Elicitation in order to present the main elicitation techniques, such as: Brainstorming, Questionnaire, Interview, Introspection, Storyboard, Storytelling, Participative Observation, Ethnography and others. Moreover, it is also covered prioritization techniques, such as: MOSCOW, First Things First and Quality Function Deployment (QFD). Duration: One module with 3 classes or 6 h of dedication.

4. Modeling in order to deal with different ways to model the requirements. Some models are general models, such as: Lexicon, Scenarios, Mindmaps, Ishikawa Diagram and others. In addition, are presented: the UML notation by introducing the Use Cases Diagram; the agile modeling by considering Product Backlog and Sprint Backlog with different granularity levels (e.g. Theme, Epic, Feature, User Story, Task and others), and the emergent modeling, such as the Goal-Oriented Modeling. Duration: Five modules with 3 classes each or 30 h of dedication.

5. Analysis in order to cover the Requirements' analysis. In this topic, it is presented requirements' verification and requirements' validation with techniques and concepts. Duration: One module with 3 classes or 6 h of dedication.

6. Pos-traceability in order to focus on traceability matrix: forward to, forward from, backward from and backward to. The idea is to deal with the trace between the

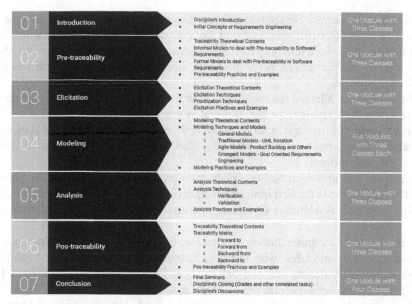

Fig. 2. Contents correlation

requirements baseline and the code. Duration: One module with 3 classes or 6 h of dedication.

7. Final to conclude the course by presenting the grades. Furthermore, a debate class is held with students to collect their opinion on the course taught. Duration: One module with 4 classes or 8 h of dedication.

The following is a brief report on the steps of the approach's cyclical refinements, considering the Participatory Action Research protocol agreed in Gil [14]:

- Data collection: the solution was evaluated through the application of questionnaires and the use of participant observation, carried out by instructors.
- Data analysis and interpretation: the data and answers of some participants to the open-ended questions were tabulated. The qualitative analysis of these data was performed in an interpretative manner, based on the brainstorming technique around the data obtained, and among the authors of this paper.
- Creation of the action plan: in order to solve demands identified in the investigative process, progress in the Project Based Learning approach was considered in the planning of each action. Considering the first version (1.0) of the approach, some of these improvements were implemented in the current school semester (in the first semester of 2019 (01/2019)), such as the use of complementary practices. One of these practices, which gave rise to an intermediate version (version 1.1), were the periodic individual evaluations, motivating individual learners' initiative, since there is greater incentive for collective activities in Project-based Learning.

Other developments were applied in the subsequent academic semester (in the second semester of 2019 (2/2019), version 2.0 of the approach, such as in the Modeling Topic the contents were divided into only three modules instead of five. This evolution reduced the number of oral presentations for this topic, since more than one content was given before each seminar.

These strategies allowed for a multi and interdisciplinary approach with an emphasis and extra time for learners to prepare for oral evaluations.

Another addition to version 2.0 was the 360° evaluation, which consists of a self-evaluation followed by the assessment of the other group members, performed after the team's oral presentation.

Therefore, this approach had two main versions, 1.0 (applied only in the Software Requirements course in the first semester of 2019 (01/2019)) and 2.0 (applied in the Software Requirements and Human-Computer Interaction courses in the second semester of 2019 (02/2019).

In the Human-Computer Interaction course, the Project-based Learning approach was also guided by modules, with lectures, focused on theoretical contents; followed by lessons to clarify doubts and oral presentations (seminar model) (see Fig. 1). Each module had a focus on a relevant topic in Human-Computer Interaction.

The main topics related to Human-Computer Interaction also are covered throughout the modules taught in the Human-Computer Interaction course.

The Human-Computer Interaction course was organized in six topics: Introduction (an initial view of the discipline and the main concepts about Human-Computer Interaction), Lifecycles Models in Human-Computer Interaction, Identifying needs and establishing requirements (elicitation techniques, user roles, user profiles etc.), Requirements Analysis, Design/Testing/Development and Conclusion.

The Requirements Analysis and Design/Testing/Development are parts of the Usability Engineering Lifecycle of Deborah Mayhew and better detailed in [19].

– Dissemination of the results: in addition to the constant documentation of the collected data, keeping track of partial results in spreadsheets and other resources, this paper presents a compilation of these results for dissemination to the specialized community.

Finally, it is worth mentioning that two scenarios were considered for the application of the Project-based Learning approach, and the Participatory Action Research modality was adopted for monitoring the application in both scenarios:

– Scenario #1:

- **What?** Application of Project-based Learning (version 1.0) in the Software Requirements subject.
- **Where?** University of Brasilia, undergraduate SE course.
- **When?** First semester of 2019 (01/2019).
- **Who?** Two instructors, PhDs in Computer Science, and students.
- **How?** By applying Participatory Action Research protocol and relying on specialized literature on Active Learning, with emphasis on Project-based Learning. First proposed version of the methodology.

- **Why?** To assess the relevance of the use of Project-based Learning (version 1.0) for the development of professional skills, promoting greater proximity between University and Market.

– Scenario #2:

- **What?** Application of Project Based Learning (version 2.0) in the subjects of Software Requirements and Human-Computer Interaction.
- **Where?** University of Brasilia, undergraduate SE course.
- **When?** Second semester of 2019 (02/2019);
- **Who?** One instructor, PhD in Computer Science, and students.
- **How?** By applying Participatory Action Research protocol and relying on specialized literature on Active Learning, with emphasis on Project-based Learning. Second proposed version of the methodology.
- **Why?** To assess the relevance of the use of Project-based Learning (version 2.0) for the development of professional skills, promoting greater proximity between University and Market.

Software Requirements and Human-Computer Interaction are mandatory courses of the fifth semester of the undergraduate course in SE at the University of Brasilia, with a workload of 4 credits each.

The Software Requirements class of the first semester of 2019 (01/2019) had 53 undergraduate students, divided into 7 groups with 7 to 9 students each, and only one group with 5 members. In terms of approval, 51 students concluded, 34 of which agreed to participate in the survey after reading and signing the free consent form, representing 66.7% of the group. The two instructors responsible for this class also agreed to participate in the research after reading and signing the free consent form.

The Software Requirements class of the second semester of 2019 (02/2019) had 58 undergraduate students, divided into 10 groups, 8 groups with 6 members and 2 groups with 5 members. In terms of approval in this class, 58 students concluded, 56 of whom agreed to participate in the survey after reading and signing the free consent form, representing 96.5% of the group. The instructor responsible for this class also agreed to participate in the research after reading and signing the free consent form.

The Human-Computer Interaction course of the second semester of 2019 (02/2019) had 65 undergraduate students, divided into 11 groups, being 10 groups with 6 members and 1 group with 5 members. In terms of approval in this class, 64 students concluded, 63 of whom agreed to participate in the survey after reading and signing the free consent form, representing 96.9% of the group. The instructor responsible for this class also agreed to participate in the research after reading and signing the free consent form.

Here are some peculiarities of this research:

– relatively large classes, around 60 (sixty) undergraduate SE students;
– predominance of male students (more than 80% in both terms), aged between 19 and 30 years old, the majority being between 20 and 22 years old (70.6%);
– heterogeneity among the students, being most of the students from the fifth semester (more than 40% in both terms), but also students of more advanced semesters and

professionals who already work in companies and return to the academy for an update/training, and
- learners with a developer profile, who find it challenging to deal with more abstract content, such as those from the Software Requirements and Human-Computer Interaction courses.

3.3 Discussion of Results

This section presents the data collected through Participatory Action Research from the perspective of undergraduate Software Engineering instructors and students.

Instructors' Perspective. In both semesters a questionnaire with multiple-choice and open-ended questions was applied. Considering the role of instructors as observers of the process in the two scenarios described above, here are some answers collected via questionnaires:

- *Instructor 01: The students were motivated to carry out very interesting projects, exploring all the content taught in class, and even going beyond, with the reading and application of extra content, indicated in complementary materials. Additionally, in class, the students showed curiosity, trying to relate the content with their professional experiences...*
- *Instructor 01: The debates held, provided greater coverage in topics of interest and scope of the course, ensuring interesting correlations with other areas of computing. It is also worth mentioning that several debates covered issues related to ethics, citizenship, accessibility, internationalization and other social and cultural aspects, which gave the students a vision that goes beyond the technical content approach.*
- *Instructor 02: Based on our experience with the Project-Based Learning approach, it promotes: (i) the awakening of leadership skills, oratory, proactive behaviour and curiosity in students; (ii) the participation of students in the construction of their knowledge, not in a passive way, waiting for knowledge to be passed exclusively by the teacher; (iii) discussions with different points of view, which enriches coverage not only of technical topics, but also of a social and cultural nature, and (iv) naturally, a multidisciplinary vision of the subject, as the projects require efforts in different strands (e.g. technical, managerial, organizational) as well as efforts related to related areas (e.g. Software Design, Software Architecture, Human Computer Interface and Software Testing) and to human and social areas.*
- *Instructor 03: Most learners liked and were motivated by the approach. It develops various skills in students, such as teamwork and dealing with conflicts generated by working in a group. It also allows the student to act as an active professional in the market. The approach requires a regular dedication from the student in order to develop the project during most of the term.*
- *Instructor 03: In this approach there is an approximation between teacher and students that allows the learner to apply knowledge in a practical project, acquiring an experience of the labor market while taking a course at the university.*
  The approach allows students, at the end of the term, to contact the teams that have commercially developed the projects to validate the artifacts produced in the course

(...) and sometimes publishing these artifacts together on the websites of reputable companies in the labor market. The validation of these artifacts alone produces a sense of reward in students.

In the answers, it is observed that instructors mention several professional skills, perceived by them, with the application of Project-based Learning in the course. The main ones were curiosity, teamwork, ethical conduct, initiative, communication, oral and written expression, among others.

In addition, instructors were asked to assign grades from 1 to 5, with 1 being the lowest value and 5 the highest value. Table 1 shows that the majority (75%) of participants gave a maximum grade (5) to the question "Does the Project-based Learning approach provide good content learning?", producing a mean of 4.8 and a standard deviation of 0.4. Scores 1, 2 and 3 were not assigned by any participant for this question.

Table 1. Development of undergraduate students' professional skills in the perception of instructors

The project-based learning approach in the course	Absolute frequency					Mean	Standard Deviation
	1	2	3	4	5		
- Provides good content learning	0	0	0	25%	75%	4.8	0.4
- Contributes to the understanding of practical aspects of SE	0	0	0	50%	50%	4.5	0.5
- Provides experiences with real and practical aspects	0	0	0	25%	75%	4.8	0.4
- Increases confidence and ability to participate in discussions with this experience	0	0	25%	25%	50%	4.3	0.8

As for the question *Does the Project-based Learning approach contribute to the understanding of the practical aspects of Software Engineering?*, instructors assigned the grades 4 and 5, resulting in a mean of 4.5 and standard deviation of 0.5.

The instructors argued, on this topic in open-ended questions, that although Project-based Learning provides a very significant approximation between theory and practice, some situations, which would be found in the performance of a Software Engineer, cannot be completely simulated in classes that are oriented by a traditional curriculum. This rigid structure imposes deadlines for activities as well as for the conclusion of the term, requiring, for example, to forego a deeper analysis about long-term practices. In a more disruptive approach, it is believed that this question could achieve a score of 5.

Instructors also attributed the question *"Does the Project-based Learning approach provide experience with questions of real and practical aspects?"* grades 4 and 5, result-ing in a mean of 4.8 and a standard deviation of 0.4. It is noticeable that the approach in fact brings theory and practice closer together and allows students to have more realistic experiences.

Finally, for the question *"Does the project-based learning approach increase confidence and ability to participate in discussions?"*, 50% of instructors rated 5, producing a mean of 4.3 with a standard deviation of 0.8.

The conclusion is that Project-based Learning develops desired professional skills in undergraduate Software Engineering students, with emphasis on a greater experience with real cases. There is concern in refining the approach to improve students' ability to participate in discussions.

Undergraduate Students' Perspective. A two-block questionnaire was applied to undergraduate Software Engineering students in both terms: (i) one focused on identifying the respondents' profile (age, gender, attending semester, among other information), and (ii) another, with questions about Project-based Learning in the courses.

The questionnaire was applied to students at the beginning of the second to last class of each subject, for the Software Requirements course in the first semester of 2019 (01/2019) and second semester of 2019 (02/2019) and for Human-Computer Interaction course only in the second semester of 2019 (02/2019). The data obtained from the participants' answers, especially in the open-ended questions, are the focus of the analysis that follows in this paper, considering the students' point of view. Here are some statements agreed by students for both applications of the approach, respectively, in the first semester of 2019 (01/2019) and second semester of 2019 (02/2019). The analysis, in these cases, is focused on observance of professional skills identified by students and documented by instructors.

– *Student 01: Working with pre-existing projects and success cases allows us to see what led them to succeed in the market;*
– *Student 02: The methodology provides the student with the application of theoretical knowledge for better comprehension. It also helps to develop the maturity to work in teams, which is very important;*
– *Student 03: The positive points revolve around practice helping the understanding of theory, the gain that hands-on and practical experience provides and the incentive for research and the student to strive to go beyond the content learned in class;*
– *Student 04: The method is great and makes learning such a vast and complex discipline a lot easier;*
– *Student 05: Positive points: gradual learning, perceptible progress along the semester, maintenance of the engagement and study of the course. Teamwork helps to develop interpersonal skills. Negative points: none;*
– *Student 06: The dynamics of the course contribute to the exchange of experiences and information between teams, as well as to the individual improvement of soft and hard skills; enabling a more practical Software Engineering course;*
– *Student 07: Development of public speaking and behavior and encourages teamwork, research and innovation;*
– *Student 08: It's quite laborious, but the result is gratifying;*

- *Student 09: Positive aspects; helping others, respect, companionship, patience and leadership. Negative aspects: sleepless nights, stress, conflicts between team members;*
- *Student 10: Positive aspects: teamwork, development of leaders and managers, greater responsibility, maturity and public speaking;*
- *Student 11: From this method, I was able to develop personal skills, such as emotional control in presentations;*
- *Student 12: Practical learning; dynamic learning; teamwork improvement; leader ship development; development of proactive behaviour, communication skills and presentation of ideas; effort and evaluation spread throughout the term.*

It is observed, in the responses, that the undergraduate SE students highlighted several professional competencies, perceived by them, with the use of Project-based Learning in the course. The key ones were: professional experience, leadership and team management, capacity for initiative, assists in problem solving, development of interpersonal skills, self-control, communication, oral and written expression, among others.

4   Conclusions and Future Work

Considering the digital age, in which technological evolution acts intensely in people's daily activities, there is also a growing need to review the curricular matrices of university courses, aiming at closer approximation between what is taught and market trends. In this sense, some authors defend active methodologies, to deal with this demand, by making use of Inverted Classrooms or project-based learning. The purpose is to allow a greater participation of undergraduate students, encouraging them to deal with real problems, and to develop desirable skills once they enter the market.

To stimulate professional skills in undergraduate SE students at the University of Brasilia, experiments in the courses of Software Requirements and Human-Computer Interaction were performed. Such practices were conducted with Participatory Action Research, in an exploratory approach throughout two terms (i.e., two scenarios of use). The research included three instructors and more than 150 students. The refinement cycles were addressed in the paper, as well as the qualitative analysis of the data, both from the instructors' and students' perspective. Analysis was conducted on an interpretative basis, and results are described in this research.

Based on the results in the observed context of the two courses, it can be stated that Project-based Learning has proved to be relevant in the development of professional skills. Among the most mentioned skills among participants are oral expression, leadership, communication, proactive behaviour, critical sense, collaboration and proximity between theory and practice. Such skills were also observed in related work.

In Grotta and Prado [20], the authors highlight the gain of more practical background in the context of computer programming. In Paschoal and Souza [21], the authors point out that the projects simulate authentic problems, and promote the development of skills such as autonomy, collaboration and critical thinking, in the studies conducted in the course of Information Systems Management. It is also emphasized that the mentioned works apply the Project-based Learning approach in subjects with a more technical profile.

The experience report described in this paper makes clear the difference between the experiences in Software Requirements and Human-Computer Interaction in comparison to the proposals of Grotta and Prado [20] and Paschoal and Souza [21], as it addresses the use of Project-based Learning in subjects, in which the topics taught are more theoretical, conceptual and on a higher level of abstraction. Therefore, it becomes a challenge to develop proactive behaviour and proximity with the practice of a SE professional. However, the success of these experiences has allowed instructors to broaden the application of this approach in other subjects of the undergraduate Software Engineering course. This has occurred for the Human-Computer Interaction course at first. In this case, it is concluded that the approach is sufficiently generalist to meet courses with similar profiles to those covered in this paper.

Finally, among the limitations of this research, the following are noteworthy: (i) the non-consideration of social aspects in the learning process, which may create, for example, cognitive gaps between learners, and (ii) the utilization of the approach in a disciplinary context, bound to evaluations that basically summarize the undergraduate student's learning in a grade at the end of the term. Such aspects will be the subject of study of this approach in the next cycles of refinement.

References

1. Masson, T.J., de Miranda, L.F., Jr., A.H.M., Castanheira, A.M.P.: Metodologia de ensino: Aprendizagem baseada em projetos (PBL). In: Anais do XL Congresso Brasileiro de Educação em Engenharia (COBENGE), Belém, PA, Brazil (2012)
2. Sales, A.B., Soares, P.M., Evangelista, da Silva Evangelista, T.: Factors influencing undergraduate software engineering course choice among students. In: Anais do Computer on the Beach, São José, SC, Brazil, pp. 009–013 (2021). https://doi.org/10.14210/cotb.v12.p009-013
3. Sales, A.B., e Silva, M.S.: Jogos sérios no processo de ensino e aprendizagem de interação humano-computador. In: Anais do XXXI Simpósio Brasileiro de Informática na Educação, pp. 552–561 (2020). https://doi.org/10.5753/cbie.sbie.2020.552
4. Barbosa, E.F., de Moura, D.G.: Metodologias ativas de aprendizagem no ensino de engenharia. In: Proceedings of International Conference on Engineering and Technology Education. Guimarães, Portugal, pp. 111–117 (2014). http://dx.doi.org/10.14684/INTERTECH.13.2014. 110-116
5. Diretrizes curriculares dos cursos de bacharelado em ciência da computação, engenharia de computação, engenharia de software e sistemas de informação e dos cursos de licenciatura em computação. In: Ministério da Educação – SESU, Brasília, DC, Brazil, pp. 1–9 (2016)
6. Kenski, V.M., Medeiros, R.A., Ordéa, J.: Ensino superior em tempos mediados pelas tecnologias digitais/higher education in times mediated by digital technologies. Trabalho Educ. 28(1), 141–152 (2019). https://doi.org/10.35699/2238-037X.2019.9872
7. Bender, W.N.: Aprendizagem Baseada em Projetos: Educação Diferenciada para o Século XXI, 1st edn. Penso, Porto Alegre (2014)
8. Minuzi, N.A., Minuzi, G.A., Santos, L.M.A., Barin, C.S.: Metodologias ativas no ensino superior: desafios e fragilidades para implementação. Redin – Rev. Educ. Interdisc. 8(1), 1–10 (2019)
9. Morán, J.: Mudando a educação com metodologias ativas. Coleção Mídias Contemp. Converg. Midiáticas Educ. Cidadania: Aproximações Jovens II, 15–33 (2015)

10. Rodrigues, L., Corrêa, E.A., Santos, B., Paz, D.P.: Metodologias ativas: sala de aula invertida: Um novo jeito de aprender. Rev. Mundi: Engenharia Tecnol. Gestão **4**(1), 133–144 (2019). http://dx.doi.org/10.21575/25254782rmetg2019vol4n1752
11. Mills, J.E., Treagust, D.F.: Engineering education - is problem-based learning or project-based learning the answer? Aust. J. Eng. Educ. **3**, 2–16 (2003)
12. Correia, W.C.C., Oliveira, G.F.: Reflexões sobre a prática da interdisciplinaridade através da metodologia *Project based Learning*: um estudo de caso no ensino de engenharia. Rev. Docência Ensino Superior **10**, 1–17 (2020). https://doi.org/10.35699/2237-5864.2020.13597
13. Neto, O.M., Soster, T.S.: Inovação Acadêmica e Aprendizagem Ativa, 1st edn. Penso, Porto Alegre (2017)
14. Gil, A.C.: Como elaborar projetos de pesquisa. 1st edn. Atlas (2018)
15. Gerhardt, T.E., Silveira, D.T.: Métodos de pesquisa, 1st edn. Editora da UFRGS, Porto Alegre (2009)
16. Sales, A.B., Serrano, M., Serrano, M.: Aprendizagem baseada em projetos na disciplina de interação humano-computador. RISTI – Rev. Ibérica Sist. Tecnol. Inf. **37**, 49–64 (2020). https://doi.org/10.17013/risti.37.49-64
17. Serrano M., Serrano M., de Sales, A.B.: Desenvolvimento de competências profissionais: relato da experiência utilizando aprendizagem baseada em projetos na disciplina de requisitos de software. Rev. Ensino Engenharia 76–81 (2021). https://doi.org/10.37702/REE2236-0158.v40p76-81.2021
18. Sales, A.B., Boscarioli C.: Teaching and learning of interface design: an experience using project-based learning approach. In: 2021 16th Iberian Conference on Information Systems and Technologies – CISTI, pp. 1–6 (2021). https://doi.org/10.23919/CISTI52073.2021.9476547
19. Mayhew, D.J.: The Usability Engineering Lifecycle: A Practitioner's Handbbook for User Interface Design, 1st edn. Morgan Kaufmann Publishers, INC., San Francisco (1999)
20. Grotta, A., Prado, E.P.: Um ensaio sobre a experiência educacional na programação de computadores: a abordagem tradicional versus a aprendizagem baseada em projetos. In: Anais do XXVI Workshop sobre Educação em Computação. SBC, Porto Alegre (2018). https://doi.org/10.5753/wei.2018.3496
21. Paschoal, L.N., Souza, S.R.S.: Uma experiência sobre a aplicação de aprendizagem baseada em projetos com revisão por pares no ensino de gestão de sistemas de informação. In: Anais do XXVI Workshop sobre Educação em Computação. SBC, Porto Alegre, RS, Brazil (2018). https://doi.org/10.5753/wei.2018.3504

Proposal for a Serious Game to Assist in the Daily Care of Children with ASD Before Covid-19

Vitor Oikawa[1] , Cibelle Albuquerque de la Higuera Amato[2]([X]) ,
and Valéria Farinazzo Martins Amato[3]

[1] Computing and Informatics Department, Mackenzie Presbyterian University, São Paulo, Brazil
[2] Developmental Disorders Department, Mackenzie Presbyterian University, São Paulo, Brazil
cibelle.amato@mackenzie.br
[3] Computing and Informatics Department and Developmental Disorders Department,
Mackenzie Presbyterian University, São Paulo, Brazil
valeria.farinazzo@mackenzie.br

Abstract. Autism Spectrum Disorder (ASD) is a condition of neurodevelopment characterized by changes in social communication, restricted interests, and repetitive behaviors. Many children with ASD need different types of intervention (behavioral, language, social, occupational, among others). Since the appearance of Covid-19 in December 2019, a state of world pandemic has been established. In Brazil, it started in March 2020. The lives of millions of people in the country have been drastically changed: schools have closed in their face-to-face mode, people began to leave home only in extreme need, and health care was changed to the virtual model. Children with autism had their appointments reduced or canceled and, after a few months, changed to an online version. The use of masks has become mandatory throughout the country. These children now need to live in a different environment than they did a long time ago. It becomes, for example, more difficult for them to understand what people say due to the use of masks. Thus, this project aims to present a serious game in which the child can train his/her ability to understand the words now spoken by people using a face protection mask, without the possibility of the visual feature of the facial face mimic. The game was validated by nine speech therapists and, subsequently, by fourteen children diagnosed with ASD who already do speech therapy sessions online. It happened during one of the sessions. Then, both groups answered a satisfaction questionnaire conducted by the speech therapist, adapted to their characteristics.

Keywords: Autism Spectrum Disorder · Serious game · Covid-19

1 Introduction

Covid-19 is a virus, discovered in 2019, which has caused quite complicated situations in people worldwide, compared to conditions of war and the occurrence of Spanish flu. In addition to the physical health problems themselves, it has triggered psychological disorders and structural changes in the world economy and how people interact [1].

© Springer Nature Switzerland AG 2021
P. H. Ruiz et al. (Eds.): HCI-COLLAB 2021, CCIS 1478, pp. 164–177, 2021.
https://doi.org/10.1007/978-3-030-92325-9_13

Since the emergence of the Covid-19 pandemic, a series of changes in society's life has been necessary for general, particularly social isolation [2]. Therefore, preventive actions are required to combat this pandemic and reduce the transmission rate, with control and protection measures such as hand hygiene, masks, and social isolation [3, 4]. However, the use of masks makes communication between people more difficult as the possibility of looking at the speaker's lips and facial mimic is lost and due to the interference and distortion of the speech sound caused by the mask.

In this context, in which the whole society faces difficulties in experiencing the pandemic, there are children and adolescents with Autistic Spectrum Disorder (ASD). ASD is a neurodevelopmental disorder, beginning in childhood, whose main characteristics are difficulties in language/communication, social interaction, and behavior [5]. For these children and adolescents, the whole scenario resulting from the Covid-19 pandemic is challenging to understand [4]. As a result, several activities were abruptly altered for these children and adolescents at the beginning of the pandemic (and have not yet wholly re-established): the face-to-face mode classes were suspended or started to operate on a student rotation basis, the speech therapy sessions were suspended and resumed in the online mode, the need of wearing a mask to go out home, among others.

While it is inconvenient for these children and adolescents to wear a mask, it interferes with their ability to communicate as there are no visual cues that can be used to facilitate the communication process.

The social impact expected for this project consists of making a digital serious game available to assist in therapeutic intervention in speech therapy sessions for better care of children and adolescents with autism before the Covid-19 pandemic.

The present study aims to: 1. validate a serious game of motivational role of performing activities within Speech Therapy sessions and how this game can be used to assist in therapeutic intervention, especially for initial training in the use of the mask and sound perception, during the pandemic phase; 2. To be applied to autistic children in speech therapy sessions and collect these children's opinions about the game through their speech therapists.

The article is organized as follows: Sect. 2 presents the theoretical basis to facilitate understanding the other sections of the work; in Sect. 3, the work methodology is explained; Sect. 4 shows the entire game development process, and Sect. 5 provides test results and discussions. Finally, in Sect. 6, the conclusions of the work are presented.

2 Theoretical Foundations

2.1 Autistic Spectrum Disorder

Autistic Spectrum Disorder (ASD) is among the mental health problems that most hinder child development [5]. A global developmental disorder that appears in the first three years of life. In addition, it affects normal brain development related to social and communication skills. The disease is marked by three fundamental characteristics: inability to interact socially; difficulty in the mastery of language to communicate or deal with symbolic games; and a pattern of restrictive and repetitive behavior [6, 7].

With this, it is possible to perceive the importance of special care for children; since discovering ASD early, it is possible to improve their personal and social development.

Recently, it is observed that the development of information technologies has been used to assist numerous practices in the health area in activities such as diagnosis, therapy, management and education, which requires the need for changes and the development of new skills by health professionals of the involved areas [8].

Piscalho and Veiga-Simão [9] indicate that a game can play an essential role in developing the child in general. It provides reflection and interrelationship between objects and events, helping the child expand the imagination and improve social, communicative and autonomy competencies.

Considering that children with autism have difficulties in responding under the control of the correct stimuli, it is important to teach the skills of playing in a structured and clean context of competing stimuli [10, 11]. Faced with a more systematic teaching, it becomes necessary to incorporate incidental education of play. Thus, the child initiates an interaction with an object or an activity that he is interested in; during the session, the professional takes advantage of this natural situation and proposes a demand, uniting teaching with play, in a natural way [11].

It is known that play is fundamental for these children and can help in teaching academic skills, such as visual-motor orientation games, for example, fitting and puzzle games [11]. On the other hand, it is also known that many ASD children have a high interest in computers and electronic games [12].

2.2 Minimal Pairs

In the minimal contrast therapy method, also known as minimal pairs, pairs of words are selected that are distinguished by a single consonant or vowel but which are produced as homonyms by the child [13]. As an example, according to Freitas and Alves [14], it is possible to say that there is a minimal pair when two phonic sequences are distinguished by a single phoneme, for example, the Portuguese words "tom" (tone) and "dom" (gift). Here, there is a minimal difference characterized by loudness, whereas /t/ is classified as an occlusive consonant segment (depending on the meeting of the posterior part of the tongue with the soft palate), alveolar (depending on whose sound is articulated at the meeting of the tip of the tongue with the dental alveoli), voiceless; the /d/ segment is classified as occlusive, alveolar, voiced. Therefore, the contrast is considered in an identical environment since the difference is found through a single sound, in the same place, in the two sound sequences. The mentioned example makes clear the distinction between the phonemes /t/ and /d/. Table 1 provides examples of minimal pairs.

The method of minimal pairs has degrees of difficulty. When the sound that distinguishes a minimal pair is presented at the beginning of the word, it is called easy; in the middle of the word, it is medium, and at the end of the word, it is difficult. There are several reasons for replacing phonemes; only two will be treated: the substitutions involving the spelling of voiced and voiceless phonemes. Some pairs of phonemes have a characteristic of differentiating themselves by the sound trait; some are voiced, and others are voiceless. The phonemes /p/, /t/, /k/, /f/, /s/, are considered voiceless since they do not present vibration of the vocal folds when produced. In turn, the phonemes /b/, /d/, /v/, /z/, are performed with vocal folds vibration, being considered, therefore, as voiced phonemes. The soundtrack corresponds to an important distinction between the pairs of these sets of phonemes: /p/ × /b/; /t/ × /d/; /f/ × /v/; /s/ × /z/ [15].

Table 1. List of minimal pairs adopted (these minimal pairs occur in the Portuguese language).

Words (in Portuguese)	Words (in Portuguese)
Pão	Mão
Fruta	Truta
Bola	Cola
Torta	Porta
Uva	Luva
Caneta	Careta

Based on the voiceless/voiced substitutions, the studied minimal pairs analyzed should be related to the environment in which the game was created in its respective phase, as the Portuguese words "pão" (bread) and "mão" (hand), "torta" (pie) and "porta" (door) belong to the bakery stage; "truta" (trout) and "fruta" (fruit), "uva" (grape) and "luva" (glove) belong to the supermarket stage; "bola" (ball) and "cola" (glue), "caneta" (pen) and "careta" (grimace) belong to the school stage.

2.3 Related Works

The use of minimal pairs is a quite common method in speech therapy sessions. In the literature, some studies were found using this method in speech therapy sessions, such as the Kera puzzle game [16]. This game makes use of minimal pairs, working as an auxiliary tool by professionals in the speech therapy field in the intervention of children with phonological disorder.

The work presented by Zorzi [15] consists of analyzing the effectiveness of the Minimal Pair Model – Modified Maximum Oppositions used in the therapy of a child with the phonological disorder in the city of Natal-RN.

Another work, developed for children in speech therapy sessions [17], aims to verify the most effective therapeutic approach for children with phonological disorders. Using two types of therapies to two distinct groups, the first based on the minimal pair model and the second on the phonetic/articulatory therapy.

Autism has always been a constant theme in the speech therapy field. As a result, some speech therapist intervention works in childhood autism were found in the literature, such as Barbosa et al. [1]. This work aims to analyze the effects of clinical listening on the parental discourse of children with autism on speech therapy teamwork at a Child and Youth Psychosocial Care Center.

Another study in this area [18] assesses the efficiency of the speech therapist therapeutic intervention for autistic children.

In the literature, no studies were found that related these two themes mentioned above, minimal pairs and autism.

3   Method

This project lasted approximately one year and involved an undergraduate student in Information Systems and a researcher in the Speech Therapy field and another researcher in Computing. Both researchers are from the Postgraduate Program in Developmental Disorders. The research took place between November 2019 and November 2020. To achieve the objectives of this project, it was necessary to carry out the following steps:

- Literature review on the topics involved (ASD and minimal pairs).
- Frequent meetings with a specialist in the Speech Therapy and Computing fields.
- Submission and approval of the project to the Research Ethics Committee, under number CAAE: 38648820.0.0000.0084.
- Implementation of the digital game, with the participation of the speech therapist in the entire development process.
- Application and testing of the game with professionals in Speech Therapy to validate that the tool has reached the minimum requirements.
- Application and testing of the game with children in the stipulated age range.
- Analysis of the results/feedback of the post-test questionnaire.

4   Game Development

The game developed is aimed at being used as an additional tool by professionals in the Speech Therapy field for the intervention of ASD children, in training their ability to understand the words now spoken by people with the use of a face protection mask, without the possibility of the visual appeal of the face, such as facial mimic. This game was developed combining the approaches of interactive software development: top-down and bottom-up, generating prototypes that are refined until an acceptable version is reached according to the requirements initially identified [19]. In this type of approach, the project's success depends on the designers knowing who their users are, that the team acts together and that the various versions are created quickly and tested. The stage of game development is set out below. This approach was used in this project to allow the game to be implemented in parts and tested by experts in an agile way.

4.1   Requirement Analysis

The elicitation of functional and non-functional requirements took place through several meetings with the specialist in Speech Therapy, the developer and the specialist in Computing. Thus, considering the target audience as children between 8 and 11 years old, the following functional requirements were considered:

- The game must provide instruction before each stage.
- The user can collect a tip (corresponds to remember the objective of that moment) in each phase.
- The game should present three different everyday scenarios to the user, namely: a bakery, a supermarket and a school.

- Each scenario must have four phases, the first phase will have a minimal pair related to the context of the scenario, the second phase will have the same minimal pair, but with a greater degree of difficulty, the third phase will have a different minimal pair related to the context of the scenario, the fourth phase will have the same minimal pair but with a higher degree of difficulty.
- The player must lose life when colliding with the enemy or if he collects a word out of the requested order.
- The game must distinguish the order of words requested, generating a loss of life if this order is not respected.
- The player must collect the words in the order in which they were requested to pass the level.
- At each new phase, more lives should be available due to the increased difficulty.

The non-functional requirements of the game are:

- The game must not have an internet connection dependency.
- The game must be run on a Windows operating system.
- The game must be intuitive.
- The game is a single user.

The game's usability requirements are:

- The game must have a design suitable for the target audience (colors, figures, texts, buttons and messages).
- The game must have audio to identify the figures suitable for the treatment.
- The game should be easy for a child with autism.
- The game should be motivating for children and adolescents with autism.
- The game cannot have objects that take the user's focus away.

4.2 Design

The game was designed to run on desktop/notebook devices with Windows operating system. The programming language used was GDscript, a Godot Engine language. The following are some key parts of the project:

- **Creation of scenarios and figures.** To develop an environment that was motivating and inviting for autistic children in the specific age group and the context of a pandemic, it was necessary to think about the most common environments that a child attend. As a result, a bakery, a supermarket and a school were obtained. Then it was necessary to look for images for the background so as not to confuse the child (without overloading written or visual information). These images were treated in such a way as to remove the background, improve the quality, blur the background, perfect the images.
- Regarding the images of the objects, there was a study of possible minimal pairs that would make sense in each proposed environment. First, all images were got from the internet (Creative Commons license) and edited. Then, these images have undergone

validation of the scenarios and objects edited by a professional in the speech therapy field.

- **Creation of audios.** The audios responsible for guiding the child to play (hunting the minimal pairs in a specific order) were recorded using the mask to give more realism to the game.
- **Gameplay creation.** Regarding the gameplay itself, it was necessary to think about funnily integrating the minimal pairs, arriving at the idea of a platform game that would have several different levels and different difficulty levels. Each day-to-day scenario contains, in each phase, minimal pairs belonging to that context. Before starting each phase, there is an instruction asking for the minimal pairs and a specific order related to the scenario.
- **Minimal pairs.** Each phase has an instruction with the respective minimal pair, increasing the difficulty in each phase passed. An example would be: "Take me bread, hand, hand, bread, in that order".

4.3 Implementation

For the research, a digital serious game will be used with some phases developed for this purpose in three different scenarios, as already mentioned (a bakery, a supermarket and a school). The game starts on a screen demonstrating the basic controls of the game (Fig. 1), then a new screen appears with a voice instructing the user to pick up objects in a certain order (Fig. 2). Then, the child has to collect them in the order he was asked, in a scenario where he needs to go up/down and jump over obstacles. The child is represented by the avatar of the boy with a mask. If he collects the wrong word or collides with an enemy, he will lose points (hearts), as shown in Fig. 3. In the same way, the child will earn stars if they get the right words. There are difficulty levels for each scenario presented in the game.

Each scenario has four phases, so when the child wins all phases, a screen will appear congratulating him (Fig. 4 and Fig. 5).

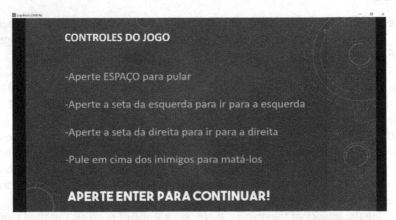

Fig. 1. Controls screen: press SPACE to jump/press the left arrow to go left/press the right arrow to go right/jump on enemies to kill them/PRESS ENTER TO CONTINUE!.

Fig. 2. The identification of the game: word search game.

The Instructions screen: Press here to listen to the instructions/PRESS ENTER TO START THE GAME.

Fig. 3. Game interaction screen, in the first phase of the bakery.

Fig. 4. The final screen of the bakery stage congratulating the user for winning the last bakery phase! Press ENTER to continue.

Fig. 5. The final screen of the supermarket stage congratulating the user for winning the last supermarket phase. Press ENTER to continue.

5   Evaluation Methodology

According to the data provided below, the game was evaluated, involving a group of professionals in speech therapy and children with ASD.

5.1   Participants

Study participants will be divided into two groups. There are nine speech therapists in the first group, whose inclusion criterion consists of exercising their profession and working with autistic children and adolescents. Fourteen children and adolescents are in the second group, aged between 8 and 11 years, whose inclusion criterion is to attend speech therapy sessions, be autistic with a medical report and who are considered able, by the specialist, to use the game. Exclusion criteria will be those not considered suitable by the speech therapist.

Failure to participate in this research (using the game) does not prevent the participants from carrying out activities planned for the speech therapy session.

The recruitment of both groups will be done for convenience since one of the project members is a speech therapist and already has contact with groups of speech therapists and children in sessions.

5.2 Local

Due to the pandemic, the research will take place online. The group of speech therapists will evaluate/validate the game at their place of convenience. For children and adolescents, the use of the game will occur in virtual speech therapy sessions that are already taking place. The research will take place in an appropriate place (of convenience for both groups) to guarantee the participants' confidentiality and privacy.

5.3 Procedures

At first, speech therapists received the executable file for installing the game on their computers. After that, they will be free to test the game for as long as they wish, but the expectation is that they will be able to navigate the game in 30 min. After that, they will be asked to answer a questionnaire about the game they evaluated (5 min) (Table 2). This questionnaire was validated by a group of speech therapists specialized in ASD.

Table 2. Usability and utility questionnaire - professional audience.

Answers
Is the game motivating for ASD children and adolescents?
Is the design adequate (Colors, Figures, Texts, Buttons and Messages)
Is the figure identification audio suitable for the treatment?
Is the game easy for an ASD child?
Is the game intuitive?
Is the game playful?
Do you believe that the game could be used for interventions in speech therapy sessions?

At the appropriate time within the session, the speech therapist applied the game so that ASD children could use it for a time not exceeding 30 min in a single session. Finally, the impressions about the use of the game by the children will be captured by a simple questionnaire that the children will answer (with the help of the speech therapist) (Table 3).

As the questionnaire will be conducted by the speech therapist, she is free to use the question in another way to be more efficient.

Table 3. Satisfaction questionnaire - children audience.

Answers
Is the game cool?
Is the game fun?
Is it an easy-understand game?
Would you play it again?
Did you understand the voice even with a mask?
Is the avatar cool?
Say things you liked about the game
Say things you did not like about the game

No information that could identify the participants was used. After analyzing the results, all those responsible for the participants will receive the return of the study through registered e-mail.

6 Results and Discussions

The methodology used to evaluate the game was composed of two parts: evaluation with speech therapists and evaluation with children, as described below.

6.1 Evaluation with Speech Therapists

The test questionnaire was answered by nine participants, being professionals in the Speech Therapy field. The responses were recorded between November 9th and 13th, 2020 and were summarized in Table 4.

After the child finished the game, the speech therapists were invited to use the game and give their opinions about the user interface, design, visual and sound effects to validate its playful, motivating, and functional character in its use in Speech Therapy sessions. Thus, a questionnaire was made available on Google Forms, containing ten multiple-choice questions, using the 5-point Likert scale.

6.2 Evaluation with Children

Fourteen children aged between eight and eleven years participated in the evaluation. After using the game for an average of 30 min, the children were asked to give their opinion on the game, using a questionnaire with ten multiple-choice questions (3-point Likert scale) and two open-ended questions. The results of the questionnaire are presented in Table 5 and the following text.

In addition to the multiple-choice questions, the children were asked questions about what they liked most about the game, among the answers are: "Everything", "To play",

Table 4. Usability and utility questionnaire - professional audience.

Questions	I definitely agree	I agree	I neither agree nor disagree	I disagree	I definitely disagree
Is the game motivating for ASD children and adolescents?	33,3%	44,4%	11,1%	11,1%	0%
Is the design adequate (Colors, Figures, Texts, Buttons and Messages)	11,1%	44,4%	33,3%	11,1%	0%
Is the figure identification audio suitable for the treatment?	11,1%	55,6%	22,2%	11,1%	0%
Is the game easy for an ASD child?		33,3%	33,3%	33,3%	0%
Is the game intuitive?	11,1%	55,6%	11,1%	22,2%	0%
Is the game playful?	11,1%	66,7%	11,1%	11,1%	0%
Do you believe that the game could be used for interventions in speech therapy sessions?	55,6%	33,3%	11,1%		

Table 5. Satisfaction questionnaire - children audience.

Questions	I agree	Neutral	I disagree
Is the game cool?	85,7%		14,3%
Is the game fun?	64,3%	28,6%	7,1%
Is it an easy-understand game?	64,3%	28,6%	7,1%
Would you play it again?	100,0%		
Did you understand the voice even with a mask?	92,9%		7,1%
Is the avatar cool?	100,0%		

"avatar", "to pick things up", "Much cool". Regarding what they liked least are: "Nothing", "the noise", "I wanted to play every day", "it's fast". It can be seen, from the children's responses, that the game had a very positive evaluation concerning the satisfaction in its use and to its visual elements, already about the sound elements, we realized that because the game is audible primarily, it even disturbed some children a little, something familiar because autistic children are more sensitive to sounds than the average population. So based on the results, small changes in the audios would be something to think. Regarding future sessions, open-ended questions will also be asked to speech therapists asking for suggestions and recommendations.

7 Conclusions

This article presented a serious game to assist speech therapy sessions with autistic children before Covid-19. All phases of the game's development cycle were presented, and tests were performed with speech therapists and children belonging to the target audience during speech therapy sessions. Both tests confirmed that the game has good usability and is an interesting resource to assist in therapeutic intervention, especially in the initial training for the use of a mask and sound perception, in this time of the pandemic.

Regarding the specific needs of children with ASD, as described in detail in the methodology, the game provided the anticipation of actions, visual support, use of realistic figures, use of everyday environments, possibility of working with communication and conversational skills in situations social.

As future work, it is possible to create more phases with different day-to-day environments, increasing difficulty levels of the minimal pairs required, and improvements in interactions with children, such as developing a virtual robot to interact in place of the audio.

Acknowledgment. The work was supported by the Coordenação de Aperfeiçoamento de Pessoal de nível superior - Brazil (CAPES) - Programa de Excelência - Proex 1133/2019.

References

1. Barbosa, A.M., de Figueiredo, A.V., Viegas, M.A.S., Batista, R.L.N.F.F.: Os impactos da pandemia covid-19 na vida das pessoas com transtorno do espectro autista. Rev. Seção Judiciária Rio de Janeiro **24**(48), 91–105 (2020). http://dx.doi.org/10.30749/2177-8337.v24n48 p91-105
2. Fundação Oswaldo Cruz –Fiocruz. Saúde mental e atenção psicossocial na pandemia Covid-19 (2020). https://portal.fiocruz.br/sites/portal.fiocruz.br/files/documentos/saude-men tal-e-atencaopsicossocial-na-pandemia-covid-19-violencia-domestica-e-familiar-na-covid-19.pdf. Accessed September 2020
3. Organização Pan-Americana de Saúde - OPAS. Organização Mundial da Saúde - OMS. Folha informativa – Covid-19 (doença causada pelo novo coronavírus) (2020). https://www.paho.org/bra/index.php?option=com_content&view=article&id=6101: covid19&Ite mid=875. Accessed 18 May 2020

4. Fernandes, A.D.S.A., Speranza, M., Mazak, M.S.R., Gasparini, D.A., Cid, M.F.B.: Desafios cotidianos e possibilidades de cuidado às crianças e adolescentes com Transtorno do Espectro Autista (TEA) frente à COVID-19. Cadernos Brasileiros Terapia Ocupacional/Braz. J. Occup. Ther. (2020). https://doi.org/10.1590/2526-8910.ctoAR2121
5. American Psychiatry Association - APA. Diagnostic and Statistical Manual of Mental disorders - DSM-5. 5 edn. American Psychiatric Association, Washington (2013)
6. Campanário, I.S.: Espelho, espelho meu: A psicanálise e o tratamento precoce do autismo e outras psicopatologias graves. Ágalma, Salvador (2008)
7. Baio, J., et al.: Prevalence of autism spectrum disorder among children aged 8 years —autism and developmental disabilities monitoring network, 11 Sites, United States, 2014. MMWR Surveill Summ. **67**(6), 1–23 (2018)
8. Fernandes, F.G., Santos, S.C., de Oliveira, L.C., Rodrigues, M.L., Vita, S.S.B.V.: Realidade virtual e aumentada aplicada em reabilitação fisioterapêutica utilizando o sensor kinect e dispositivos móveis. Universidade Federal de Uberaba-UNIUBE, Minas Gerais (2014)
9. Piscalho, I.A.D., Simão, A.M.V.: Promoção da autorregulação da aprendizagem das crianças: proposta de instrumento de apoio à prática pedagógica. Nuances: estudos sobre Educação **25**(3), 170–190 (2014). http://dx.doi.org/10.14572/nuances.v25i3.3163
10. Strain, P.S.: LRE for preschool with handcaps: what we know and what we should be doing. J. Early Intervent. **14**(4), 291–329 (1990). https://doi.org/10.1177/105381519001400401
11. Carvalho, O.M.F.: Do uso de jogos digitais com criança autista: estudo de caso. Autismo: Vivências e caminhos 77 (2016). https://doi.org/10.5151/9788580391329-10
12. Aguiar, E.C., Gomes, V.O., e Sarinho, V.T.: QuizTEA - Uma proposta de desenvolvimento de quiz digitais para indivíduos portadores do transtorno do espectro autista. In: XVII Brazilian Symposium on Computer Games and Digital Entertainment (SBGames) (2018). https://doi.org/10.5753/sbcas.2019.6262
13. Pagliarin, K.C., Keske-Soares, M.: Abordagem contrastiva na terapia dos desvios fonológicos: considerações teóricas. Rev. CEFAC **9**(3), 330–338 (2007). https://doi.org/10.1590/S1516-18462007000300006
14. Freitas, A.M.A., Alves, G.C.: Consciência fonológica: a utilização de jogo digital como estratégia para o ensino de Língua Portuguesa. Letras Letras **32**(2), 83–108 (2016)
15. Zorzi, J.L.: As trocas surdas sonoras no contexto das alterações ortográficas. Soletras (15) (2008). https://doi.org/10.14393/LL63-v32n2a2016-5
16. Figueiredo, K.O., Cardenuto, R.R.: KeRa Puzzle: Jogo Digital Educacional para Apoio à Intervenção Fonoaudiológico. Rev. Ibérica Sist. Tecnol. Inf. Lousada Ed. (E41), 503–515 (2021)
17. Giacchini, V., Mota, H.B., Mezzomo, C.L.: Diferentes modelos de terapia fonoaudiológica nos casos de simplificação do onset complexo com alongamento compensatório. Rev. CEFAC **13**, 57–64 (2011). https://doi.org/10.1590/S1516-18462011000100008
18. Tamanaha, A.C., Chiari, B.M., Perissinoto, J.: A eficácia da intervenção terapêutica fonoaudiológica nos distúrbios do espectro do autismo. Rev. Cefac **17**, 552–558 (2015). https://doi.org/10.1590/1982-021620156314
19. Sommerville, I.: Software Engineering. 9th edn. (2011). ISBN-10, 137035152, 18

Specified Ontologies in User Tags to Graphical User Interface Hedonistic Type Based on Sentiment Analysis

Alberto Ochoa-Zezzatti[1] , Jaime Muñoz-Arteaga[2] , Paulo N. M. Sampaio[3]([✉]) ,
and Laura M. Rodríguez Peralta[4]

[1] Universidad Autónoma de Ciudad Juárez, Ciudad Juárez, México
alberto.ochoa@uacj.mx
[2] Universidad Autónoma de Aguascalientes, Aguascalientes, México
jaime.munoz@edu.uaa.mx
[3] Graduate Program in Computing and Systems, University of Salvador (UNIFACS), Salvador, Bahia, Brazil
paulo.sampaio@unifacs.br
[4] Faculty of Information Technologies and Data Science, Universidad Popular Autónoma del Estado de Puebla, Puebla, México
lauramargarita.rodriguez@upaep.mx

Abstract. In this research, some promising initial results are described from induced ontologies labels related to a Hedonistic Graphical User Interface with vocabularies. These results were selected using Cultural Algorithms based on desire intentions using some model assumptions. The usefulness of ontology aspects as a supplement to a labeling system that brand and model results and also demonstrates clearly its usability specification. Proposing a revised probabilistic model using ontologies to induce seed ontology aspects and describe how the model can be integrated into the community's logistics labeling. Most hedonistic interfaces do not have an appropriate model that can correctly measure the assessment of having made a suitable match. Therefore, there is no model of user satisfaction associated with the search for a virtual dating center, which is why we propose a way to analyze the labels associated with an experience in a hedonistic interface and its associated satisfaction considering ontologies and an innovative metaheuristic. This metaheuristic allows to group-specific characteristics considering attributes associated with archetypes of male escorts.

Keywords: Hedonistic GUIs · Cultural algorithms · Ontology · Automatic tagging based on emotion threshold

1 Introduction

In this research, some promising initial results from induced ontologies labels related with a Hedonistic GUI (Graphical User Interface) with vocabularies are described - they were selected using Cultural Algorithms based on desire intentions using some

© Springer Nature Switzerland AG 2021
P. H. Ruiz et al. (Eds.): HCI-COLLAB 2021, CCIS 1478, pp. 178–191, 2021.
https://doi.org/10.1007/978-3-030-92325-9_14

model assumptions. The usefulness of ontology aspects as a supplement to a labeling system that brand and model results to consider a group of users that require sensorial interactions through a hedonistic GUI. Proposing a revised probabilistic model using ontologies to induce seed ontology aspects and describe how the model can be integrated into community's logistics labeling.

Most hedonistic interfaces do not have an appropriate model that can correctly measure the assessment of having made a suitable match, and therefore there is no model of user satisfaction associated with the search for a virtual dating center, which is why we propose a way to analyze the labels associated with an experience in a hedonistic interface and its associated satisfaction taking into account ontologies and an innovative metaheuristic that allows to group specific characteristics considering attributes associated with archetypes of male escorts. In recent years, there has been a rapid growth in the use of labeling applications, both in the number of labeling applications associated with pictures as well as in the number of users participating in communities labeling. This growth currently exceeds our understanding of how the entries are efficient and productive for a range of applications and users are made. Labeling systems are often placed in opposition to the taxonomic models and two types they are commonly cited:

1. The user interfaces for annotation based on a closed, hierarchical vocabulary are clumsy and inflexible, and;
2. A strict concept tree that does not reflect its use and intention. The first criticism is valid but can be easily treated with dynamic ontologies and better mechanisms for UI.

Much of the second review is not so much an issue with taxonomy (ontology) itself, but rather with the problematic models that force users to put concepts into a single hierarchy. Most of these issues can be treated using ontologies aspects that separate the various aspects of scoring attempt. Some common facets used in recording media include the location, the associated activity or event, several aspects of painting (people, flora, wildlife, objects, etc.) and especially in the context shares, given by emotional response. Labels provide a simple and straightforward mechanism to create annotations denoting a variety of aspects, and also provide direct means of shipment on a search. The search to identify a global optimum for a subject is specific, it is easier to converge when using tags associated with the descriptors, that is why this affects additional resources that consider runtime aspects to be able to properly monetize the user considering the prevalence of the visual aspect in their interaction with users (This can partially mitigate a UI that fits an aligned vocabulary). On the other hand, when an initial search returns a lot of results, labels do not support intuitive and efficient models or the refinement of the question. In the best case, users can refine currently a search near using clusters (statistical) related concepts. Although it is sometimes useful to clustered operation, it is very difficult to assess. In [1] the distinction between polythetic clusters (in which members of the cluster share a certain proportion of system characteristics) and monothetic clusters in which all members share a common characteristic described. As a consequence, in [1], the authors discuss how users can more easily understand the monothetic clusters. Therefore, polythetic clusters are difficult to label, compared to monothetic clusters which are easier to label and be adapted to several common interface paradigms such as directed navigation few hierarchies for refinement of the question, among others, as is possible analyzed with our proposed model named "Remarenm" (Recovery Matching rent men) in Fig. 1.

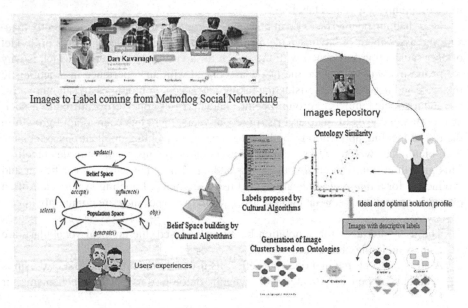

Fig. 1. Proposal model of this research.

In [2] different aspects of search mechanisms have been explored, as well as in [3, 4], which demonstrate the usefulness of search interfaces for image search. Although some in the community that brand labels resist the taxonomy, including del.icio.us (http://del. icio.us) recently added "packages" - while it's purely organizational (packages do not support the ontological semantics), the feature recognizes the problems of organization to scale a model brand labels. It is believed that users should not have to choose among models based purely on taxonomic label models with closed vocabularies. Therefore, a model that balances techniques statistical natural language processing with domain knowledge to induce ontology that can be balanced on the final answer is explored. The goal of this work is to propose a system that preserves the flexibility of the interface for tagging annotation while meeting the power and usefulness of an ontology aspect in the search and display interface associated with a holistic model in the search of a continuous interaction with the final user. Initial results from a system based on symbolic logic for considered variables in the form of a model based on a recurring tagging system or presented in a Hedonistic GUI (Rentonline), demonstrating the potential for the technique to induce the appropriate ontology for a search and display the user interface. The rest of this research describes the approach, the test set using cultural algorithms and evaluation, coupled with a proposal for a model refine a search, swim in different profiles and compare with users in a same population group and how it would fit into the logistics of a community marked by labels and in this Hedonistic GUI.

2 Related Research

An extensive literature review was carried out to determine similarity models for the selection of persons based on generic descriptors, since the concept of beauty is more cultural than mathematical and can only be associated with symmetry values, see is possibly understand in Eq. 1. Figure 2 depicts a simple statistical model of symbolic logic in which X presupposes if described:

$$P(X \mid Y) \geq 0.7 \text{ and } P(Y \mid X) \leq 1 \tag{1}$$

Beauty calculates:
Tag's descriptors 0.94
Mathematical symmetry 0.91
Similar experiences 0.90
Romantic speech 0.87

Fig. 2. Statistic model for beauty.

To do this in [1] this model of co-occurrence applies to the terms of the concept extracted from retrieved documents for a leading question (use a search "query" is helpful to adjust the terms domain). In [5] the same technique to assist (i.e., professionally annotated) photographs of a historical data collection suit associated with male escorts. The resulting taxonomies are quite noisy (i.e., many of the proposed pair's assumption is incorrect), especially since the domain vocabularies are focused by the original questions. The results are presented in Table 1 as a baseline. Although not function properly, these models generate the taxonomy that reflects the actual use, and thus satisfy properly labeling applications. Many other researchers have experimented inducing ontology using statistical techniques including Natural processing language [4, 6, 7]. Some of these [6, 7] depend at least in part of grammatical speech, because this can only be applied in the context of natural language. Other [4] seeks to match concepts to existing ontologies such as Data Word Team; these models may be inherently less noisy, but since WordNet is based on vocabulary in standard English, this can be difficult to adapt such models to dynamic vocabulary and sometimes idiosyncratic emerging labeling applications (e.g., for names of events).

Table 1 presents the results obtained using the same technique adapted to contribute to the photographs of a historical collection [4]. In Table 1 we can note that the resulting taxonomies are quite noisy because many of the proposed pairs of presupposition are incorrect, especially because the vocabularies of the domain are focused on the original questions. Despite this, this kind of models generate the taxonomy that reflects the real use, and in this way, they adequately satisfy the applications for labeling. In addition, there had been attempts to match concepts to existing ontologies such as Word Net; these models can be intrinsically less noisy, but since Word Net is based on standard English vocabulary, this can make the adaptation of stories difficult in dynamic and idiosyncratic vocabulary that emerges in labeling application [8].

Table 1. Comparative studies compared by strategies and stratagems in [4].

Paper	BDI	Multi agent	Ontol ogies	Labe ling	Model of emotion	Art and Aesthetics	Year	Title
Wenlan Luo [9]	X	X	X	✓	✓	X	2018	Applying multi-label techniques in emotion identification of short texts
T. Keskin [10]	X	X	X	X	X	✓	2018	Behavioral and autonomic responses to real and digital reproductions of works of art
N. Chen [11]	X	X	X	X	X	✓	2018	Introduction: Art and the brain: From pleasure to well-being
Lim et al.[12]	X	X	X	X	✓	✓	2021	Characterizing the emotional response to art beyond pleasure: Correspondence between the emotional characteristics of artworks and viewers' emotional responses
(Ochoa et al.)	✓	✓	✓	✓	✓	✓	2021	This research

3 Exploratory Approach

A. Pass Assumption proposed in [4] labeling system to a Hedonistic GUI model was adapted by adjusting the statistical thresholds to denote the ad hoc use, and adding the filter control for highly idiosyncratic vocabulary. So potentially it includes X if:

$$P(X \mid Y) \geq t \text{ and } P(Y \mid X) < t \geq D_{min} \, D_x, \, D_y \geq \geq D_{min} \, D_{min} \, U_x, \, U_y \geq D_{min} \tag{2}$$

Where: t is the tendency of co-occurrence, Dx is the number of documents in which the term x occurs, and may be greater than a minimum value Dmin, and Ux is the number of users using x in at least one image annotation, and may be larger than a minimum value Umin. Filter input documents (i.e., photos), requiring a minimum of 2 terms of the label so that the co-occurrence outside fixed. A series of experiments were conducted, varying the parameters t, Dmin, and Umin. a balance that minimized the error rate and maximized the number of proposed pairs assumption was sought. Using more stringent threshold values for the co-occurrence (approaching 0.9) substantially reduces the rate of error, but dramatically reduces the number of proposed peers. Useful values were between 0.7 and 0.8, under comparable value were determined empirically as in [1]. The model is more sensitive to changes in Umin, which Dmin. Umin set to any value below 5 produced many highly idiosyncratic terms in noisy pairs of fancy; a useful range was 5 to 20. Values Dmin diverges from 5 to 40, and proved useful as a means of a fine the value. Both values were increased slowly while the number of documents was increased. With the entry static below 1 million photos, the vocabulary was less stable and so the model was more sensitive to the parameters.

B. Pruning and tree reinforcement Once the statistics of co-occurrence is calculated, pairs of candidate terms are selected using the specified constraints. Then a graph of possible co parent-child relationships built, and filters out the co- occurrence of nodes with the ancestors that are logically about his father. Once the statistics of co-occurrence is calculated, the candidate term pairs are selected using the specified constraints. Subsequently, a figure of possible relationships father-son is built, and filtering out the co-occurrence of nodes with the ancestors that are logically about his father. That is, for a given term relationship should be strengthened. We increased the weights of each accordingly. Finally, with every leaf on the tree the best path is chosen to root, given the weights (reinforced) of the co-occurrence for potential parents of each node, and we join paths in trees. With its systems sufficiently large document, many of the trees that result is quite broad - example, cities with points of interest. A disproportionate number of erroneous trajectories substructures single instance (singleton) and a second hearing (doubleton), with respect to the sub-structures larger observed, and filtering these out together. This is justified since the total number of trees the candidate was too big for these runs (from 500 to more than 3,000 pairs candidates meet with a basic assumption and the criterion of infiltration), and since the ultimate goal is to provide enough structure to assist in making sense and navigation guide through the collection. A secondary goal is to improve the search terms inferring father for images with terms of the child, and in this sense some recoveries are certainly sacrifice in infiltration outside the singleton and doubleton trees. It is thought that users' trees assumption will be more sensitive to the precision recovery, but this aspect of the model should be evaluated in studies of large-scale user.

4 Data Set and Analysis

A snapshot of the data meta-base Rentonline during a longitudinal time April 2019- April 2021 was used (see Fig. 3). To this date, it had a total of 787 of updated images, and around 7000 thousand entries in total. Approximately 5 million of these images were marked as "non-public" so were excluded from the experimental system. The tables were modified by anonymizing for all user data (including photo identifications) and all images with less than 2 terms were filtered. This resulted in a set of tests about 1700 images. The associated vocabulary was limited to 200K and 5000 pairs were generated in total (an exact number is not available because filtering some while reducing the use went Cultural Algorithms proposed a better candidate to be select for our model). Using this technique, Evolutionary Computation determine the cultural aspects of the community to evaluate. Among annotations, Rentonline, vocabulary is contrary regarding limits spelling and term (e.g., "Los Angeles" shows often as they can be analyzed as two terms "the" and "angels" because an interface something -Intuitive input label). In addition, there are many idiosyncratic terms of the annotation. The latter vary from those described personal events as a phrase on a label ("mybestfriend's dog" - possibly indicating some confusion. These different attributes are possible in order to determine when a male escort is more adequate to a specific public as presented in Fig. 3.

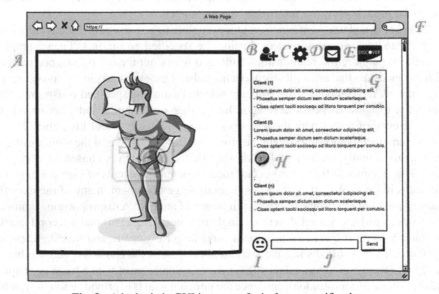

Fig. 3. A hedonistic GUI in terms of wireframe specification.

Considering a previous review in the literature – in particular related to a group of metrics applied to differentiate from traditional GUI – we consider the following aspects of a Hedonistic Interface:

A: In this area of the screen, the "Escort boys" are featured, and some suggestions of physical characteristics and idioms are filtered. When a subject is no more available, a more adequate replacement is automatically sought, most of the cases using the Random Forest algorithm.
B: In Hedonistic Interfaces, in order to build an adequate monetization model, it necessary the existence of multishow events, where a group of "subscribers" are able to specify the duration and presentation mode of the show. In this virtual room, the subscribers are basically voyeuristic, and they can exchange group messages as Word Cloud messages. In our literature review we considered the application of Group Sentiment Analysis.

C: Adjustments associated with sounds, background music and even consider setting the lights from the source of the signal, specifying semiautomatic controls, most of the "Escort boys" are adjusted in a "no nudity" but provocative clothing to try to identify origins and tastes of the possible "subscribers", the origin and duration, are analyzed in real time to specify a pattern of individual and collective behavior.

D: The messages are "monetized" and they are associated with time (minutes), that is, it is required to have a set of virtual money that is translated into service points, this allows indicating the type of message and its associated complexity to attract attention from the "Escort boy".

E: Related to sound alerts in order to specify the waiting times associated with a particular "Escort boy" and determine the sequence of messages, which are particularized for each session and the response ranking determined by previous behavioral indicators.

F: Specifies the user's view control, this includes an eye tracking model associated with the performances related to each "Escort boy".

G: Interactions of up to seven lines of each subscriber and specifications of an individual "private" session, this is where "Sentiment Analysis" is done and descriptive considerations are sought with ideas contributing the subject for continuous improvement of his performance. In this type of platform everything is ranked.

H: Cognates of customer categories, to specify who is a prominent subscriber based on the opinion of the Escort boys.

I: Group of emoticons associated with the most recurrent behaviors with the user's performance and evaluated by a longitudinal aspect of their performance. The most recurrent are: 😿 😈 😄 😿 😽 🙉 😬

J: Rapid incidence texts during the performance and short texts very similar to those of Twitter, in fact the accounts have threads to determine criteria specifications of more than one user.

The trees were evaluated that were manually. Each proposed assumption couple was marked as correct, inverted, related, synonym (including the language in common terms variants as flower "/" blume "/" fleur "/" bloem, among others), or noise (entirely wrong) demonstrates several examples of the types of trees generated many of the concepts of the son "Los Angeles" are near or points of interest.

A great variety of descriptors are (possibly) related to a particular scenario of experience and it is an example of entropy resulting from a statistical model associated with the identification of the best descriptor for a label. On the opposite, the second example is more particular, since each of the child nodes is a hyponym of a concept of fragility such as the label "crystal", although perhaps an art historian would create himself as a domain model of a semantic field of descriptors of a scene. The label "etéreo", that is why for the representation of a set of individuals such as the representation of symmetry (beauty) in use within the Rentonline community and associated with visual aspects, descriptors of emotions and texts associated with interaction with the user. Therefore, based on our experience with this work, it is easier to associate descriptors with an image that allows recommending an experience for a given scenario and this is because the Hedonist GUI has as its primary guideline "monetize the experience with escort boys".

The experience presented in [13], describes how images are recorded and retrieved as easily as possible by emphasizing various aspects of the keyword. Instead, activity and pictures community Rentonline also seem to emphasize another aspect that might be described best as emotion or response. In this research the results of a large proportion of shared vocabulary are attached to the names of places, which, when correctly labeled, can adequately identify an episode in time and be used with a refined model to produce more balance with other aspects.

For location, a combination of names of geographical coordinates associated with relevant temporal aspects as well as points of interest that characterize the place was considered. So, we consider "Los Angeles" a reasonable father of "Chinese Theater". As a pure type of relationship, it does not hold, however, in order to locate a picture, it is entirely reasonable. Also, "Los Angeles" can relate to, but is not a parent of the "muni" or "streetfair". For generic terms like "lake" and "park" instances of lakes or parks could be reasonably considered as children. As for images, more typical relations were used: "dog" with a specific breed is considered, "food" "kimchee" and "creamcheese" where "restaurant" related only. In a large photo sharing environment such as Rentonline, personal relationships are less useful for the question, so almost all personal names as noise in any context of the pair considered. Table 2 presents the results for models related to the assumption of the results compared.

Table 2. Comparison of results

Model	Average Relations	Correct	Relationship/Same*	Error	Average another aspect
A [1]	?	23%	49%	8%	19%
B [5]	105	15%	10%	0.2%	43%
C (Proposed by authors)	750	43%	37%	3.87%	36,7%

*Relation between specialized tags with another specific topic.

In [1] reported a high "aspect of" numbers, and attributed this at least partly because of the question's vocabulary-limiting. In [5] similar to our application, it is presented and is so useful bottom line is provided. it is believed that the model would be made better if it were applied to the entire vocabulary of their data set rather than a focused question. Both [1] and [5] seems to contain an inconsistency in the statistical model (the second term should be expressed as $P(X \mid Y) < 0.8$ and not $P(X \mid Y) < 1$, although this may be an error typographical coderivative in the articles.

5 Proposed Model

The initial results are very promising and give rise to additional research. The proposed model produces sub-structures that reflect different aspects in general, however it cannot categorize conceptual aspects. It has planned a series of changes to the model to address this.

A. Migrating to a pure probabilistic model are currently working to express the assumption, construction pruning the tree, and classification appearance together in a unified probabilistic model, similar to what is proposed in [7]. A probabilistic model should be more robust, and incorporate concepts such as: the number of authors uses a "label" as a property scale attribute rather than a simple threshold as in the current model. Also, if better support for misspellings and repetitions is desired, we believe that the interface currently used by Rentonline can be more useful to support the suggestion that the labels 'repository (e.g., del.icio.us -which was discontinued in 2017, although there are plans to restore it in 2021). Representing the ontology graph as coderivative concepts that have multiple tags can be associated with spellings variables in a probabilistic manner. The most common spelling is the natural label.

B. Exploring morphological analysis and morphological tools is also carried out, nevertheless, they focus on the potential of combining aspects. The initial analysis of the data indicates that certain morphological techniques (such as removing the plural and the gerund form verbs) may be appropriate to some and not to others.

   This detail of the set of identifiers can be related to a complex and large problem with the assumption of a component when it is in common use - such as with the descriptor "taciturn" which can contextualize a Gen Z lifestyle - people tend to name (neither too general nor too specific) generic concepts. In particular, they use unspecific generic concepts such as "country" or "mainland" for location and "mammal" or "plant" for an image. In the results, for example, certain country names were specified and rarely are placed under cities. However, these higher ontological concepts are freely available in the form of geographical dictionaries associated with contextual indicators and common taxonomies. It plans to specify our new model car with these top model of a specific domain (DUMOs) ontologies. This will address the inherent weakness in the assumption, serving another purpose as well. Specified ontology top level structure, can enforce the model aspect that makes the most sense for users; since it is an entry in the model, you can easily test variations on this with the user base.

C. Moderation community support while the model is expected to reduce noise (errors) in our findings, it is believed that the model can be improved by deploying not a fully automated process, but rather as a productivity tool. Many labeling applications have an established model for the community, including enthusiasts' moderators for secondary popular domains. If the statistical model may suggest ontology to a set of advisors, they need only to approve or reject the proposed relationships. Once a baseline is established, it requires little effort from advisors to maintain the current fresh ontology, reflecting the current use. The statistical model reflects community use, with moderators acting as supervisors and to balance a specific feature in our model with pleasure and determine a correlation between cost and satisfaction.

   Many hedonistic interface search engines require a combination of visual aspects (images and videos of male escorts) and sentiment analysis of user experiences, as is proposed in [10], for this reason it is very important to build a descriptive model which considers several aspects to evaluate.

As results of our model, we proposed a numerical prediction associated with each male escort, as presented in Fig. 4.

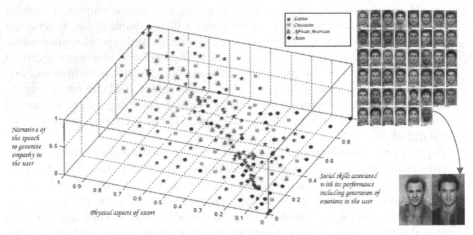

Fig. 4. Numerical prediction plotting location of each male escort based on a representation of Symbolic Capital.

6   Conclusions and Future Research

This paper described assumptions-based ontologies to induce the use of labelling produced a promising initial results model. We expect that further refinement to this model improves accuracy, and also induces to ontological aspects. The results support most

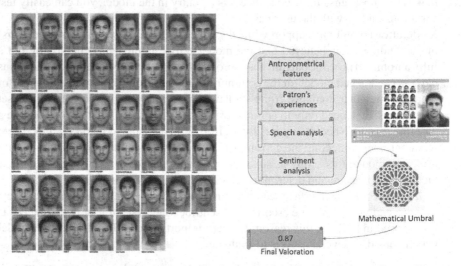

Fig. 5. Propose model to determine the final valuation of a Male issue on Rentonline-

Fig. 6. Neuromarketing components associated with the Hedonism experience in a GUI.

effective search and browser interfaces, and can be reasonably integrated into existing models of community moderators as enthusiasts' balancers who determine if a physical feature or personality characteristic can be associated with each male escort. In our future research it is important to propose a multicriteria analysis model which consider different attributes to determine the most relevant group of features related to a correct selection of a particular issue in order to specify a better experience, using the model proposed in Fig. 5.

Also, with the advent of Neuromarketing technology, it will be possible to improve the identifiers of the guideline associated with the satisfaction of the experience, each device that is used to identify emotions during the experience allows to determine strategies and stratagems associated with the intention of extending the positive effect of the interaction in a Hedonist GUI, as depicted in Fig. 6.

Another aspect analyzed and that should be of great interest is to understand through a structural equation the way in which the tracking of a cult object, such as a musical group, is selected, because in the Hedonistic Interfaces it is sought that the music is an important aspect of the appropriate description and that it remains for a longer time in the collective imagination of the users as can be seen in Fig. 7.

Finally, a very important aspect is to determine the regional tastes associated with LGBT films and specialized magazines - as can be seen in Fig. 8 - this will allow each user to have a suitable escort prototype ready so that the Hedonist Interface can gain knowledge of the user group and proactively determine strategies and stratagems suitable for client satisfaction.

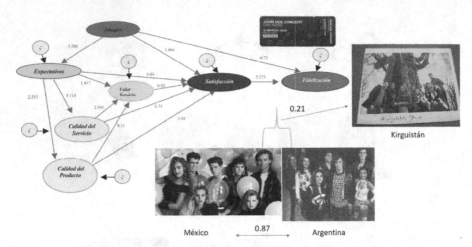

Fig. 7. Structural equation model to determine the following of a musical band and associated with the experience of the users' collective.

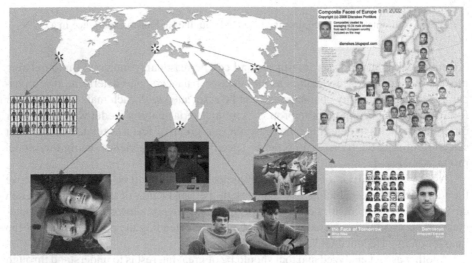

Fig. 8. Retrospective mosaic of user preferences for seven regions of the world, based on textual preferences, and likes associated with LGBT magazines and movies.

Acknowledgments. K. Valadez collaborator in Rentonline, for access to mirror the target database in a Hedonistic GUI.

References

1. Sanderson, M., Croft, B.: Deriving concept hierarchies from text. In: Proceedings of the 22nd Conference of the ACM Special Interest Group in Information Retrieval, pp. 206–213 (1999)

2. Dumais, S., Cutrell, E., Cadiz, J., Jancke, G., Sarin, R., Robbins, D.: Stuff I've Seen: a system for personal information retrieval and re-use. SIGIR Forum (ACM Special Interest Group on Information Retrieval). 72–79 (2003). https://doi.org/10.1145/860435.860451

3. Hearst, M.: User interfaces and visualization. In: Baeza-Yates, R. Ribeiro- Neto, B. (eds.) Modern Information Retrieval, pp. 257–323. ACM Press, New York (1999)

4. Yee, K.-P., Swearingen, K., Hearst, M.: Faceted metadata for image search and browsing. In: Proceedings of the SIGCHI Conference on Human Factors in Computing Systems, pp. 401–408 (2003)

5. Clough, P., Joho, H., Sanderson, M.: Automatically organizing images using concept hierarchies. In: Proceedings of Multimedia Information Retrieval (2005)

6. Hearst, M.: Automatic acquisition of hyponyms from large text corporation. In: Proceedings Of COLING 92, Nantes (1992)

7. Mani, I., Samuel, K., Concepcion, K., Vogel, D.: Automatically inducing ontologies from corpora. In: Proceedings of CompuTerm 2004: 3rd International Workshop on Computational Terminology, COLINGO 2004, Geneva (2004)

8. Allam, H., Bliemel, M., Al Amir, O., Toze, S., Shah, K., Shoib, E.: Collaborative ontologies in social tagging tools: a literature review of natural folksonomy. In: 2020 Seventh International Conference on Information Technology Trends (ITT), pp. 126–130 (2020). https://doi.org/10.1109/ITT51279.2020.9320894

9. Luo, W.: A study on diversified emotional interaction mode of users. In: Stephanidis, C. (ed.) HCI 2018. CCIS, vol. 851, pp. 420–428. Springer, Cham (2018). https://doi.org/10.1007/978-3-319-92279-9_56

10. Keskin, T.: Pricing of games as a service: an analytical model for interactive digital services with hedonistic properties. In: Proceedings of the 51st Hawaii International Conference on System Sciences 2018. Hawaii International Conference on System Sciences 2018, Manoa, HI (2018). https://doi.org/10.24251/HICSS.2018.165

11. Chen, N.: Acceptance of social robots by aging users: towards a pleasure-oriented view. In: Rau, P.-L.P. (ed.) CCD 2018. LNCS, vol. 10911, pp. 387–397. Springer, Cham (2018). https://doi.org/10.1007/978-3-319-92141-9_30

12. Lim, C.-K.: An emotional tactile interaction design process. In: Kurosu, M. (ed.) HCII 2021. LNCS, vol. 12762, pp. 384–395. Springer, Cham (2021). https://doi.org/10.1007/978-3-030-78462-1_30

13. Naaman, M., Harada, S., Wang, Q., Garcia-Molina, H., Paepcke, A.: Context geo-referenced data in digital photo collections. In: MULTIMEDIA '04: Proceedings of the 12th Annual ACM International Conference on Multimedia, pp. 196–203 (2004). https://doi.org/10.1145/1027527.1027573

Towards a Definition of a Learning Model of Business Simulation Games Based on the Analysis of Response from Physiological Devices

Cleiton Pons Ferreira[1,2,3](✉) ⓘ, Carina Soledad González-González[1] ⓘ,
and Diana Francisca Adamatti[2] ⓘ

[1] Universidad de La Laguna, San Cristóbal de Laguna, Spain
{alu0101382166,carina.gonzalez}@ull.edu.es
[2] Universidade Federal do Rio Grande, Rio Grande, Brazil
dianaada@gmail.com
[3] Instituto Federal de Educação Ciência e Tecnologia do Rio Grande do Sul, Rio Grande, Brazil

Abstract. Business simulation games have been adopted as a learning strategy by companies and universities. However, real-time monitoring and analysis of the use of these resources has not been sufficiently studied. This work presents initial results of a research whose final objective is to present the definition of an optimized model of simulators for organizational environments, based on the analysis of user experience supported by physiological feedback devices and neuroscientific concepts. The first collections carried out with participants from Brazil and Spain during the experimentation with three games point to important design, and usability elements that are meaningfull and stimulating for its users, such as the graphical interface, the interaction of resources and easy visualization. Based on these results and future collections, it is expected to structure the proposal of a tool model capable of preparing and motivating professionals to develop the skills and technical knowledge required by the world of work.

Keywords: Business Simulation Game · Electroencephalography · Eye Tracking · Hemoencephalography · Learning · Neuroscience

1 Introduction

The search for the best academic training of its students, increasingly aligned with the needs of organizations, has led educational institutions to use support tools in the development and improvement of knowledge, skills and competences. In addition to the need to improve virtual learning environments reinforced by the COVID-19 pandemic, the importance of a more scientific look at the possible contributions of Business Simulation Games (BSG) in this scenario arises [1].

Considering BSG as a serious game, research shows that to meet the learning requirements, its development goes beyond resources such as interactivity, immersion, engagement and loyalty to the real situation [2] and includes aspects such as: objective goals of

© Springer Nature Switzerland AG 2021
P. H. Ruiz et al. (Eds.): HCI-COLLAB 2021, CCIS 1478, pp. 192–207, 2021.
https://doi.org/10.1007/978-3-030-92325-9_15

the game, experimental challenges, evaluation and constant feedback on the apprentice's performance, which makes the evaluation complex, since there is no predefined object, but an experimentation environment with the possibility of errors and successes, in which it is necessary to evaluate the whole process beyond the result [3]. In addition, there are few studies, and even less of quantitative character, on the contribution of these tools to the cognitive and socioemotional aspects of their users, today considered essential for professionals [4, 5].

The proposal of this work arises when presenting a multidisciplinary study involving the areas of Computation, Game Design, Education and Neurosciences so that, together, they can contribute elements that support the development of serious games that are increasingly closer to the reality that involves the organizational processes of a company, and thus can be used as a learning resource. The scientific hypothesis presented in this research in progress is that, from a data collection using physiological devices as an assessment method during the user experience with BSG, considering the most relevant aspects in the design and usability of these tools, it is possible to define a system model interactive business environment that is more attractive to the learner and more trustworthy for those who apply it, whether in an educational institution or in the company itself. It is expected, from the signs of use of the biological signal collection devices:

- Recognize suggestive patterns observed by stimuli offered at different times and levels during the use of different types of BSG, observed through the respective devices;
- From the analysis of the results obtained, propose a model that can be used as a reference in the BSG project, highlighting the most important aspects that should be considered in its development.

2 Background

2.1 Approaching Serious Games and Neuroscience for A Better Learning

The development of skills and competences necessary for the current generation of students, has been recommended by recognized institutions around the world. Studies point out the importance of continuous improvement in aspects such as creativity, high-level thinking, collaboration and the ability to analyze problems and make decisions for professional success [5–7].

The great and current challenge of teaching is to establish the balance between practice and theory, as normally the knowledge developed in academia is limited to a static view of organizations and as an ordered set of activities, without considering any possible changes in business models. A solution that presents itself to solve the problem is the Serious Games, designed to improve the learning experience for students [8], but in practice only a small part of the knowledge acquired by apprentices in the classroom can actually be applied in labor life [9]. To reverse this reality the Serious Games are gaining a relevant space in learning environments, including business applications. In these virtual systems, the learner can experience situations in specific environments, addressing different aspects of the organization, constructing new models of processes in which they interact as a key character, so that the planning and decision-making exercise is more important than the result [10]. It is also associated with the use of serious games, the development of skills such as motivation, analytical thinking, knowledge transfer, knowledge retention, adaptive learning, attitude and behavioral change [11] and may favor the acquisition and future evocation of the content, offering elements that can support the reconstruction of a context.

In a Neuroscientific perspective, when dealing with something different and unexpected, the brain seeks to connect to an existing network, in which the information received will be integrated, increasing the potential for retaining information, considering that a new information makes sense, or has meaning, when it fits in a predefined neuronal pattern [4, 12, 13]. Another important aspect of behavior is a close correlation between brain functions and emotions. In particular, the limbic system, the paralimbic system, the vegetative nervous system, and the reticular activating system are involved in processing and controlling emotional reactions [14].

From an affective point of view, the serious game helps in the development of technical skills, abilities and intellectual capacities, achieved through the integration of functional areas, reinforcing the integration of learning. At the same time, group-level learning is achieved through games that explore team dynamics that make learning independent and help develop interpersonal skills [11]. Specific scientific investigation by neuroscientists have helped to create models and give great insights about simulation and serious to support advanced learning, such as an increase in brain volume and plasticity with its use [15–17], and also highlight the development of skills such as coordination, memory and visual acuity.

2.2   Definition and Elements of Business Simulation Games (BSG)

Serious Games and Simulators are digital tools designed for a purpose other than entertainment and fun (without necessarily excluding such characteristics), involving the use of gamification technologies and methodologies to deal with real-world situations with the purpose to teach or train. According to [18], "A simulation is a working representation of reality; it may be an abstracted, simplified or accelerated model of a process. It purports to have a relevant behavioral similarity to the original system". The same author also highlights that simulation and serious game "Combines the features of a game (competition, cooperation, rules, participants, roles) with those of a simulation", and concludes that "A serious game is a simulation game if its rules refer to an empirical model of reality".

The BSG constitutes a concrete example of an e-learning method in management training [19] because it presents virtual representations of real business environment that allow students to manage companies in risk-free situations and provide an overall view of corporate strategic functions and allow students to address educational contents in interactive and attractive ways [20]. Each business game that incorporates any of the features of the "business world" should be considered a BSG. All business games could be considered a BSG and should be categorized as "simulation game" or "serious game", except in case that the tool offers erroneous teaching and virtual environments that manifest professedly unrealistic reactions to a player's choices [21]. A BSG can be used as a learning tool, simulating market trends or corporate behaviors to provide strategic view [22], be it a new business or already established.

The first and more recognized classification established for the BSG [22], considered that this tool under the design aspect can present itself as: total enterprise or functional interacting or noninteracting, and computer or noncomputer; and according to their expected use: as a part of a general management training program; for selling new techniques or procedures, or for conducting research.

As an effective learning method, simulators must develop and/or improve skills, besides supporting the assessment of results and providing feedback to the users [23], what does it mean include aspects related to the fidelity, verification and validation of the model and of the tool itself, such immersion, interactivity and non-linearity [24] including others like sequential nature of decisions, user interface and appearance [21]. With regard to the systematization of research on the modeling of a game, the Taxonomy of Computer Simulations [25] and then adapted for the BSG [21] considers the following macro-categories: Environment of application; Design elements of user interface; Target groups, Goals & Feedback; User relation characteristics; Characteristics of the simulation model.

Considering the high level of complexity and multiplicity of operational and project requirements that are presented, it is essential to consider the possibility of investigating new methodologies and devices to monitor and analyze the user experience of BSG, contributing with important elements to guide its design and success as a learning tool.

2.3   Human-Computer Interaction Devices Supporting the BSG User Experience

The use of Human-Computer Interaction (HCI) devices applying physiological and neuroscientific techniques has been allowing studies involving the disciplines of psychophysics, cognitive neuroscience, and computer science, to understand and explore the effective benefits of technologies for human learning processes, including simulators and games.

A recent research addressed the most prominent methods in this field [26], highlighting the Electroencephalography (EEG) and Eye tracking (ET) considered the two support techniques most used and with more effective response in the business context [27–30], and that the following will be presented its forms of operation, functionalities, limitations and possible contributions in the context of the BSG.

Another emerging technique that has been solidifying and deserves attention, due to its relative simplicity and low cost, is Hemoencephalography (HEG), a procedure based on measuring blood flow and capable of evaluating dependent functions of the prefrontal cortex of the brain [31]. For a better understanding, the basic working principle of each of the three techniques is presented below:

I) Electroencephalography (EEG). Electroencephalography, based on EEG data, has been one of the most used methods for capturing and analyzing non-invasive brain signals. To capture the signals, a cap is inserted in the individual's head, and electrodes are attached to it, which easily make contact and capture brain stimuli, from tiny electrical activity changes in the brain during a predefined activity. The moment the neuron is activated, it becomes polarized, generating an action potential that can be transmitted to other neurons, thus generating the circulation of information and showing the electrical activity of the brain, which in sequence is captured by the electrodes and sent for the electronic module that performs data filtering and treatment [32]. The records obtained through the electrodes show the intensity of the brain waves obtained from the scalp. Modern EEG devices have a high temporal resolution, capable of measuring activity every millisecond, and a good precision spatial resolution. The devices are normally portable and are currently sold at relatively affordable prices in some models, allowing the use of this equipment to be more widespread [33]. The use of EEG in the areas of emotion recognition and mental effort has been used in many types of research. The temporal resolution of EEG is high, meaning that changes in brain activity can be detected milliseconds after effectively they occur. However, the spatial resolution of EEG is limited, but it is possible to identify the general source of EEG, providing information about the types of mental processes that are occurring [26]. In an important investigation [34], several methods were proposed to extract useful information from the observed human EEG activities. In other studies, EEG measurements have been used to research the user response to games [35, 36], and field experts discussed the methodological advancements within player experience and playability research considering EEG as a good measure for cognitive processing [37].

II) Eye-Tracking (ET). Eye-Tracking is a method that can directly and continuously record visual attention, often employed to explore the attention bias [29]. The most well-known ET equipment uses a device that emits infrared rays into the user's eyes (infrared light is used to avoid discomfort of the user with strong light) which in turn hits the pupil and returns to the device, allowing accurately calculate where the person is looking and also measure eye movements such as fixations, sights, and regressions. However, there are already ET systems that use the computer's own WebCam and that, despite a lower precision, are beginning to be an alternative adopted for ocular measurement, due to its low cost. Also known as "SearchGazer", it has been used for remote online studies and experiments, especially in the context of web search [38].

The ET devices have been used in diagnostic applications, through the extraction of data from record eye movements and the associated visual behavior, giving a diagnosis very fast [39]. The following metrics can be collected through ET, during system evaluation of a predefined activity [40], for performance measures: Efficiency and Effectiveness; for process measures: Number of fixations and Fixation, Attentional switching and Scanpath similarity. This is an indicator of position and sequence similarity among different viewers, normally used for comparisons between expert and novice. The study of monitorated tasks by ET provides patterns of activity that reflect the interactions among the stimulus, the receptive-field activating region, the temporal response characteristics of the neuron, and the retinal positions and image motions imparted by the eye displacements. The diversity of the activity patterns suggests that during natural viewing of a stationary scene some cortical neurons are carrying information about saccade occurrences and directions whereas other neurons are better suited to coding details of the retinal image, offers the dual benefit of monitoring brain activity as well as oculomotor function [40]. Considering the reported functionalities, currently the eye-tracking systems have been used in fields such as marketing [29, 30], analysis of the usability of a system and games [41], and more recently in human behavior and Neuroscience studies [40, 42], including the use of EEG and ET devices in a joint and complementary way [41].

III) Hemoencephalography (HEG). HEG is a technological mechanism that uses infrared light to measure the flow of oxygen through the skull. HEG technology uses the property of biological tissue to spread and drive some types of radiant energy in the form of wavelengths. Specifically, HEG uses a low-frequency infrared light source and a receiver connected to a 3-cm handkerchief for evaluation of the activation of the prefrontal cortex [31]. This is a technique for measuring brain signals considered relatively new in scientific circles. To have a dimension of the number of investigations related to the subject, a search was carried out in two recognized databases (on June 4, 2021), only with the word "Hemoencephalography", and the results yielded the following: PUBMED (11 articles) and Web of Science (20 articles). A first look at this small number of published works, all in the health area, mainly in behavioral analysis of people with disabilities, many of them indicate relevant results in both cognitive and emotional aspects [31, 43–45], highlighting the enormous potential of this technique, in addition to highlighting the benefit of its low cost [31] [44], which may be a good indicator that it may be applicable in the study with BSG.

3 Methods

This is a mixed investigation with quantitative and qualitative data generation, defined as the verification and comparison of data obtained through different informants, using different collection instruments, applied at different times [46]. Using the multiple method, it is possible to mix, invert and explore different types of data to better understand the event under study.

While many questions or problems are of a type that presuppose one form of research [qualitative or quantitative] rather than another, not all problems preclude multiple approaches and some lend themselves positively to using a mixed approach [47].

Data collection is being carried out with students and professors of engineering courses and, therefore, it is characterized as a case study [48]. To achieve the objectives of the full investigation, the following steps are being taken:

- Survey of some existing BSGs in the serious games and simulation market;
- Analyze the main features and usage variations of each simulator;
- Selection of simulation tool(s) for data acquisition, considering the possibility of choosing different projects and usage models;
- Data acquisition. Data will be collected through different HCI devices;
- Image and data processing for each tool evaluated according to the device(s);
- Validation of results in the light of Neuroscience, also using qualitative research with participants, as a criterion for comparing the positive and negative aspects and limitations that each tool presents;
- Proposal of a BSG model that will serve as a reference for the development of new learning environments and update the existing ones.

3.1   The Devices Used in the Experiments

The data collection during the use of the BSG intends, until the end of the complete research, to use the following possible physiological devices, individually or together: **I) Actichamp**[1].**(EEG1).**It is a modular amplifier system that integrates several final components for EEG (electroencephalogram) analysis. The equipment has a 32-channel module in combination with ActiCap electrodes, which is a cap placed on the scalp, which has the channels exposed in the 10–20 international standard, where 32 electrodes are inserted to obtain data. Signals acquired through electrodes and sensors are amplified, digitized and then transferred to the computer via a USB input, allowing data to be stored and viewed [49]. This equipment was made available by the Social and Environmental Simulation Laboratory (LAMSA), of FURG – Brazil.

II) Tobii X60 Eye Tracker[2].**(ET1).**This equipment records eye movement at 60 Hz (60 times per second) using a corneal reflection tracker connected to a computer. Tobii Studio software is used to manage recordings during a task and to generate look metrics. The Tobii fix filter was used where a fix is defined as eye movement below the speed limit of 0.42 pixels/ms. A move above this speed is defined as a draw. To determine attention to each part of the screen, areas of interest (AOI) were established using a rectangular drawing tool. This equipment was provided by the Computer and Systems Engineering Laboratory (LAB I3MA), ULL-Spain.

III) ET Web Cam (ET2). Online system for ET developed by Realeye[3]., in license-to-use format for capturing images through the user's Webcam and storing data in the cloud using the computer. The average spatial precision of the chosen tool (113 px) is consistent with the stimuli in motion and sufficient to replicate results in the fixation relationships of the human face [50] The recording and data collection, with a time limit of 10 min, starts after an eye calibration procedure in viewpoints positioned at different points. The system used provides, in the website of the developer, heat maps of fixations obtained from images recorded during the test with the participant.

IV) ET Pupil Labs (ET3). Pupil Core Tracking Glasses (Pupil Labs, Germany)[4]. provide a modifiable, secure and lightweight (~23g) device and an open source data collection and analysis platform. The equipment consists of two ocular cameras (200 Hz each) and a scene camera (60 Hz). A real-time tracking algorithm is used to detect the shape and position of the pupil. ETG uses a model-based approach to estimate gaze that fits image-detected pupil parameters in optical modeling and estimates the optical axis orientation of the eye relative to the RF eye camera. To estimate the relative position of the three cameras, a calibration is needed, where a series of markers are displayed around the screen at a distance where the user moves his head slowly while fixating on a marker [51]. This equipment was provided by the Computer and Systems Engineering Laboratory, ULL-Spain.

---

[1] Actichamp: https://www.brainproducts.com/.

[2] Tobii: https://www.tobiipro.com/.

[3] Realeye: https://www.realeye.io/.

[4] Pupil Labs: https://pupil-labs.com/.

V) HEG Alpha[5].(HEG1) Is a device that reveals the brain metabolism through a direct relationship with the use of oxygen by the brain, which consists of an adaptable headband near infrared (nIR), containing a transmitter and an optical receiver. It utilizes the fact that more oxygenated blood has a more reddish color. The equipment sends pulses of red and infrared light through the skull to the cortex below and measures the level of oxygen in the blood by comparing the intensity between red light and infrared light. The lights emitted by the red and infrared LEDs are sent alternately at a sampling rate of 480 Hz [52].

3.2 Script of Tasks of the Experiments and Ethical Aspects

The tasks during each of the experiments basically consist of:

- Answer a pre-test questionnaire containing questions about the participant's profile and their perceptions about the use of the BSG;
- Watch or read a tutorial on how to use the simulator, presenting the basic operating principles and simulator features;
- Position the devices and make calibrations / adjustments for the tests with each participant (Brazil and Spain);
- Carry out the proposed activity using the BSG;
- Answer a post-test questionnaire, which contains questions about the learning experience after using the BSG, as well as aspects related to the features and design elements of the tool.

The experiment is being developed at different times in Brazil and Spain, and adapting its operation according to some particular local issues, such as choosing the most appropriate BSG to the reality of each collection (language, available time) and the device(s) collection available in each country. To carry out the activities, the BSG and all supporting material (manuals and tutorials) are being made available to the participant in their official language or English.

Although data collection is performed in a non-invasive way, but considering that the research involves people, this project was presented and approved by the Ethics Committees of the Universities of Brazil (FURG) and Spain (ULL).

3.3 The Experiment Format for Each Chosen BSG

Experiment 1: The BSG Wholesale Warehouse. A simulator developed by the company Anylogic[6]. was chosen, which was made available in a free version for academic use. The model called 'Wholesale Warehouse' simulates a logistical environment, receiving goods in large volumes, storing them and then distributing them to retailers. A first collection was carried out with the EEG1 device in Brazil, with 2 students from the Engineering course. A second collection was carried out with the ET1 in Spain with 2 students also from Engineering courses. Data collection was limited to 15 min, where

---

5 Alpha: https://www.hegalpha.com/.
6 Anylogic: https://www.anylogic.com/.

volunteers had time to familiarize themselves with the situation proposed in the simulator of up to 5 min and the rest of the time was used to make the necessary changes to solve the problem of an imbalance between entry and exit of goods to avoid overcrowding in the warehouse.

Experiment 2: The BSG OGG Industrial. This Serious Game developed by OGG[7]., occurs in the form of a competition between industries in the same field (in the test a market of water purifier manufacturers was simulated), contemplating decisions on: production, sales and marketing, human and financial resources. Online, each round is equivalent to 3 months of life for each company. The students can access from their home, just using a computer with internet. Due to the complexity of developing the concepts involved in process management, the BSG was played in the form of a course in 17 weeks, in which in the last 3 weeks each of the 22 participants (engineering students) was responsible for making the company's decision, monitored by ET2.

One of the main reasons for choosing both the BSG and the ET device was to allow the collection to be carried out without the student's displacement from their home, in view of the issue of the Covid-19 Pandemic. The Data collection was limited to 10 min, which was the collection ET2 system timeout, but could be repeated for another 10 min if the participating student still needed more time to make decisions. In this case, it was necessary to recalibrate the device. A new collection is being planned to take place with another group of participants, using the ET2 and EEG1 measuring devices simultaneously.

Experiment 3: The BSG Mc Donald's. McDonald's is a serious video game of strategy, designed by Molleindustria[8]., that provides knowledge of managing a company in a more playful way, in which the player assumes the role of director of the McDonald's corporation and has to control from the production process to the sale of products, always looking for the best result. In addition to the normal day-to-day decisions in the business world, the player has other options that involve ethical aspects. A first collection was recently carried out with the ET3 and HEG1 devices in Spain with 7 students and 3 professors from undergraduate and graduate engineering courses. Data collection was limited to 20 min, including tutorial reading time. If the game ended during this time, the participant would restart the game until the time limit was completed. A repetition of the experiment is planned with participants from Brazil, using the ET2 and EEG1 devices.

4 Partial Results

This is an ongoing study that is in the data collection phase, and the results obtained are still initial. However, the follow-up of the experiments carried out already allow for some important subsidies to the research.

From the Heat Maps obtained with the EEG1 during Experiment 1 with the BSG Wholesale Warehouse, at times with greater brain activation in the intermediate phase of

---

[7] OGG: https://ogg.com.br/.

[8] Molleindustria: http://www.molleindustria.org/.

the test performed by the 2 Brazilian participants, and supported by the Neuroscientific representation of brain functions used as a reference [4], allowed to identify that the participants mainly resorted to the regions located in the Frontal Lobo: Responsible for the functions of operational memory of objects and spatial memory; visuospatial attention; Figurative and analytical reasoning. It was also identified that, near the end of the task, the participants mainly resorted to the regions located in the Occipital and Parietal Lobo: Responsible for movement perception functions; Speed perception; Analytical view; Visuospatial attention (in conjunction with Frontal Lobo).

The regions located in Lobo Frontal were visibly less activated in relation to previous stages of using the simulator, considering that they were informed that time was closing and that they would no longer be able to promote significant changes.

The fixation/saccade maps generated with the 3 Spanish participants, for the same Experiment 1, but using the ET1 device for data collection, showed that two of them focused mainly on the images, and that the screen area relative to the adjustable variables of the simulator was of significantly low interest by the participants. The participant who achieved a better performance in the simulation was able to balance his fixation on various points on the screen and defined a more efficient strategy for solving the problem. The heat map of one of the participants shows that he didn't even see some parts of the settings screen, which is justified, when reporting in the post-test questionnaire, that he did not understand the use of a feature explained in the tutorial.

The results obtained with the EEG signals allowed us to identify that the BSG, due to its constructive and design characteristics: - It favored the acquisition and evocation of content, identified through the activity of Lobo Frontal areas linked to memory and figurative and analytical reasoning, mainly in the phase of building the strategy to be adopted in the game by the participant; - Enabled constant interactivity by promoting actions that required perception of movement and speed, analytical vision and visuospatial attention, by activating areas of the Occipital and Parietal Lobo, more intensely in the final phase of the game when making decisions quickly and efficiently are essential for success in the task;

The same experiment with the ET allowed us to identify, by monitoring eye tracking, that the BSG provided a formulation of individual and different strategies that lead to success, stimulating the participants' creativity and attention.

From the analysis of the 5 questionnaires (Brazil and Spain) together with the EEG an ET data recorded from the BSG user experience, it was observed that none of the volunteers had great knowledge or professional experience in the field of logistics, but they all ended up establishing valid strategies to solve the proposed problem, which allows us to infer, when associated with quick familiarization with the simulator and brain and ocular activation, that practical knowledge in the area is not a preponderant factor for the use of a simulator, as long as it offers resources to facilitate the learning of the subject. Also, all participants considered as important features in a simulation software, in the crossover between the pre- and post-test answers: - Identification of results; - Unexpected situations; - Actions available in the user interface.

This qualitative perception, associated with the results of brain and eye activation, highlights that the simulator must present clear and objective results, dynamic motivational factors and constant interaction with its users.

The still initial analysis of heat maps and facial expression provided by ET2 in the Experiment 2 with the BSG OGG Industrial, in triangulation with the questionnaire responses, allowed us to identify that decision-making took place in less time when previously discussed in groups. In reading visual information, the amount of time for decision making depends on the amount of information the brain needs, because the more non-visual information (knowledge) the individual has, the less visual information he will need [53]. One of the participants stated that digital strategy games amuse him, but he said he felt stressed in carrying out the activities involved in the simulator, which can justify the lack of fixation on the screen at various times during the activity, in line with neuroscientific studies that suggest that negative emotions and stress negatively affect attentional mechanisms [54].

The Heat Map of some participants is clearly more accentuated on the sales and marketing page, indicating an intense focus on results and concern with ranking, reinforcing that intrinsic motivation can be modified by extrinsic factors and positive Competent Emotional Stimuli generates emotional states that support attention, involvement and acceptance behaviors [55].

The Experiment 3 with the BSG Mac Donald's and the respective data collection with ET3 and HEG1 with students and teachers from Spain was carried out recently, but the data has not yet been analyzed, however the follow-up during the tests already allows inferring some contributions for this study:

– In general, there was a significant change in blood oxygenation by the HEG1 in the prefrontal cortex of the participants associated with negative results and endgame.

The situation is repeated when the participant immediately faces unexpected situations when accessing a different screen in the game. In this case, simultaneous monitoring by ET3 shows an increase in the number of fixations, which suggests an increase in the level of attention trying to understand the new situation and defining a solution.

– As the measurement of the HEG signal has been monitored since reading the game tutorial, it is possible to identify that the oxygenation level increases as the participant starts to play and establishes itself in the form of concentration at levels that vary according to their involvement with the BSG, in line with the flow concept which means the completely engaging state of mind when immersed in an activity [56].

5 Conclusions

This work presents an excerpt from a Doctoral Thesis that aims to develop an optimized BSG design model from data collection with HCI devices monitoring the user experience. The different devices used, separately or together, in tests with participants in Brazil and Spain, following the use of games with different resources, design elements and proposed tasks, are providing the creation of a large set of information, the result of these experiments. A complete analysis and crossing of these data, including the answers to the pre- and post-test questionnaires, applied to all participants, will allow obtaining consistent results to achieve the proposed objectives. Although the experiments have not yet been fully concluded, the collections already carried out with three different BSGs allowed the partial analysis of some results and some important preliminary conclusions.

The results obtained with Experiment 1, using an EEG device for real-time monitoring during the use of the BSG, made it possible to understand, through the activation of specific areas of the brain, that a game that aims to simulate a real environment in a predominantly visual precise way:

– Constantly offer tasks that require memory recall and provoke figurative and analytical reasoning for decision making;
– Provide perception of time and space so that decisions are coherent with realities and stimulating for the formulation of strategies;

The analysis of brain activation also adds to the results of the questionnaires before and after the experiment applied to the participants, which highlighted the importance of an easy interaction and understanding of the player's role as a motivational factor.

The Experiment 2, using an ET device, allowed to identify by the time of eye fixation of the participants on BSG OGG screens, and user's perceptions, how much is relevant that the game presents:

– Elements that encourage competitiveness to increase the learner's motivation;
– Feedback information about your game performance and freedom to define different ways to achieve a goal, encouraging reflection, critical thinking and strategic behavior;
– Reliability with regard to results and an adequate level of information that provides exploration of scientific content in a complex way and linked to situations similar to real contexts;
– Possibilities for socializing and sharing ideas with others that enable social-emotional development.

The Experiment 3, carried out recently with the ET and EEG devices, has not yet started its analysis, however, a first look at the results shows the importance of having used two collection devices simultaneously and complementary, which allowed identify in more detail, for example, specific moments and situations in the game that generated changes in the participant's attentional state.

The partial results are, so far, aligned with the objective established for the research, which is, based on the signs of use of physiological signal collection devices, to propose a model that can be used as a reference in the BSG project, highlighting the most important elements that should be considered in its development. The methodological strategy of analyzing different BSG has been providing insights into the importance of characterizing the universe of these games to define their relevant characteristics. At the same time, measurements with different physiological devices in the same game have contributed a lot to the identification of design aspects that present meaning to the user, in different moments of the game. Based on this perception, as a future work, it is intended to repeat experiments 1 and 2 using two collection devices, to further improve the quality of the data generated, in addition to carrying out Experiment 3 with participants in Brazil. Afterwards, a crossing of information will be carried out to finally establish the proposed design model.

Finally, it is necessary to highlight how important it has been to be aware of the technologies available on the market to assist in research. Although it is pertinent to carry out a comparative study between the various devices used, using the HEG1, it was possible to monitor brain behavior in a simpler way. with a larger number of participants. With the ET2, it was possible to carry out the tests even with the limitations caused by the COVID-19 pandemic. Anyway, knowing and taking advantage of these new devices and sensors and using them in an integrated way for neurofeedback is very important to discover and increasingly improve the digital business learning tools.

Acknowledgments. We would like to thank the ULL and FURG, which through a cooperation agreement between the two institutions, has allowed to advance research on the user experience with BSG through the support of biofeedback devices. We would also like to thank the Instituto Federal de Educação, Ciência e Tecnologia do Rio Grande do Sul (IFRS), which has enabled the author Cleiton Pons Ferreira to integrate and contribute to this group of studies.

References

1. Zulfiqar, S., Al-Reshidi, H.A., al Moteri, M.A., Feroz, H.M.B., Yahya, N., Al-Rahmi, W.M.: Understanding and predicting students' entrepreneurial intention through business simulation games: a perspective of covid-19. Sustainability, Switzerland. 13, 1–27 (2021). https://doi.org/10.3390/su13041838
2. McGlarty, K.L., Orr, A., Frey, P.M., Dolan, R.P., Vassileva, V., McvAy, A.: A Literature Review of Gaming in Gaming. Gaming in Education, 1–36 (2012)
3. Ratwani, K.L., Orvis, K., Knerr, B.: Game-Based Training Effectiveness Evaluation in an Operational Setting. 34 (2010)
4. Lent, R.: Cem bilhões de neurônios: conceitos fundamentais de neurociência. São Paulo: Atheneu, São Paulo (2001)
5. Santos, D., Primi, R.: Desenvolvimento socioemocional e aprendizado escolar: uma proposta de mensuração para apoiar políticas públicas (2014).https://doi.org/10.1017/CBO9781107415324.004
6. Bontinck, G., Isik, Ö., Van den Bergh, J., Viaene, S.: Unlocking the potential of the process perspective in business transformation. In: La Rosa, M., Loos, P., Pastor, O. (eds.) BPM 2016. LNBIP, vol. 260, pp. 161–176. Springer, Cham (2016). https://doi.org/10.1007/978-3-319-45468-9_10
7. Prifti, L., Knigge, M., Löffler, A., Hecht, S., Krcmar, H.: Emerging business models in education provisioning: a case study on providing learning support as education-as-a-Service. Int. J. Eng. Pedagogy (iJEP). 7, 92 (2017). https://doi.org/10.3991/ijep.v7i3.7337
8. Monk, E.F., Lycett, M.: Measuring business process learning with enterprise resource planning systems to improve the value of education. Educ. Inf. Technol. 21(4), 747–768 (2014). https://doi.org/10.1007/s10639-014-9352-6
9. Baldwin, T.T., Pierce, J.R., Joines, R.C., Farouk, S.: The elusiveness of applied management knowledge: A critical challenge for management educators. Acad. Manage. Learn. Educ. 10, 583–605 (2011). https://doi.org/10.5465/amle.2010.0045
10. Barçante, L.C., Pinto, F.C.: Jogos de negócios: revolucionando o aprendizado nas empresas. Impetus, Rio de Janeiro (2003)
11. Abdullah, N.L., Hanafiah, M.H., Hashim, N.A.: Developing creative teaching module: business simulation in teaching strategic management. Int. Educ. Stud. 6, 95–107 (2013). https://doi.org/10.5539/ies.v6n6p95

12. Gazzaniga, M., Heatherton, T., Halpern, D.: Ciência psicológica. Artmed Editora (2005)
13. Izquierdo, I.: Memória. Porto Alegre: ArtMed (2002)
14. Bălan, O., Moise, G., Petrescu, L., Moldoveanu, A., Leordeanu, M., Moldoveanu, F.: Emotion classification based on biophysical signals and machine learning techniques. Symmetry. **12**, 21 (2019). https://doi.org/10.3390/sym12010021
15. Green, C.S., Bavelier, D.: exercising your brain: a review of human brain plasticity and training-induced learning. Psychol Aging. **23**, 692–701 (2008). https://doi.org/10.1037/a00 14345.Exercising
16. Kühn, S., et al.: The neural basis of video gaming. Transl. Psychiatry. **1**, (2011). https://doi. org/10.1038/tp.2011.53
17. Kühn, S., Gleich, T., Lorenz, R.C., Lindenberger, U., Gallinat, J.: Playing super mario induces structural brain plasticity: Gray matter changes resulting from training with a commercial video game. Mol. Psychiatry **19**, 265–271 (2014). https://doi.org/10.1038/mp.2013.120
18. Ruohomaki, V.: Viewpoints on learning and education with simulation games. In: Riis, J.O. (Ed.) Simulation Games and Learning in Production Management, pp. 14–28. Chapman & Hall, London, UK (1995)
19. Siddiqui, A., Khan, M., Akhtar, S.: Supply chain simulator: a scenario-based educational tool to enhance student learning. Comput. Educ. **51**, 252–261 (2008). https://doi.org/10.1016/j. compedu.2007.05.008
20. García, J., Cañadillas, I., Charterina, J.: Business simulation games with and without supervision: an analysis based on the TAM model. J. Bus. Res. **69**, 1731–1736 (2016). https://doi. org/10.1016/j.jbusres.2015.10.046
21. Greco, M., Baldissin, N., Nonino, F.: An exploratory taxonomy of business games. Simul. Gamin. **44**, 645–682 (2013). https://doi.org/10.1177/1046878113501464
22. Eilon, S.: Management Games. Journal of the Operational Research Society. **14**, 137–149 (1963). https://doi.org/10.1057/jors.1963.22
23. ABNT: NBR ISO 10015: Gestão da qualidade - Diretrizes para treinamento (2001)
24. Benyon, D.: Designing Interactive Systems: A comprehensive guide to HCI, UX and interaction design (2013)
25. Maier, F.H., Größler, A.: What are we talking about? - a taxonomy of computer simulations to support learning. Syst. Dyn. Rev. **16**, 135–148 (2000). https://doi.org/10.1002/1099-172 7(200022)16:2%3c135::AID-SDR193%3e3.0.CO;2-P
26. Bell, L., Vogt, J., Willemse, C., Routledge, T., Butler, L.T., Sakaki, M.: Beyond self-report : a review of physiological and neuroscientific methods to investigate consumer behavior. **9**, 1–16 (2018).https://doi.org/10.3389/fpsyg.2018.01655
27. Arico, P., Borghini, G., di Flumeri, G., Sciaraffa, N., Babiloni, F.: Passive BCI beyond the lab: current trends and future directions. Physiol. Meas. **39**, (2018). https://doi.org/10.1088/ 1361-6579/aad57e
28. Teo, J., Chia, J.T.: EEG-based excitement detection in immersive environments: An improved deep learning approach. In: Nifa, F., Lin, C., Hussain, A. (eds.) 3RD International Conference on Applied Science and Technology (ICAST 2018). Amer Inst Physics, Georgetown, Malaysia (2018). https://doi.org/10.1063/1.5055547
29. Burger, C.A.C., Knoll, G.F.: Eye tracking: possibilidades de uso da ferramenta de rastreamento ocular na publicidade. Fronteiras - estudos midiáticos. **20**, 340–353 (2018). https://doi.org/ 10.4013/fem.2018.203.07
30. Oliveira, J.H.C., Giraldi, J.M.E.: Neuromarketing and its implications for operations management: an experiment with two brands of beer. Gestao e Producao. **26** (2019). https://doi. org/10.1590/0104-530X3512-19
31. Serra-Sala, M., Timoneda-Gallart, C., Pérez-Álvarez, F.: Clinical usefulness of hemoencephalography beyond the neurofeedback. Neuropsychiatr. Dis. Treat. **12**, 1173–1180 (2016). https://doi.org/10.2147/NDT.S105476

32. Eysenck, M.W., Keane, M.T.: Manual de Psicologia Cognitiva. Artmed: Porto Alegre, Porto Alegre (2010)
33. Kugler, M.: Uma contribuição ao desenvolvimento de interfaces cérebro-computador utilizando potenciais visualmente evocados (2003)
34. Wolpaw, J.R., et al.: Brain-computer interface technology: a review of the first international meeting. IEEE Trans. Rehabil. Eng. **8**, 164–173 (2000). https://doi.org/10.1109/tre.2000.847807
35. Salminen, M., Ravaja, N.: Oscillatory brain responses evoked by video game events: the case of super monkey ball 2. Cycberpsychol. Behav. **10**, 330–338 (2007). https://doi.org/10.1089/cpb.2006.9947
36. Sheikholeslami, C., Yuan, H., He, E.J., Bai, X., Yang, L., He, B.: A high resolution EEG study of dynamic brain activity during video game play. In: Annual International Conference of the IEEE Engineering in Medicine and Biology – Proceedings, pp. 2489–2491 (2007). https://doi.org/10.1109/IEMBS.2007.4352833
37. Nacke, L.E.: Affective Ludology: Scientific Measurement of User Experience in Interactive Entertainment (2009). http://www.bth.se/fou/forskinfo.nsf/Sok/ca7dff01c93318fdc1257646004dfce1/$file/Nacke_diss.pdf%5Cnhttp://phd.acagamic.com/
38. Papoutsaki, A., Laskey, J., Huang, J.: SearchGazer: Webcam Eye Tracking for Remote Studies of Web Search. In: Chiir 2017: Proceedings of the 2017 Conference Human Information Interaction and Retrieval. 17–26 (2017). https://doi.org/10.1145/3020165.3020170
39. Li, J., Sun, S., Zhang, L.: An Improved Classification Model for Depression Detection Using EEG and EyeTracking Data Jing Zhu, Zihan Wang, Tao Gong, Shuai Zeng, Xiaowei Li*, Member, IEEE, Bin Hu*, Member, IEEE, Jianxiu Li, Shuting Sun. Lan Zhang. (2020). https://doi.org/10.1109/TNB.2020.2990690
40. Duchowski, A.T.: Eye Tracking Methodology (2017). https://doi.org/10.1007/978-3-319-578 83-5
41. Cuesta-cambra, U., Rodríguez-terceño, J.: El procesamiento cognitivo en una app educativa con electroencefalograma y «Eye Tracking». Comunicar. XXV, 41–50 (2017)
42. Carvalho, M., Oliveira, L.: Emotional design in web interfaces. Observatorio. **11**, 14–34 (2017). https://doi.org/10.15847/obsobs1122017905
43. Serra-Sala, M., Timoneda-Gallart, C., Pérez-Álvarez, F.: Evaluating prefrontal activation and its relationship with cognitive and emotional processes by means of Hemoencephalography (HEG). J. Neurother. **16**, 183–195 (2012). https://doi.org/10.1080/10874208.2012.705754
44. Scd, H.T., et al.: Increase of cerebral blood oxygenation using Hemoencephalography (HEG): an efficient brain exercise therapy intentional increase of cerebral. J. Neurotherapy : Inv. Neuromodulation, Neurofeedback Appl. Neurosci. Intentional, 37–41 (2008). https://doi.org/10.1300/J184v08n03
45. Kamali, A.M., Saadi, Z.K., Yahyavi, S.S., Zarifkar, A., Aligholi, H., Nami, M.: Transcranial direct current stimulation to enhance athletic performance outcome in experienced bodybuilders. PLoS ONE **14**, 1–20 (2019). https://doi.org/10.1371/journal.pone.0220363
46. Denzin, N.K., Lincoln, Y.S. (eds.) Handbook of Qualitative Research . 3rd ed. Thousand Oaks, CA: Sage 2005 (2006)
47. Lankshear, C., Knobel, M.: Digital Literacies: Concepts, Policies and Practices (2008)
48. Yin, R.K.: Estudo de Caso: Planejamento e Métodos. Bookman, Porto Alegre, RS (2015)
49. Bastos, N.S., Adamatti, D.F., de Carvalho, F.A.: Development of logic skills in high school students: a propostal based on neuroscience. Braz. J. Comput. Educ. **24**, 53 (2016)
50. Semmelmann, K., Weigelt, S.: Online webcam-based eye tracking in cognitive science: a first look. Behav. Res. Methods **50**(2), 451–465 (2017). https://doi.org/10.3758/s13428-017-0913-7

51. Lewien, R.: GazeHelp: exploring practical gaze-assisted interactions for graphic design tools. In: ACM Symposium on Eye Tracking Research and Applications, pp. 1–4. ACM, New York, NY, USA (2021). https://doi.org/10.1145/3450341.3458764

52. Rodrak, S., Wongsawat, Y.: On the classification of EEG/HEG-based attention levels via time-frequency selective multilayer perceptron for BCI-based neurofeedback system (2012)

53. Smith, F.: Leitura para além dos olhos. Leitura significativa. Tradução Beatriz Affonso Neves. Porto Alegre: Artmed (1999)

54. Izquierdo, I.: Questões sobre Memória. Unisinos, São Leopoldo (2004)

55. Damásio, A.: O mistério da consciência: do corpo e das emoções ao conhecimento de si. Editora Companhia das Letras (2015)

56. Tsai, M.-J., Huang, L.-J., Hou, H.-T., Hsu, C.-Y., Chiou, G.-L.: Visual Behavior, flow and achievement in game-basedlearning.pdf. Comput. Educ. **98**, 115–129 (2016). http://dx.doi.org/10.1016/j.compedu.2016.03.011

User Experience Evaluation in MOOC Platforms: A Hybrid Approach

Ana Poma(✉) 📵, Germania Rodríguez 📵, and Pablo Torres 📵

Computer Science and Electronic Department, Universidad Técnica Particular
de Loja, Loja, Ecuador
{alpomax,grrodriguez,pvtorres}@utpl.edu.ec

Abstract. Massive Open Online Course (MOOCs) have become one of the most popular trends in global education, however, most of them do not meet users' expectations and satisfaction. The objective is to identify existing publications regarding User Experience (UX) evaluation in MOOC platforms in order to discover trends and identify different evaluation approaches such as existing evaluation methods, techniques or tools, as well as how they are classified and combined. For this purpose, the systematic mapping approaches of Petersen et al. (2015) and the Systematic Literature Review (SLR) of Torres et al. (2018) are employed. The systematic mapping sample corresponds to 33 relevant articles and 21 primary studies of the SLR process. The findings reveal that both usability and UI are most frequently evaluated, however, attention needs to be paid to other MOOC technology criteria such as MOOC videos. Therefore, it is necessary to consolidate existing findings for future research.

Keywords: MOOC · Massive Open Online Courses · UX · User experience · Usability · Evaluation

1 Introduction

User Experience (UX) from the simplest perspective is defined in how people feel when they use a product or service [1], which is fundamental for the success or failure of any product in the market [2]. On the other hand, Massive Open Online Courses (MOOCs) have become one of the most popular trends in online education, attracting millions of students every year, achieving great popularity among several universities [3], which offer MOOCs through various prestigious platforms such as Coursera, Udacity, edX, among others.

The main factors affecting UX in MOOC platforms are the quality of the content (related to the field of education) and the technical aspects of the platform [4–8]. Regarding the first factor, Meyer et al. [9] points out that the possible causes of the attrition rate are related to the principles of instructional design. Regarding the second factor, in [10–13] they mention that the main problems contributing to attrition in MOOCs are poor usability and User Interface (UI) design. Frolov and Johansson [5] mention that

© Springer Nature Switzerland AG 2021
P. H. Ruiz et al. (Eds.): HCI-COLLAB 2021, CCIS 1478, pp. 208–224, 2021.
https://doi.org/10.1007/978-3-030-92325-9_16

poor design results in poor usability and poor usability can have a negative impact on UX and, moreover, on task achievement and completion within MOOCs.

Several studies indicate that research on UX evaluation in MOOC platforms is essential to achieve learning success [6, 14, 15]. Therefore, the objective of the present study is to conduct a search for scientific contributions that have been made to evaluate UX and/or UX factors in MOOC platforms from a technological point of view, identifying research trends in this area, as well as the methods, techniques and/or tools that have been proposed or used. To achieve this objective, a hybrid methodology is applied that combines the proposals of systematic mapping in software engineering by Petersen et al. [16] and the systematic literature review applied to engineering and education by Torres et al. [17], in order to know and organize the results of existing research in a quantitative and qualitative way.

To make explicit the work done, this article has been structured in the following sections: Sect. 2 describes the user experience, Sect. 3 describes the methodology used to perform the literature review and its application, Sect. 4 shows the results obtained, Sect. 5 presents the discussion and finally Sect. 6 the conclusions and recommendations.

2 User Experience (UX)

There is currently no consolidated and accepted definition of what UX is, however, the definition presented by ISO 9241–11:2018 [18] is one of the most complete: "UX refers to user perceptions and responses resulting from the use and/or anticipated use of a system, product or service". There are several models that have been developed to describe the different categories and factors that make up the UX [19–21] in addition to the definition of UX presented in ISO 9241:11–2018 [18], which present a global perspective of UX (Fig. 1); understanding by category the components: context, user and system, and factors such as perception, usability, etc.

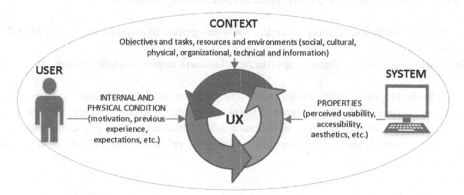

Fig. 1. Categories and factors that make up the UX and their interaction. Based on [18–21].

3 Methodology

A hybrid methodology is applied that combines the proposals of systematic mapping in software engineering by Petersen et al. [16] and the systematic literature review (SLR) applied to engineering and education by Torres et al. [17]. The main reason for combining these two proposals is that the mapping is oriented to software engineering [16] and is complemented by the SLR [17] which is oriented to the education domain, additional according to [22] a mapping study preceding an SLR provides a valuable basis for future research and for performing a well-founded SLR.

The phases selected according to each methodology have been grouped into three stages: planning, development and presentation as an adaptation of the stages proposed by Torres et al. [17].

3.1 Planning

The *research questions (RQ)* for the systematic mapping correspond to general questions with the objective of classifying and organizing the relevant literature of the types of contributions that have been developed to evaluate the UX in MOOC platforms and discover research trends. These are described below:

RQ1: What is the frequency of publication of studies evaluating UX in MOOC platforms?
RQ2: MOOC platforms and/or MOOC components that have been evaluated?
RQ3: Which MOOC platforms have been evaluated per year?
RQ4. Which categories within the technological dimension of MOOCs have been evaluated?
RQ5. Which articles evaluate UX and/or its associated factors?

The research questions for SLR respond to specific questions related to the results of the empirical studies and correspond to the following questions:

RQ6: What methods, techniques and/or tools are applied to evaluate the UX in MOOC platforms?
RQ7: How are these evaluation approaches classified, applied and/or combined?

The development of the *conceptual mentefact* was used to represent the main concepts of the research for the creation of the semantic search structure of relevant articles, as well as discrimination based on inclusion and exclusion criteria [17]. Using the conceptual mentefact, the general domain covering the research area can be delimited as shown in Fig. 2.

3.2 Development

The development stage identifies three phases: search strategy, selection process, data extraction and quality assessment. The *search strategy* consists of defining keywords, selecting databases (DB) of interest and defining the review protocol (inclusion and

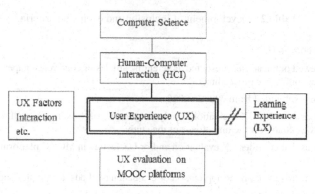

Fig. 2. Conceptual mentefact - UX in MOOC platforms. Based on De Zubiría (1996) cited in [17].

exclusion criteria). Keywords are formulated on the basis of the research questions; conceptual mentefact; PICO criteria, synonyms from Thesaurus [23]; acronyms/acronyms of the keywords are also considered as shown in Table 1.

Table 1. Keywords to perform the semantic search.

No	Computer Science		
	Human Computer Interaction (HCI)	Population	Intervention
1	UX	*MOOC*	evaluat*
2	user* experience*	Massive* Open Online Course*	assess*
3	usab*		research*
4	accessib *		appraise*
5			measur*

The choice of the *search strategy* was made through the search in databases (DBs) related to the field of study are: IEEE Xplore, Scopus and ACM Digital Library.

The *review protocol* corresponds to the inclusion and exclusion criteria that will serve as the basis for the search and selection of articles of interest. Both mapping and SLR share some inclusion and exclusion criteria (Table 2), however, they are different in terms of objectives and data analysis. The systematic mapping requires obtaining an overview of the research area, as well as discovering research gaps and trends according to the general research questions, so it is not convenient to narrow down the search so much; while SLR synthesizes evidence by analyzing the results and demonstrating empirical evidence according to the specific research questions.

The search strings and the number of studies found for each database are shown in Table 3. It should be noted that an advanced search was performed, specifically on titles, abstracts and keywords.

Table 2. Development of inclusion and exclusion criteria.

No	Inclusion criteria (IC)
IC1	Peer-reviewed publications, presented as scientific articles or conference papers in scientific journals or conference proceedings
IC2	Publications submitted from 2008 to 2020
IC3	Publications in which UX evaluation is only one element of the study, as well as publications in which UX evaluation is the main focus of the study
IC4	Publications that consider UX evaluation and/or UX factors in MOOC platforms or any of their components
IC5	Publications that mention the application of evaluation methods, techniques and/or tools
No	Exclusion criteria (EC)
EC1	Publications that are not in the area of Computer Science
EC2	Publications that are not available in English
EC3	Publications duplicated from other publications
EC4	Publications that refer to learning experience (LX) or content evaluation according to the pedagogical dimension
EC5	Publications that do not apply to the area of higher education and are not related to xMOOCs (based on university courses)
EC6	Publications that are not available in full text
EC7	Publications that do not demonstrate empirical evidence

Table 3. Search scripts applied to databases according to inclusion and exclusion criteria.

DB	Search script	Results obtained
SCOPUS	TITLE-ABS-KEY (("*MOOC*" OR "massive* open online course*") AND ("user* experience*" OR ux OR usab* OR accessib*) AND (evaluat* OR assess* OR research* OR appraise* OR measur*)) AND (LIMIT-TO (SRCTYPE, "p") OR LIMIT-TO (SRCTYPE, "j")) AND (LIMIT-TO (DOCTYPE, "cp") OR LIMIT-TO (DOCTYPE, "ar")) AND (LIMIT-TO (SUBJAREA, "COMP")) AND (LIMIT-TO (LANGUAGE, "English")))	55
IEEE Xplore	(("Abstract": "MOOC" OR "Abstract": "massive open online course") AND ("Abstract": "user experience" OR "Abstract": ux OR "Abstract": usab* OR "Abstract": accessib*) AND ("Abstract": evaluat* OR "Abstract": assess* OR "Abstract": research* OR "Abstract": appraise* OR "Abstract": measur*))	32
ACM Digital Library	Abstract:((((("user experience" OR "UX" OR usab* OR accessib*) AND ("MOOC" OR "massive open online course") AND (evaluat* OR assess* OR research* OR appraise* OR measur*)))) AND filter: {Article Type: Research Article, Publication Date: (01/01/2008 TO 09/30/2020)}	18
Total		105

The number of publications included and excluded is shown in Fig. 3 according to each stage of the selection and quality assessment process. To ensure that the results for the final sample of base articles for SLR are accurate, quality assessment is then applied to the set of 23 primary studies, based on [24] to describe and score the quality criteria (QC) as follows: QC1: Is the motivation for conducting UX assessment and/or its associated factors clearly stated? QC2: Is the process for applying the assessment approach(es) clearly described? QC3: Do the assessment approach(es) present verifiable results of their application. CQ4: Are the evaluation approach(es) available for download or consultation in the study itself or on any external resource (e.g., websites). The quality criteria were scored as follows:(Y - yes) if the QC is fully or explicitly met. (P - partially) if the QC is partially or implicitly met. (N - no) if the CQ is not defined or cannot be easily inferred. The scoring procedure is as follows: $Y = 1$, $P = 0.5$, $N = 0$. The results of the quality analysis indicate that there are 14 studies that scored 4 points, i.e., they meet all quality criteria. There are 7 studies that scored 3.5 points, due to the fact that most of them meet QC4 partially. In [27, 28] and [29] the items of the applied techniques were not well specified in the study, so some items had to be collected from the discussion and results section of each study. Finally, 2 studies obtained a score of 3 points because they did not comply with QC4, so they were excluded from the list for the SLR.

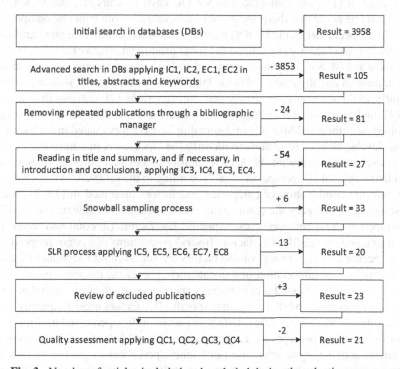

Fig. 3. Number of articles included and excluded during the selection process.

Therefore, the final sample corresponding to the systematic mapping corresponds to 33 primary studies covering the research area and 21 relevant research articles (referred to as base articles) corresponding to the SLR for the evaluation of UX in MOOC platforms. Both the search strategy process and the selection and quality assessment process were defined by one researcher and subsequently reviewed by another researcher individually. Consensus meetings were held between the two researchers to discuss and assess the quality of the findings, when there was any disagreement, it was discussed until an agreement was reached. Finally, the results were reviewed by a third researcher to validate the consistency of the results obtained.

4   Results

4.1   Systematic Mapping Process

Regarding RQ1, the search for articles of interest was conducted from 2008 to September 2020, with a growing interest focused on the evaluation of UX in MOOC platforms, and this trend will continue to increase in the following years. In addition, the different selected studies are well represented by prestigious conferences and journals that correspond to the Computer Science field, due to the fact that most of them have JSR index. Regarding RQ2, there are studies that evaluate MOOC platforms in general (14), MOOC courses (11), tools integrated in MOOC environments (5), and MOOC videos (5). It should be noted that there are studies that evaluate more than one component at a time. With respect to RQ3, the MOOC platforms most frequently evaluated are Coursera (11), edX (8), and Udacity (5), among the most prominent. To answer RQ4, technological criteria and MOOC indicators proposed in [32] are considered. The technological criterion most frequently evaluated is the UI (15), as for the MOOC indicators, the most frequently evaluated are: control of video clip functions (4), collaborative discussion tools (4), and providing a transcript of the videoconference (3). Table 4 illustrates the technological criteria and MOOC indicators that have been evaluated in the base articles.

The development of RQ5 aims to identify the UX factors that have been evaluated through user interaction with the MOOC platform. For this purpose, a study is conducted from a global UX perspective, i.e., according to the ISO 9241-11:2018 definition of UX and the combination of categories and factors presented in [19–21] and [11]; understanding by category the components: user, system and context; and the UX factors grouped in those categories: user-specific UX factors (internal and physical state of the user), system-specific UX factors (users' perceptions of system properties), and context-specific factors. Context-of-use factors are not taken into account in the present study due to lack of information in this category. Therefore, the user-specific UX factors most frequently assessed are: previous experiences, motivation, attitudes, expectations, and engagement; while the system-specific UX factors most frequently assessed are: usability, opinions/feedback, satisfaction, accessibility, perceived usefulness, interaction effectiveness, perceptions, continuance intention, behavior (includes emotional engagement and feelings), interaction efficiency, perceived interest, intention to recommend, emotions, quality, and confirmation (fulfillment of intention or fulfillment of expectations).

Table 4. Technological criteria and indicators for MOOC platforms.

ID	Technological criteria	References	f
TC1	MOOC platform user interface	[12, 15, 25, 33–44]	15
I1.1	Provide search box to find different learning materials	[40]	1
I1.2	Help systems should focus on reducing "user errors"	[40]	1
TC2	Interface and video content	[11]	1
I2.1	Control video clip functions: play, repeat, full screen, slow down, stop and pause	[29, 33, 44, 45]	4
I2.2	Provide a transcript of the video conference	[33, 44, 46]	3
I2.3	Clear sound	[44]	1
I2.4	Use short video clips	[33]	1
I2.5	Synchronize video conference and video transcript	[46]	1
TC3	Social and learning tools	[37]	1
I3.1	Collaborative discussion tools	[30, 37, 47, 48]	4
I3.2	Link to social networking tools such as "Facebook and Twitter"	[37]	1
I3.3	Online participant list available to assist learners in synchronous discussions	[37, 48]	2
I3.4	Videoconferencing tools to allow learners in different locations to communicate with teachers	[37]	1
TC4	Learning analytics	[26, 31]	2
I4.1	Performance reporting to learners	[37]	1
I4.2	Statistics on course activities	[37]	1

TC= Technological Criterion; I = Indicator.

4.2 SLR Process

From the results of the systematic mapping, two specific questions are developed for SLR with the aim of finding, critically evaluating and aggregating articles of relevance to the present research area. With respect to RQ6 there are methods focused on evaluating usability (inquiry, inspection and user testing), UX (general method of UX web principles and those evaluating behavior, feedback and emotions), as well as general research methods, as indicated in Table 5.

As for the techniques found in the primary studies, they correspond to techniques that evaluate UX and usability in MOOC platforms, which are presented in Table 6.

Table 5. Methods that evaluate the UX in MOOC platforms.

ID	Methods	References	*f*
M1	Inquiry method	[12, 25, 27, 28, 36, 38, 43, 44]	8
M2	Inspection method	[4, 15, 34, 37, 41, 46]	6
M3	User test method	[25, 36, 38, 43, 44]	5
M4	Research models	[44, 48, 49]	3
M5	Experimental method	[25, 43]	2
M6	Convenience sampling method	[27]	1
M7	Judgmental sampling method	[27]	1
M8	Method of analyzing user behavior by observing facial expressions	[36]	1
M9	Method of text mining of course comments to obtain emotion and emotional theme recognition	[47]	1
M10	Method of general principles of web UX by applying the failure coefficient influencing UX	[4]	1
M11	Behavioral sequential analysis method	[29]	1
M12	Home page UI design content analysis method	[43]	1

Table 6. Techniques that evaluate the UX in MOOC platforms.

ID	Techniques	References	*f*
T1	Usability testing	[25, 36, 38, 43, 44]	5
T2	Questionnaire post-test	[25, 28, 36, 43, 44]	5
T3	Survey	[27, 33, 42, 48, 49]	5
T4	Questionnaire pre-test	[12, 25, 27, 28]	4
T5	Observation	[25, 36, 38, 44]	4
T6	Interviews	[27, 38, 43]	3
T7	Questionnaire post-task	[25, 43]	2
T8	Standards inspection	[4, 34]	2
T9	Retrospective survey	[38]	1
T10	Thinking out loud	[44]	1
T11	Heuristic evaluation	[37]	1
T12	Accessibility guidelines	[46]	1

Regarding the tools applied in the primary studies to assess UX in MOOC platforms, they are detailed in Table 7. It should be noted that this study focuses on standardized questionnaires as tools used to assess UX and usability.

Table 7. Tools that evaluate the UX in MOOC platforms.

ID	Tools	References	∫
H1	SUS (System Usability Scale)	[12, 25, 38]	3
H2	eXaminator	[34, 35]	2
H3	SortSite	[4, 34]	2
H4	Pingdom	[4]	1
H5	achecker	[4]	1
H6	UMUX-Lite (Usability Metric for UX – Lite)	[12]	1
H7	SEQ (Single Ease Question)	[25]	1
H8	ASQ (After- Scenario Questionnaire)	[43]	1
H9	VisAWI (Visual Aesthetics of Website Inventory)	[43]	1
H10	Pleasure	[43]	1
H11	Testbirds Company Questionnaire	[12]	1
H12	TAM (Technology Acceptance Model)	[42]	1
H13	CSUQ (Computer System Usability Questionnaire)	[43]	1
H14	aDesigner	[34]	1
H15	Chrome Developer Tools - Accessibility Audit	[35]	1
H16	WAVE	[35]	1

Once the evaluation approaches (methods, techniques and tools), the UX factors (user-specific and system-specific), as well as the MOOC platforms evaluated in general, their technological criteria and MOOC indicators have been extracted, the information is classified in tables according to the base article to which they refer. Table 8 corresponds to user-specific UX factors, Tables 9, 10 and 11 correspond to system-specific UX factors.

Table 8. Evaluation of the user's own UX factors (internal and physical state of the user).

UX factors	MOOC platform	MOOC course	TC1	I2.1
Previous experiences	[36] M1, M3, M8, T2, T5, T1 [27] M7, T6 [48] M4, T3	[28] M1, T4		
Attitudes	[27] M6, T3		[36] M1, M3, M8, T2, T5, T1	[29] M11
Expectations	[48] M4, T3	[28] M1, T4		
Motivation	[27] M6, M7, T3, T6	[33] T3		

Table 9. Evaluation of system-specific UX factors (user perceptions of system properties) of MOOC platforms and courses in general.

UX factors	MOOC platform	MOOC course
Usability	[4] M10, T8, H3, H4, H5	[28] M1, T2
Perceptions	[27] M1, M6, M7, T3, T6	
Satisfaction	[48] M4, T3	[49] M4, T3 [28] M1, T2
Perceived usefulness		[49] M4, T3
Accessibility	[4] M10, T8, H3, H4, H5	[35] H2, H15, H16
Behavior		[49] M4, T3
Perceived interest		[49] M4, T3
Intention to continue use	[48] M4, T3 [27] M6, T3, T6	[49] M4, T3
Intention to recommend		[49] M4, T3
Perceived openness	[48] M4, T3	
Flow experience		[49] M4, T3
Confirmation		[49] M4, T3 [28] M1, T2
Effectiveness of the interaction	[48] M4, T3	
Efficiency of the interaction	[4] M10, T8, H3, H4, H5	

Table 10. Evaluation of system-specific UX factors (user perceptions of system properties) of the MOOC platform UI.

UX factors	TC1 – MOOC platform UI	
Usability	[36] M1, M3, M8, T2, T5, T1 [25] M1, M3, M5, T2, T5, T7, T4, T1, H1, H7 [38] M1, M3, T5, T8, T9, T1, H1 [12] M1, T4, H1, H6, H11	[42] T3, H12 [43] M1, M3, M5, M12, T2, T7, T1, H13 [44] M1, M3, M4, T2, T5, T10, T1
Perceptions	[12] M1, T4, H1, H6, H11	[43] M1, T6
Emotions	[36] M3, M8, T2, T5, T1	[43] M1, M3, M5, T2, T1, H10
Satisfaction	[36] M1, M3, M8, T2, T5, T1 [38] T6	[12] M1, T4, H1, H6, H11 [43] M3, M5, T2, T7, T1, H13, H8
Perceived usefulness	[42] T3, H12 [43] M3, M5, T2, T7, T1, H13	[44] M1, M3, M4, T2, T5, T10, T1
Accessibility	[34] M2, T8, H3, H2, H14 [15, 37, 41] M2	[44] M1, M3, M4, T2, T5, T10, T1
Behavior	[12] M1, T4, H1, H6, H11	
Perceived interest	[44] M1, M3, M4, T2, T1	
Intention to continue use	[36] M3, T2, T1 [42] T3, H12	[44] M4, T2
Intention to recommend	[36] M3, T2, T1 [44] M4, T2	
Quality	[43] M1, M3, M5, T2, T7, T1, H13	
Findability	[44] M1, M3, M4, T2, T5, T10, T1	
Perceived difficulty	[25] M1, M3, M5, T2, T5, T7, T4, T1, H1, H7	
Aesthetics	[43] T2, H9	
Perceived enjoyment	[42] T3, H12	
Effectiveness of the interaction	[25] M1, M3, M5, T2, T5, T7, T4, T1, H1, H7	[43] M1, M3, M5, T2, T7, T1, H8
Efficiency of the interaction	[25] M1, M3, M5, T2, T5, T7, T4, T1, H1, H	[43] M1, M3, M5, T2, T7, T1, H8

Table 11. Evaluation of system-specific UX factors (user perceptions of system properties) of MOOC indicators.

UX factors	I2.1	I2.2	I2.3	I2.4	I2.5	I3.1	I4.2
Usability	[44] M4, T2		[44] M4, T2				[37] T11
Satisfaction						[48] M4, T3	
Perceptions	[33] T3	[33] T3		[33] T3			
Accessibility		[46] M2, T12 [44] M4, T2			[46] M2, T12		
Perceived interest		[47] M9					
Emotions						[47] M9	

5 Discussion

Through the results obtained from the systematic mapping it has been possible to discover research trends, such as studies that develop and integrate collaborative discussion and learning analysis tools within MOOCs. Through the application of SLR it has been possible to determine that there are both methods and techniques mainly focused on usability evaluation, and that the most frequently evaluated technological criterion is the UI. There are also important scientific contributions that combine several evaluation approaches to assess different aspects of MOOC platforms, such as the collection of demographic data and their previous experience with MOOCs, followed by user testing that allows to obtain both qualitative and quantitative feedback through the application of questionnaires, think aloud, emotion recognition, observation, etc., at the end additional data is collected on how the user felt when interacting with the platform through interviews, open-ended questionnaires, etc.. The fulfillment of expectations is also evaluated after a longer period of use. There are studies that perform comparative analysis between MOOC platforms, other studies apply heuristics to evaluate the usability of the UI and guidelines to evaluate accessibility. Another proposed approach is the application of research models that evaluate the relationships between different UX factors and how they influence satisfaction, intention to continue use and intention to recommend. Therefore, these models represent a valuable basis for discovering the aspects that influence UX in MOOC platforms. On the other hand, there are important tools to assess UX among which standardized questionnaires such as SUS, CSUQ, UMUX-LITE, etc. stand out. Through the SLR application process, important UX evaluation approaches and how to combine them to evaluate different aspects related to MOOC platforms are collected, which were presented in Sect. 4.2 and correspond to the main findings in the present research.

6   Conclusions and Recommendations

The present research reveals the different UX evaluation approaches applied in the context of MOOCs, which can be useful to evaluate general UX or specific UX factors, applied both to MOOC platform or courses as well as to specific MOOC components such as videos or embedded tools. It should be noted that the findings reveal the application of evaluation methods, techniques and tools focused on MOOC technology criteria; which demonstrate verifiable results of their application.

Due to the heterogeneity of MOOCs, it is not advisable to develop a standard form of evaluation, however, the present review could help to inform about existing evaluations that can be combined and/or used depending on the needs, environments and available resources.

The methodology proposed for the present research provides a useful means to extract relevant information for future research, according to the interest and adoption of MOOCs especially in HEIs, and which is continuously increasing over the years.

References

1. Soegaard, M.: The Basics of User Experience Design: A UX Design Book by the Interaction Design Foundation (2002)
2. Morville, P.: The 7 Factors that Influence User Experience, Interaction Design Foundation (2018). https://www.interaction-design.org/literature/article/the-7-factors-that-influence-user-experience
3. Rabahallah, K., Mahdaoui, L., Azouaou, F.: MOOCs recommender system using ontology and memory-based collaborative filtering. In: ICEIS 2018 – Proceedings of the 20th 20th International Conference on Enterprise Information Systems, vol. 1, no. Iceis, pp. 635–641 (2018)
4. Pascual, J., Castillo, C., García, V., González, R.: Method for analysing the user experience in MOOC platforms. In: 2014 International Symposium on Computers in Education. SIIE 2014, pp. 157–162 (2014). https://doi.org/10.1109/SIIE.2014.7017722
5. Frolov, I., Johansson, S.: An Adaptable Usability Checklist for MOOCs: A usability evaluation instrument for Massive Open Online Courses (2014)
6. Hakami, N., White, S., Chakaveh, S.: Motivational factors that influence the use of MOOCs: learners' perspectives: a systematic literature review. In: CSEDU 2017 – Proceedings of the 9th International Conference on Computer Supported Education, vol. 2, no. Csedu, pp. 323–331 (2017). https://doi.org/10.5220/0006259503230331
7. Wautelet, Y., Heng, S., Kolp, M., Penserini, L., Poelmans, S.: Designing an MOOC as an agent-platform aggregating heterogeneous virtual learning environments. Behav. Inf. Technol. 35(11), 980–997 (2016). https://doi.org/10.1080/0144929X.2016.1212095
8. Cruz-Benito, J., Borras-Gene, O., Garcia-Penalvo, F.J., Blanco, A.F., Theron, R.: Learning communities in social networks and their relationship with the MOOCs. Rev. Iberoam. Tecnol. del Aprendiz. 12(1), 24–36 (2017). https://doi.org/10.1109/RITA.2017.2655218
9. Meyer, R., Gaskill, M., Vu, P.: Rating user interface and universal instructional design in MOOC course design. Rev. Int. des Technol. en pédagogie Univ. J. Technol. High. Educ. 12(2), 62–74 (2015). https://doi.org/10.18162/ritpu-2015-v12n2-01
10. Zaharias, P., Poylymenakou, A.: Developing a usability evaluation method for e-learning applications: beyond functional usability. Int. J. Hum. Comput. Interact. 25(1), 75–98 (2009). https://doi.org/10.1080/10447310802546716

11. Xiao, J., Jiang, B., Xu, Z., Wang, M.: The usability research of learning resource design for MOOCs. In: 2014 IEEE International Conference on Teaching, Assessment and Learning for Engineering (TALE), pp. 277–282 (2014). https://doi.org/10.1109/TALE.2014.7062640
12. Korableva, O., Durand, T., Kalimullina, O., Stepanova, I.: Usability testing of MOOC: Identifying user interface problems. In: ICEIS 2019 – Proceedings of the 21st International Conference on Enterprise Information Systems, vol. 2, no. Iceis, pp. 468–475 (2019). https://doi.org/10.5220/0007800004680475
13. Korableva, O., Durand, T., Kalimullina, O., Stepanova, I.: Studying user satisfaction with the MOOC platform interfaces using the example of coursera and open education platforms. In: ACM International Conference Proceeding Series, pp. 26–30 (2019). https://doi.org/10.1145/3322134.3322139
14. Veletsianos, G., Collier, A., Schneider, E.: Digging deeper into learners' experiences in MOOCs: participation in social networks outside of MOOCs, notetaking and contexts surrounding content consumption. Br. J. Educ. Technol. **46**(3), 570–587 (2015). https://doi.org/10.1111/bjet.12297
15. Azhar, T.F., Kasiyah, Santoso, H.B.: Evaluation of instructional and user interface design for MOOC: Short and free futureLearn courses. 2019 International Conference on Advanced Computer Science and information Systems. ICACSIS 2019, pp. 425–434 (2019). https://doi.org/10.1109/ICACSIS47736.2019.8979754
16. Petersen, K., Vakkalanka, S., Kuzniarz, L., Feldt, R., Mujtaba, S., Mattsson, M.: Guidelines for conducting systematic mapping studies in software engineering: an update. In: 12th International Conference on Evaluation and Assessment in Software Engineering. EASE 2008, vol. 64, pp. 1–18 (2015). https://doi.org/10.1016/j.infsof.2015.03.007
17. Torres-Carrión, P.V., Gonzalez-Gonzalez, C.S., Aciar, S., Rodriguez-Morales, G.: Methodology for systematic literature review applied to engineering and education. In: IEEE Global Engineering Education Conference EDUCON, vol. 2018-April, pp. 1364–1373 (2018). https://doi.org/10.1109/EDUCON.2018.8363388
18. "ISO 9241-11:2018(en), Ergonomics of human-system interaction—Part 11: Usability: Definitions and concepts (2018). https://www.iso.org/obp/ui/#iso:std:iso:9241:-11:ed-2:v1:en. Accessed 25 July 2020
19. Arhippainen, L., Tähti, M.: Empirical evaluation of user experience in two adaptive mobile application prototypes. In: Proceedings of the 2nd International Conference on Mobile and Ubiquitous Multimedia, pp. 27–34 (2003). http://www.ep.liu.se/ecp/011/007/ecp011007.pdf
20. Morville, P.: User Experience Design (2004). http://semanticstudios.com/user_experience_design/. Accessed 29 July 2020
21. Roto, V., Law, E., Vermeeren, A., Hoonhout, J.: Abstracts collection demarcating user experience. In: Dagstuhl Seminar Proceedings, pp. 1–26 (2011)
22. Petersen, K., Feldt, R., Mujtaba, S., Mattsson, M.: Systematic mapping studies in software engineering. In: 12th International Conference on Evaluation & Assessment in Software Engineering. EASE 2008, pp. 1–10 (2008)
23. Synonyms and Antonyms of Words—Thesaurus.com. https://www.thesaurus.com/. Accessed 03 Aug 2021
24. Kitchenham, B., Pearl Brereton, O., Budgen, D., Turner, M., Bailey, J., Linkman, S.: Systematic literature reviews in software engineering - a systematic literature review. Inf. Softw. Technol. **51**(1), 7–15 (2009). https://doi.org/10.1016/j.infsof.2008.09.009
25. Tsironis, A., Katsanos, C., Xenos, M.: Comparative usability evaluation of three popular MOOC platforms. In: IEEE Global Engineering Education Conference, EDUCON, vol. 10-13-Apri, no. April, pp. 608–612 (2016). https://doi.org/10.1109/EDUCON.2016.7474613
26. Ruipérez-Valiente, J.A., Muñoz-Merino, P.J., Pijeira Díaz, H.J., Ruiz, J.S., Kloos, C.D.: Evaluation of a learning analytics application for open edX platform. Comput. Sci. Inf. Syst. **14**(1), 51–73 (2017). https://doi.org/10.2298/CSIS160331043R

27. Nurhudatiana, A., Anggraeni, A., Putra, S.: An exploratory study of MOOC adoption in Indonesia. In: ACM International Conference on Proceeding Series, pp. 97–101 (2019). https://doi.org/10.1145/3337682.3337690
28. Rabin, E., Kalman, Y.M., Kalz, M.: An empirical investigation of the antecedents of learner-centered outcome measures in MOOCs. Int. J. Educ. Technol. High. Educ. 16(1), 1–20 (2019). https://doi.org/10.1186/s41239-019-0144-3
29. Liu, M.C., Yu, C.H., Wu, J., Liu, A.C., Chen, H.M.: Applying learning analytics to deconstruct user engagement by using log data of MOOCs. J. Inf. Sci. Eng. 34(5), 1175–1186 (2018). https://doi.org/10.6688/JISE.201809_34(5).0004
30. Fu, S., Wang, Y., Yang, Y., Bi, Q., Guo, F., Qu, H.: VisForum: a visual analysis system for exploring user groups in online forums. ACM Trans. Interact. Intell. Syst. 8(1) (2018). https://doi.org/10.1145/3162075
31. Rohloff, T., Sauer, D., Meinel, C.: Student perception of a learner dashboard in MOOCs to encourage self-regulated learning. In: TALE 2019 - 2019 IEEE International Conference on Engineering, Technology and Education (2019).https://doi.org/10.1109/TALE48000.2019.9225939
32. Fahmy Yousef, A.M., Chatti, M.A., Schroeder, U., Wosnitza, M.: What drives a successful MOOC? An empirical examination of criteria to assure design quality of MOOCs. In: 2014 IEEE 14th International Conference on Advanced Learning Technologies, ICALT 2014, no. July, pp. 44–48 (2014). https://doi.org/10.1109/ICALT.2014.23
33. Mamgain, N., Sharma, A., Goyal, P.: Learner's perspective on video-viewing features offered by MOOC providers: Coursera and edX. In: 2014 IEEE International Conference on MOOC, Innovation and Technology in Education (MITE), pp. 331–336 (2014). https://doi.org/10.1109/MITE.2014.7020298
34. Iniesto, F., Rodrigo, C.: Accessibility assessment of MOOC platforms in Spanish: UNED COMA, COLMENIA and Miriada X, pp. 169–172 (2014). https://doi.org/10.1109/SIIE.2014.7017724
35. Calle-Jimenez, T., Sanchez-Gordon, S., Luján-Mora, S.: Web accessibility evaluation of massive open online courses on Geographical Information Systems. In: IEEE Global Engineering Education Conference EDUCON, no. April, pp. 680–686 (2014). https://doi.org/10.1109/EDUCON.2014.6826167
36. Pireva, K., Imran, A.S., Dalipi, F.: User behaviour analysis on LMS and MOOC. In: 2015 IEEE Conference on e-Learning, e-Management e-Services, IC3e 2015, no. March 2019, pp. 21–26 (2015). https://doi.org/10.1109/IC3e.2015.7403480
37. Jiménez-González, S.G., et al.: Heuristic Approach to Evaluate Basic Types of Interactions-Communications in MOOCs (2016)
38. Sharfina, Z., Santoso, H.B., Isal, R.Y.K., Aji, R.F.: Evaluation and Improvement of Indonesian Massive Open Online Course (MOOC) Interaction Design of MOOC X, pp. 888–893 (2017)
39. Paiva, A.D.S., Das Neves, A.J.W.A., Ramos, B.O., De Macedo, C.M.S., Domingues, F., Bueno, J.: Usability analysis of three massive online open course platforms. In: Proceedings of the International Conference on WWW/Internet 2017 Applied Computing 2017, no. May 2020, pp. 135–141 (2017)
40. Azami, H.H.R., Ibrahim, R.: Development and evaluation of Massive Open Online Course (MOOC) as a supplementary learning tool: an initial study. Int. J. Adv. Comput. Sci. Appl. 10(7), 532–537 (2019). https://doi.org/10.14569/ijacsa.2019.0100773
41. Hanifa, M.R., Santoso, H.B., Kasiyah: Evaluation and recommendations for the instructional design and user interface design of coursera MOOC platform. In: 2019 International Conference on Advanced Computer Science and Information Systems. ICACSIS 2019, no. 2014, pp. 417–424 (2019). https://doi.org/10.1109/ICACSIS47736.2019.8979689

42. Tao, D., Fu, P., Wang, Y., Zhang, T., Qu, X.: Key characteristics in designing massive open online courses (MOOCs) for user acceptance: an application of the extended technology acceptance model. Interact. Learn. Environ., 1–14 (2019).https://doi.org/10.1080/10494820. 2019.1695214

43. Liu, S., Liang, T., Shao, S., Kong, J.: Evaluating localized MOOCs: the role of culture on interface design and user experience. IEEE Access **8**, 107927–107940 (2020). https://doi.org/ 10.1109/ACCESS.2020.2986036

44. Nurhudatiana, A., Caesarion, A.S.: Exploring User Experience of Massive Open Online Courses (MOOCs), pp. 44–49 (2020). https://doi.org/10.1145/3383923.3383968

45. Nishchyk, A., Sanderson, N.C., Chen, W.: How elderly people experience videos in MOOCs. In: Proceedings of the 19th International Conference on Engineering and Product Design Education (E&PDE17), Building Community: Design Education for a Sustainable Future, no. September, pp. 686–691 (2017)

46. Acosta, T., Zambrano-Miranda, J., Luján-Mora, S.: Analysis of the accessibility of educational videos in massive open online courses. In: EDULEARN19 Proceedings, vol. 1, no. July, pp. 8321–8331 (2019). https://doi.org/10.21125/edulearn.2019.2076

47. Liu, Z., Zhang, W., Sun, J., Cheng, H.N.H., Peng, X., Liu, S.: Emotion and associated topic detection for course comments in a MOOC platform. In: 2016 International Conference on Educational Innovation through Technology (EITT), pp. 15–19 (2016).https://doi.org/10. 1109/EITT.2016.11

48. Chen, C., Lee, C., Hsiao, K.: Comparing the determinants of non-MOOC and MOOC continuance intention in Taiwan Effects of interactivity and openness (2018). https://doi.org/10. 1108/LHT-11-2016-0129

49. Lu, Y., Wang, B., Lu, Y.: Understanding key drivers of MOOC satisfaction and continuance intention to use. J. Electron. Commer. Res. **20**(2), 105–117 (2019)

User Interface Adaptation through Ontology Models and Code Generation

Amani Braham[1,3]([✉]) [iD], Maha Khemaja[2] [iD], Félix Buendía[3] [iD], and Faiez Gargouri[4] [iD]

[1] University of Sousse, ISITCom, 4011 Sousse, Tunisia
[2] University of Sousse, 4000 Sousse, Tunisia
[3] Universitat Politècnica de Valencia, 46022 Valencia, Spain
fbuendia@disca.upv.es
[4] University of Sfax, 3029 Sfax, Tunisia
faiez.gargouri@usf.tn

Abstract. The development of adaptive user interfaces becomes increasingly complex due to the rapid growth of interaction devices. This has promoted a great interest towards the study of adaptive user interface in the Human Computer Interaction (HCI) field. Consequently, various model-driven approaches have been introduced to further such fields. However, these approaches did not make use of semantic models and thus did not support knowledge reuse for representing user interfaces and adaptation rules. To tackle these issues, we present in this work the user interface generation component that concerns the development of adaptive user interfaces from ontology models. In this regard, a model driven approach along with ontology models represent the main artifact of the proposed component to allow knowledge reuse and to improve the semantics of the generated user interfaces. To illustrate the feasibility of the present component, we provide a concrete case study that highlights the adaptation of the generated user interfaces in different contexts of use.

Keywords: HCI · Interface design and generation · Adaptive interface · Multimodal interface · Ontology model · Model driven

1 Introduction

Currently, users are surrounded by a broad range of Human Computer Interaction (HCI) devices [1]. The extensive use of these devices resulted in a growing interest in the study of user interfaces. Moreover, the context of use of such devices evolves over the time with the capability of the technology embedded in these devices. This has promoted a widespread interest in the design of user interfaces, within the HCI research community, to support the variability of the context of use, including the platform, the user, and the environment. In this sense, the adaptation of user interfaces has been introduced as a solution to meet the requirements of users in different contexts of use [2]. In general, user interface adaptation is defined as the process of adapting the interface according to different context criteria. Adaptive user interfaces introduce broad challenges to HCI design and challenge the development of user interfaces. In this regard, several research

© Springer Nature Switzerland AG 2021
P. H. Ruiz et al. (Eds.): HCI-COLLAB 2021, CCIS 1478, pp. 225–236, 2021.
https://doi.org/10.1007/978-3-030-92325-9_17

studies have been proposed to deal with user interface adaptations denoting various interface design aspects.

In this sense, various Model Driven Engineering (MDE) approaches have been proposed. These approaches highlight the use of models as the main artifacts for transforming models into final source code. Among these approaches, we can mention methods that are based on TERESSA [3], MARIA [4], UsiXML [5], and IFML [6] to support user interface modeling and transformation. Under this context, the use of model-driven methods oriented to the adaptation to the target software is possible [7]. Model-driven approaches can also provide the adaptation of user interfaces to the context of use based on parameterized transformations [8]. Despite the fact that existing model-driven approaches provide the possibility of modeling user interfaces and transforming models to a source code, they do not make use of semantic models and do not support knowledge reuse for representing user interfaces and adaptation rules. Consequently, there is a need to enhance the semantic of the developed interfaces within model-driven approaches. One such method to deal with these concerns is the use of ontologies that represent a solution to allow sharing knowledge [9] and improve the semantic of the developed applications [10]. Here, the contribution of this work focuses on extending model-driven approaches with semantic models in order to generate adaptive user interfaces. To this end, we present a user interface generation component that allows the development of adaptive user interfaces based on model-driven approach and ontology models. The proposed ontology models provide a formal specification of user interfaces, users' context, along with adaptation rules.

The remainder of this paper is structured as follows: Sect. 2 examines the related work. Section 3 provides an overview of the proposed solution. Section 4 introduces a case study example that highlights an example of user interface model adaptation and source code generation. Finally, Sect. 5 outlines the conclusions and further research work.

2 Related Work

Many works in the field of user interface development and adaptation have been reported in the literature. In the following, we briefly provide an overview of relevant works that deal with user interface adaptation and user interface code generation, and discuss their limitations regarding our main challenges.

Many researchers have provided MDE approaches for the development of adaptive user interfaces. In this context, Bouchelligua et al. [8] present a model driven engineering approach for user interface adaptation to the context of use based on parameterized transformations [11]. These parameters constitute the context of use and are considered at the level of the transformation of an abstract user interface into a concrete user interface. In their work, authors develop a context meta-model that is used in the adaptation process. Similarly, Ghaibi et al. [12] present a model-driven method for generating adaptive user interfaces according to user preferences and capabilities. In their work, adaptations are applied to the generation process of the Cameleon Reference Framework [7]. Besides, the adaptation rules are integrated in the development of accessible user interfaces at design-time. Moreover, in [13], authors provide a model driven approach for adapting user interfaces taking into account the accessibility context. The adaptation of user interface models is achieved based on meta-model transformation.

Other works rely on rule-based adaptation techniques for adapting the final user interface. These methods require the use of adaptation models that identify how the user interface is changed according to the change of the context of use. In this sense, Miñón et al. [14] propose an approach for integrating adaptation rules into the process of user interface development. In particular, they develop the Adaptation Integration System that focuses on integrating accessibility requirements in model-based user interfaces. Their proposed system provides adaptation services that can be applied at both design-time and run-time. Nevertheless, their system has the problem of conflict that can arise when the context model and the adaptation rules identify an element with the same semantic. Another example is the work proposed by Yigitbas et al. [15]. In their work, authors provide a model-driven approach for the development of self-adaptive user interfaces. They introduce a new modeling language, including the ContextML and AdaptML for context management and user interface adaptation, respectively. Context information is extracted at runtime and used for selecting adaptation rules.

Various works focus on the generation of the user interface source code. For instance, the work of Schuler et al. [16] presents a framework named RUMO. Their framework is used for the generation of multi-platform user interfaces. It provides the possibility to define rules, which introduce application specific constraints, to be used for transforming a user interface model to a specific platform. In particular, their rules introduce application specific constraints. Another work, presented by Bouraoui et al. [17], introduces a model driven approach for developing adaptive user interfaces that are adapted to various platform. It allows the generation of user interfaces based on some transformation techniques. These techniques enable the transformation from abstract accessible user interface model to executable user interfaces. Other model-driven methods introduce Domain Specific Language (DSL) to take advantage of incorporating domain knowledge in models [18]. In this context, Sabraoui et al. [19] propose a model driven development approach that relies on DSL. Their approach allows developers to automatically generate native graphical user interface code for android applications. Similarly, Rieger et al. [20] introduce a model-driven approach that integrates accessibility concerns into the development of cross-platform mobile applications. Their proposed approach is based on the definition of specialized domain specific languages.

The work presented in [14] is based on the Advanced Adaptation Logic Description Language (AAL-DL) to define the adaptation rules. Other works [12, 15] use the domain-specific language to define the abstract user interface adaptations. Here, in this work, we propose the use of ontologies to provide a formal representation of user interfaces, the context and adaptation rules. Moreover, in [14], adaptation rules are applied to the concrete user interface. In [8, 13, 16], adaptations are based on parameterized transformations. Rather than that, the integration of adaptation rules, considered in this work, is achieved on the level of the user interface ontology model. Finally, in contrast to the aforementioned works, our proposed solution considers the extension of model-driven approach with ontology models to generate adaptive user interfaces.

3 Proposal

In Fig. 1, we present the global AUIDP framework [21, 22] that contributes to the development of adaptive user interfaces. In this work, we focus on the user interface generation component that is part of the user Interface Code Generator using DEsign Patterns (ICGDEP) system (Fig. 1b). The main target of the present component is to (i) allow the integration of adaptation rules within the user interface model according to users' current context, and (ii) generate the source code that corresponds to the adaptive user interface model. The user interface model is obtained from the pattern integration component of the ICGDEP system. In this work, the user interface model is identified as an ontology model that is composed by a set of user interface design pattern fragments.

As illustrated in Fig. 2, the present user interface generation component requires as input a user interface ontology model. We distinguish three main phases for generating the source code within the present component, regarding user interface model adaptation

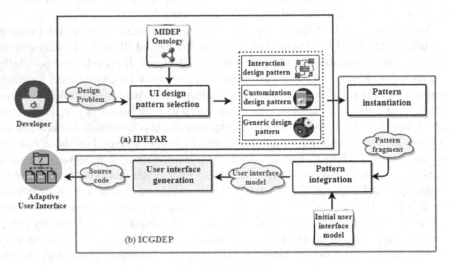

Fig. 1. The global AUIDP framework.

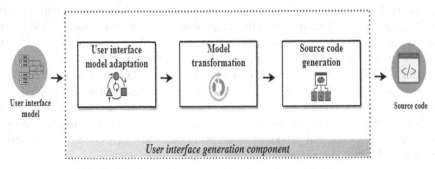

Fig. 2. User interface generation component main phases.

phase, model transformation phase, and source code generation phase. The description of each phase is introduced in the subsections below.

3.1 User Interface Model Adaptation Phase

The first phase, within the proposed component, represents the main contribution of this work. It is in charge of applying adaptation rules on the user interface ontology model. The architecture of this first phase is illustrated in Fig. 3.

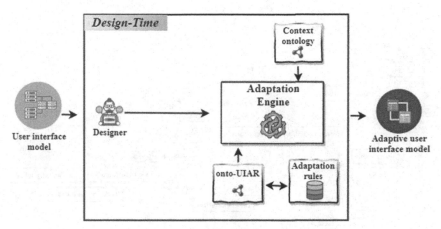

Fig. 3. Architecture of the user interface model adaptation phase.

The design-time level, within the user interface adaptation phase, is responsible for achieving design-time adaptations. At this level, software developers are involved in the adaptation phase; they interact with the user interface generation component. In particular, they define a list of context information, which are supported by adaptation rules, and provide the adaptation engine the desired context information. Moreover, the adaptation engine receives the current context and the user interface model in order to provide as a result an adaptive user interface model. To achieve this purpose, the adaptation engine retrieves adaptation rules, which are mostly related to the user's context, and applies actions, provided by the adaptation rules, on the user interface ontology model. In particular, the adaptation engine uses ontology model adaptation services to allow the management of ontology models. The adaptation rules are formally presented in the onto-UIAR (ontology for User Interface Adaption Rules). Some examples of these rules and the onto-UIAR ontological model are outlined in Table 1 and Fig. 4, respectively.

230   A. Braham et al.

Table 1. A partial list of adaptation rules.

Rule	Condition	Action
walkingRule	The user is walking or driving	Change to vocal modality
darkEnvRule	The environment is dark/ Light brightness level is low	Change font color to white and background color to black
lowVisionRule	The user has low vision	Increase the size of interface elements

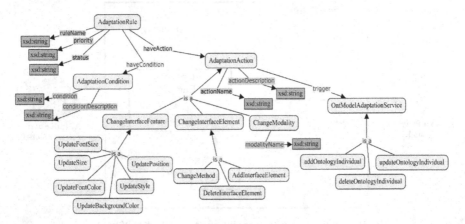

Fig. 4. Onto-UIAR ontological model.

3.2 Model Transformation Phase

The adaptive user interface model generated from the first phase, which is an ontology model, is provided to the model transformation phase. The architecture of this phase is illustrated in Fig. 5. Two main modules are considered to fulfill the transformation phase, including the retrieval engine and the OntoPIM transformer.

- The retrieval engine is in charge of applying a set of queries to retrieve ontology instances, which correspond to the current context, from the adaptive user interface ontology model. This engine generates a query result document that is used as input in the second module.
- The OntoPIM transformer is responsible for transforming the query results, obtained from the previous module, into a PIM GUI (Platform Independent Model Graphical User Interface). The obtained PIM GUI model represents the specification of the GUI independently of the target platform and it is consistent with our DSL considered in the following step.

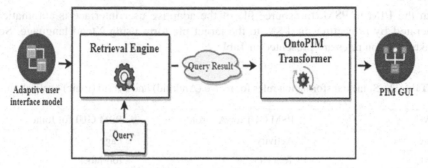

Fig. 5. Architecture of the model transformation phase.

3.3 Source Code Generation Phase

The last phase within the user interface generation component concerns the generation of source code. The PIM, obtained from the model transformation phase, represents an instance of a DSL meta-model named MIDEP DSL. The MIDEP DSL is a domain specific language that we have developed using Xtext [23]. It is related to the user interface module within the MIDEP ontology [21, 22]. As illustrated in Fig. 6, the PIM is first transformed to PSM (Platform Specific Model) using Xtend Language [24]. Each element in the PIM is associated with a specific PSM element. After the transformation

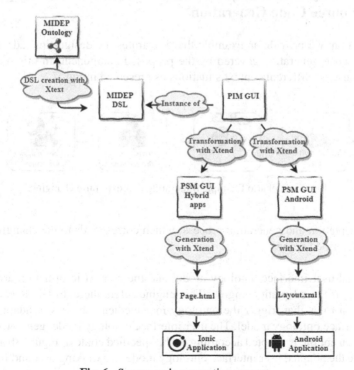

Fig. 6. Source code generation process.

from the PIM to PSM, the source file of the adaptive user interface is automatically generated by projecting the PSM to the target platform using Xtend language. Some transformation rules are presented in Table 2.

Table 2. Some transformation rules for native (Android) and hybrid (Ionic) applications.

PIM	PSM GUI for Android	PSM GUI for Ionic
Page	Activity	Page
Text	TextView	Ion-label
Input Type = text Type = password Type = email Type = number	EditText InputType = text InputType = password InputType = email InputType = number	Ion-input Type = text Type = password Type = email Type = number
Button	Button	Button ion-button
Spacer	View	Br

4 Case Study: An Example of User Interface Model Adaptation and Source Code Generation

In this section, we provide an example that illustrates the design-time adaptation and the source code generation covered by the proposed component. In this scenario, we consider a user in different context situations as presented in Fig. 7

Fig. 7. Scenario Example illustrating context of use changing.

The adaptation and generation process, which corresponds to the changing context of use is described below.

- The initial user interface ontology model and the context information are provided as input for the adaptation engine. This engine infers the onto-UIAR and retrieves adaptation rules that trigger the ontology management services to adapt the initial user interface ontology model. The user interface ontology model generated from the adaptation engine is adapted according to the specified context. Figure 8b and Fig. 9b illustrate the adapted user interface ontology model for walking user and for eyewear user, respectively.

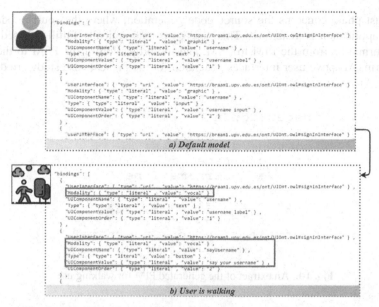

Fig. 8. Excerpt of the user interface ontology model for walking user.

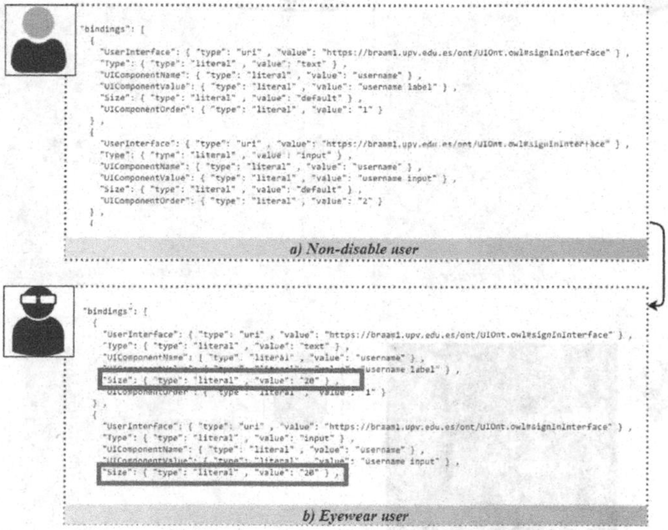

Fig. 9. Excerpt of the user interface ontology model for eyewear user.

- The resulting adaptive user interface ontology model is used as input is the transformation phase. In this phase, the OntoPIM transformer converts the ontology model to a PIM that is consistent with our MIDEP DSL. An extract of the resulted PIM for walking users is illustrated in Fig. 10.

- The last phase concerns the source code generation, where the source code of an Ionic application is generated. This process is automatically fulfilled based on the transformation from the PIM to PSM, and the projection of the PSM to the target platform. Adaptive user interfaces generated for the present case study are depicted in Fig. 11.

```
page SignIn
{
component-elements[
text username
 title "username label"
   size 'default' ,
button sayUsername
   size 'default'
{ title "say your username"
 } ,
```

Fig. 10. An extract of the generated PIM for walking user.

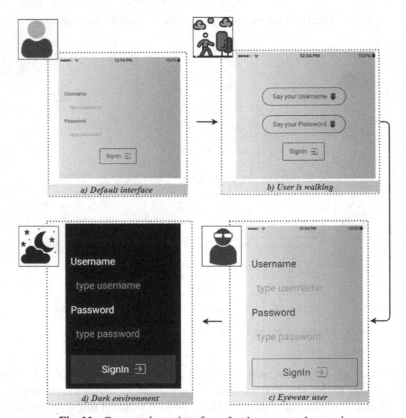

Fig. 11. Generated user interfaces for the presented scenario.

5 Conclusion

In this work, we presented the user interface generation component, which is part of the global AUIDP framework, for the development of adaptive user interfaces. In this component, we extended a model-driven approach with semantic models to generate adaptive user interfaces that are more related to the current context of use. The present semantic models raise the specification of user interfaces, users' context, and adaptation rules. Thus, they enable sharing knowledge and enhance the consistency of the developed interfaces. On the basis of the specified models, the adaptation of the user interfaces and the generation of the final source code are automatically fulfilled at design-time for software developers. To illustrate the adaptation of user interfaces to different contexts of use, we presented a concrete case study that highlights the feasibility of the presented component. In ongoing research, we plan to cover the run-time level in order to enable the generation of adaptive user interfaces to final users.

References

1. Carbonell, N.: Ambient multimodality: towards advancing computer accessibility and assisted living. Univ. Access Inf. Soc. **5**(1), 96–104 (2006). https://doi.org/10.1007/s10209-006-0027-y
2. Akiki, P.A., Bandara, A.K., Yu, Y.: Adaptive model-driven user interface development systems. ACM Comput. Surv. **47**(1), 9:1–9:33 (2014).https://doi.org/10.1145/2597999
3. Berti, S., Correani, F., Mori, G., Paterno, F., Santoro, C.: TERESA: a transformation-based environment for designing and developing multi-device interfaces. In: Conference on Human Factors in computing Systems, CHI 2004 extended abstracts on Human factors in computing systems, Vienna, Austria, pp. 793–794 (2004). https://doi.org/10.1145/985921.985939
4. Paternò, F., Santoro, C., Spano, L.D.: MARIA: a universal language for service-oriented applications in ubiquitous environment. ACM Trans. Comput.-Hum. Interact. **16**(4), 1–30 (2009). https://doi.org/10.1145/1614390.1614394
5. Limbourg, Q., Vanderdonckt, J., Michotte, B., Bouillon, L., Florins, M.: USIXML: a user interface description language supporting multiple levels of independence. In: ICWE Workshops, pp. 325–338 (2004)
6. Brambilla, M., Fraternali, P.: Interaction Flow Modeling Language Model-Driven UI Engineering of Web and Mobile Apps with IFML. The OMG Press, Morgan Kaufmann (2014)
7. Calvary, G., Coutaz, J., Thevenin, D., Limbourg, Q., Bouillon, L., Vanderdonckt, J.: A unifying reference framework for multi-target user interfaces. Interact. Comput. **15**(3), 289–308 (2003). https://doi.org/10.1016/S0953-5438(03)00010-9
8. Bouchelligua, W., Mahfoudhi, A., Benammar, L., Rebai, S., Abed, M.: An MDE approach for user interface adaptation to the context of use. In: Bernhaupt, R., Forbrig, P., Gulliksen, J., Lárusdóttir, M. (eds.) HCSE 2010. LNCS, vol. 6409, pp. 62–78. Springer, Heidelberg (2010). https://doi.org/10.1007/978-3-642-16488-0_6
9. Gruber, T.R.: Toward principles for the design of ontologies used for knowledge sharing. Int. J. Hum. Comput. Stud. **43**(5–6), 907–928 (1995). https://doi.org/10.1006/ijhc.1995.1081
10. Chen, H., Perich, F., Finin, T., Joshi, A.: SOUPA: standard ontology for ubiquitous and pervasive applications. In: The Proceedings of the First Annual International Conference on Mobile and Ubiquitous Systems: Networking and Services (Mobiquitous 2004), Boston, MA, 22–25 August (2004). https://doi.org/10.1109/MOBIQ.2004.1331732

11. Vale, S., Hammoudi, S.: Context-aware model driven development by parameterized transformation. In: Proceedings of MDISIS (2008)
12. Ghaibi, N., Dassi, O., Ayed, L.J.B.: A tool support for the adaptation of user interfaces based on a business rules management system. In: Proceedings of the 29th Australian Conference on Computer Human Interaction, pp. 162–169 (2017). https://doi.org/10.1145/3152771.315 2789
13. Zouhaier, L., Hlaoui, Y.B., Ayed, L.J.B.: Users interfaces adaptation for visually impaired users based on meta-model transformation. In: 2017 IEEE 41st Annual Computer Software and Applications Conference (COMPSAC), vol. 1, pp 881–886 (2017). https://doi.org/10.1109/COMPSAC.2017.258
14. Miñón, R., Paternò, F., Arrue, M., Abascal, J.: Integrating adaptation rules for people with special needs in model-based UI development process. Univ. Access Inf. Soc. **15**(1), 153–168 (2015). https://doi.org/10.1007/s10209-015-0406-3
15. Yigitbas, E., Jovanovikj, I., Biermeier, K., Sauer, S., Engels, G.: Integrated model-driven development of self-adaptive user interfaces. Softw. Syst. Model. **19**(5), 1057–1081 (2020). https://doi.org/10.1007/s10270-020-00777-7
16. Schuler, A., Franz, B.: Rule-based generation of mobile user interfaces. In: 2013 10th International Conference on Information Technology: New Generations, pp. 267–272. IEEE (2013). https://doi.org/10.1109/ITNG.2013.43
17. Bouraoui, A., Gharbi, I.: Model driven engineering of accessible and multi-platform graphical user interfaces by parameterized model transformations. Sci. Comput. Program. **172**, 63–101 (2019)
18. Mernik, M., Heering, J., Sloane, A.M.: When and how to develop domain-specific languages. ACM Comput. Surv. (CSUR) **37**(4), 316–344 (2005). https://doi.org/10.1145/1118890.111 8892
19. Sabraoui, A., Abouzahra, A., Afdel, K., Machkour, M.: MDD approach for mobile applications based on DSL. In: International Conference of Computer Science and Renewable Energies (ICCSRE). IEEE 2019, pp. 1–6 (2019). https://doi.org/10.1109/ICCSRE.2019.880 7572
20. Rieger, C., Lucrédio, D., Fortes, R.P.M., Kuchen, H., Dias, F., Duarte, L.: A model-driven approach to cross-platform development of accessible business apps. In: Proceedings of the 35th Annual ACM Symposium on Applied Computing, pp. 984–993 (2020). https://doi.org/10.1145/3341105.3375765
21. Braham, A., Khemaja, M., Buendía, F., Gargouri, F.: UI design pattern selection process for the development of adaptive apps. In: The Thirteenth International Conference on Advances in Computer-Human Interactions ACHI, Valencia, Spain, pp. 21–27 (2020)
22. Braham, A., Buendía, F., Khemaja, M., Gargouri, F.: User interface design patterns and ontology models for adaptive mobile applications. Pers. Ubiquit. Comput. (2021). https://doi.org/10.1007/s00779-020-01481-5
23. Xtext. https://www.eclipse.org/Xtext/documentation/index.html. Accessed 02 May 2021
24. Xtend. https://www.eclipse.org/xtend/documentation/index.html. Accessed 02 May 2021

User-Centered Design Approach for a Machine Learning Platform for Medical Purpose

Alicia García-Holgado[1]([⊠]) [iD], Andrea Vázquez-Ingelmo[1] [iD],
Julia Alonso-Sánchez[1] [iD], Francisco José García-Peñalvo[1] [iD], Roberto Therón[1] [iD],
Jesús Sampedro-Gómez[2] [iD], Antonio Sánchez-Puente[2] [iD], Víctor Vicente-Palacios[3] [iD],
P. Ignacio Dorado-Díaz[2] [iD], and Pedro L. Sánchez[2] [iD]

[1] GRIAL Research Group, Research Institute for Educational Sciences, University of
Salamanca, Salamanca, Spain
{aliciagh,andreavazquez,juliaalonso,fgarcia,theron}@usal.es
[2] Cardiology Department, Hospital Universitario de Salamanca, SACyL. IBSAL, Facultad de
Medicina, University of Salamanca, and CIBERCV (ISCiii), Salamanca, Spain
{jmsampedro,asanchezpu}@saludcastillayleon.es, {acho,
plsanchez}@usal.es
[3] Philips Healthcare, Alicante, Spain
victor.vicente.palacios@philips.com

Abstract. Machine learning is increasingly present in different sectors. Decision-making processes that occur in all types of companies and entities can be improved with the use of AI algorithms and machine learning. Furthermore, the application of machine learning algorithms enables the possibility of providing support to automate the undertaking of complex tasks. However, not all users who want to use machine learning are skilled enough from a technological and data science point of view to use many of the tools that are already available on the market. In particular, the health sector is taking advantage of AI algorithms to enhance the decision-making processes and to support complex common activities. Nonetheless, physicians have the domain knowledge but are not deeply trained in data science. This is the case of the cardiology department of the University Hospital of Salamanca, where the large amount of anonymized data makes it possible to improve certain tasks and decision-making. This work describes a machine learning platform to assist non-expert users in the definition and application of ML pipelines. The platform aims to fill data science gaps while automatizing ML pipelines and provides a baseline to integrate it with other developed applications for the cardiology department.

Keywords: Machine learning · User-centered design · Cardiology · Focus group · ML pipelines

1 Introduction

Machine Learning (ML) applications are continuously growing in different fields. The application of ML algorithms enables the possibility of providing support to automate the undertaking of complex tasks.

© Springer Nature Switzerland AG 2021
P. H. Ruiz et al. (Eds.): HCI-COLLAB 2021, CCIS 1478, pp. 237–249, 2021.
https://doi.org/10.1007/978-3-030-92325-9_18

One of the main fields which is benefiting from the application of these algorithms is the health field. The health context involves several tasks including diagnosis, classification, disease detection, segmentation, assessment of organ functions, etc. [1–3], that can be partly automated and enhanced through artificial intelligence support.

Moreover, datasets are constantly being generated through several sources, which provides enough volume of data to apply these kinds of algorithms. However, the application of ML is not trivial; it is necessary to rely on data science and programming skills to select the proper algorithm and preprocess the datasets accordingly.

Given the benefits that can be derived from the application of ML in the medical domain, it is crucial to democratize knowledge regarding algorithms and pipelines, as it could enable non-expert users to support their decision-making processes with AI.

In this work we present a ML platform to assist non-expert users in the definition and application of ML pipelines. The main challenge of this platform is to provide a proper user interface to ease the understanding of the outcomes and processes involved in ML pipelines. For these reasons, we followed a user-centered design approach to capture requirements and needs from a variety of users profiles, including AI experts and non-experts.

The rest of the paper is structured as follows. Section 2 outlines related applications and works to assist users in ML and data science tasks. Section 3 describes the ML platform proposal. Section 4 details the user study carried out to validate the conceptual application, followed by Sect. 5, in which the results are summarized. Finally, Sect. 6 presents the conclusions derived from this work.

2   Related Works

Several tools are already developed for supporting ML processes. We can organize them in three categories. First, tools for developers and data scientist which provide libraries for creating ML applications. For example, TensorFlow, which is a ML system that operates at large scale and in heterogeneous environments [4], helping researchers push the state-of-the-art in ML and developers easily build and deploy ML powered applications. Another example is Apache Mahout, a library for scalable ML on distributed dataflow systems [5]. In this category, we can also include libraries for Python such as PyTorch, Scikit-learn or Keras.io, and cloud services such as Google Colab, which is a serverless Jupyter notebook environment [6].

Second, there are applications that target experts and at the same time provide tools for non-specialist users. There several applications provide visual environments that support the visual definition of ML models.

For example, Weka, a collection of ML algorithms for data mining tasks. It has four environments, specifically, it has a visual interface, Knowledge Flow, that enables users to specify a data stream by graphically connecting components representing data sources, preprocessing tools, learning algorithms, evaluation methods, and visualization tools [7, 8].

RapidMiner Studio provides tools for building ML workflows in a comprehensive data science platform. It has the Visual Workflow Designer tools to create ML workflows, each step is documented for complete transparency. This part of the tool allows to connect the data source, automated in-database processing, data visualization as well as the Model Validation process [9].

SPSS by IBM includes a product for supporting visual data science and ML. The main work area in SPSS Modeler is the stream canvas, an interface to build ML streams connecting nodes [10].

Another example is KNIME Analytics Platform. It provides tools for creating visual workflows for data analytics with a graphical interface, without the need for coding. KNIME is a modular environment, which enables easy visual assembly and interactive execution of a data pipeline [11].

On the other hand, the ML has started to introduce in primary and secondary education. This has prompted the development of tools to help non-expert users, such as children, to perform simple ML processes using a visual interface. In particular, there are two tools that are noteworthy. LearningML [12], a tool to foster computational thinking skills through practical AI Projects, and Machine Learning for Kids. Both tools are based on a simple pipeline used to train models and an integration with Scratch to use the trained model.

As can be seen, there are plenty of powerful applications focused on easing the application of ML algorithms as well as educational tools to understand these complex workflows. However, our application context asks for a customized tool with specific requirements related to the health sector and more emphasis on providing an educational experience to those unskilled users while using the platform. The next sections will outline these requirements and our approach to address the necessities regarding the automatization of ML pipelines in this domain.

3 Platform Definition

3.1 The Problem

As introduced before, the health sector is taking advantage of AI algorithms to enhance the decision-making processes and to support complex common activities such as image segmentation, disease detection, identification of risk factors, etc. However, to benefit from these algorithms, it is important to rely on robust data science skills. In fact, in the health sector, it is necessary to rely both on data science skills as well as on domain knowledge to get the most out of the application of AI pipelines in the health sector.

Having both data science skills and domain knowledge is very powerful, but it is also very difficult, as physicians are not usually (deeply) trained in data science, and data scientists might not be specialized in specific domains. For these reasons, it is necessary to fill these skills and domain knowledge gaps, which is usually addressed by having multidisciplinary teams.

However, bringing AI and data science concepts closer to physicians would be more efficient, as they would be less dependent of data scientists. The presented tool lay its foundations on this specific issue: to fill data science gaps while automatizing ML pipelines.

Section 2 proved that there are already plenty of tools that address the automatization of AI and data science pipelines, but the necessity of adapting them to the user needs identified in the medical sector asks for a customized tool. In fact, although these tools are mostly generic and powerful, we want to focus on enhanced interactivity to improve the engagement of physicians while still providing all the benefits derived from the introduction of ML pipelines in medical departments, as well as an integrated on-going training during the use of the tool's features.

Moreover, by developing this customized platform, we can also focus on the integration of these services with other developed applications for the cardiology department of the University Hospital of Salamanca (such as the CARTIER-IA platform [13, 14]), fostering the creation of a robust technological ecosystem [15, 16].

3.2 User Needs

The development of the tool follows a user-center approach. The users have been categorized into two groups. The main user group is physicians. They have knowledge or interest in AI/ML and have data. Moreover, they do not have enough knowledge of programming or using AI algorithms. These users are also characterized by a wide age range and different levels of digital competence, which also influence in the user needs.

The secondary user groups are students and ML experts. Medical students neither do they have knowledge of programming, but they are mostly young, and it is supposed that they have more experience with digital tools. Regarding ML experts, they have knowledge of AI/ML as well as programming skills, however they are not domain experts.

The needs of physicians and medical students are mainly focused on:

- Getting a tool to apply AI/ML in medical datasets without technical expertise and with limited knowledge of ML.
- Visualizing and analyzing medical data.
- Learning about data analysis and its usefulness and benefits in medicine.
- Learning about ML algorithms in a practical way.
- Being able to use a ML application that allows a detailed data visualization and help in interpreting the data.

On the other hand, the needs of ML experts lie in facilitating the integration of algorithms in ML pipelines. Furthermore, we also identify customization as a need. They need to modify the parameters and heuristics of a ML algorithm and learn from the results of their tests.

3.3 Main Scenarios

User scenarios are stories about people and their activities [17]. We have identified five scenarios that cover the goals and questions to be achieved through the tool. The scenarios are mainly focused on supplying the needs of the physicians, the main user group.

First, the pipelines definition. The platform interface will allow the definition of ML pipelines through graphical elements and interactions, to materialize the tasks defined using a programming approach such as those develop using Luigi, the Python module to build complex pipelines of batch jobs. Users will be able to customize the pipeline and access the intermediate results, as well as save configurations for sharing or later use.

The second scenario covers the algorithm training. Users of the platform will be able to train various algorithms by providing some input data. The platform will allow the user to choose the type of algorithm and configure the parameters associated with it. It is proposed that the algorithm and parameter selection process will be guided by a series of heuristics based on existing literature (although it is also proposed that expert users can add or modify these heuristics) depending on the scheme, the problem to be solved and the volume of data entered.

The third scenario is focused on visualization and interpretation of the results. Various metrics and results will be obtained after training is completed depending on the algorithm or ML model used. These results can be ROC curve plots, cut-off points with specificity/sensitivity/etc. values, variable importance, etc. The platform will assist users in the process of interpreting these results through visualizations, annotations, and explanations.

The next identified scenario will support the data checking and visualization. Users will also be able to check and visualize the input data, to explore it. Moreover, the platform will provide feedback regarding the potential problems of the dataset and the feasibility of using different algorithms on the input data.

Finally, the last scenario is related to the use of heuristics. This scenario addresses two objectives, one focused on medical students without ML knowledge and other for ML experts. First, the use of heuristics through a rule-based recommender will be a functionality to use the platform as a didactic tool. The feature will provide a guided process during the definition of pipelines, selection and training of algorithms, interpretation of the results, etc., to provide an educational component in the platform itself for those users who are not experts in AI or programming.

Secondly, the heuristics are also for ML expert users, who may be physicians, data scientists or developers. Particularly, we have identified customization as the main need for ML experts. For this reason, the platform will allow the modification of heuristics. The basic heuristics will be based on existing literature [18, 19], but expert users will be able to modify them through XML documents or a graphical interface, being able to store several versions of the heuristics used in the platform.

4 Concept Validation

The test phase was focused on validating the application to make sure works well for the people who will use it. In particular, the process was focused on and identifying the design requirements using the feedback of the primary and secondary users (physicians and ML experts).

The concept validation includes the development of a high-fidelity prototype [20] using Adobe XD together a remote focus group [21] with final users testing the digital prototype remotely and answering questions related to usability in order to identify problems and discover new requirements.

4.1 The Prototype

The ML platform aims to assist non-expert users in the definition and application of ML pipelines. The platform will also support the integration with other developed tools.

There are three profiles when logging in: regular user, expert, and administrator. The regular user can perform all the tasks that we have mentioned above that represents the main functionality of the application. The expert also has access to the heuristics used by the application and can review and modify them. The administrator can perform all these tasks and manages user accounts and validate them.

The tool is divided into different screens that bring together all the functionality (Fig. 1). We can distingue three groups of screens. First, the homepage which provides information about the platform and the user access. The platform is totally private, so that access to it is protected by user registration and login. In addition, the user sign-in involves a validation process, so users apply for a new account and administrators have to approve it.

The next set of functionality focuses on project management within the platform. Users (both regular and experts) will create ML projects. Each project is mainly a pipeline with one or more inputs and one or more outputs. The platform allows saving the projects in a personal area (Fig. 2), so user can reuse them so many times as needed. Users can also download projects to have a copy or even send them to another user using any other media (email, shared folder, etc.). Users can upload those projects to their accounts

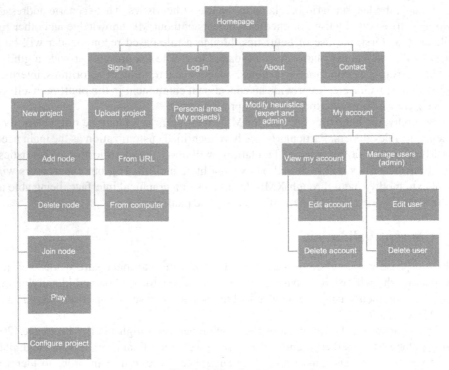

Fig. 1. Main site flows.

through their personal area using an URL to a shared space or a zip file located in the computer.

Furthermore, the personal area also contains a main functionality for expert users and administrators; an interface to manage the heuristics. Experts can modify the parameters and heuristics of a ML algorithm and learn from the results of their tests.

Finally, most of the functionality is in the project editor (Fig. 3). The editor allows creating a new pipeline or editing an existing one. This interface is divided into three main parts. First, a top bar with provides access to the personal area and user account. It also has a button to reset the project.

Second, a toolbar containing all the nodes that can be added to the pipeline grouped by categories: data, data preparation, data processing, visualization, ML algorithms and evaluation. The design is conceived to be able to add new nodes over time. Moreover, the toolbar provides tools for join nodes, configure, execute, and save the project.

The toolbar has two views, a simplified view for expert users or those with more experience in the use of the platform, and a detailed view showing the name of all nodes and categories.

The last and principal part of this interface is the workspace, a blank area to build the pipeline connecting different nodes (Fig. 3). Each node has inputs and outputs; it produces an output, a set of results, which are the input to the next node. A node can be connected with several nodes, for example, a visualization node to get a visual analysis

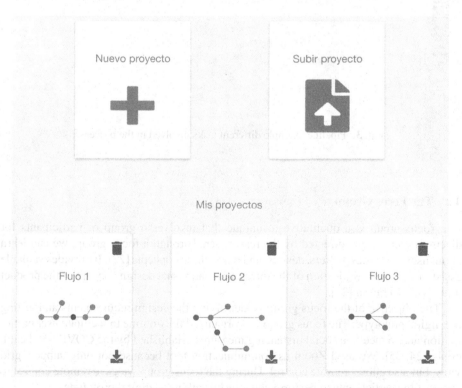

Fig. 2. Saved ML pipelines (projects) in the user's personal area.

of the intermediate results and a node to apply an algorithm to that dataset. The nodes have also different visual marks to provide useful information:

- A warning mark in those cases in which there are missing information, a problem in the execution of the node or a recommendation to improve the configuration of the node.
- A result mark to indicate that this node produces as output a set of intermediate results that can be retrieved when the pipeline is executed.
- A suggestion mark to provide additional information and support regular users without ML knowledge.

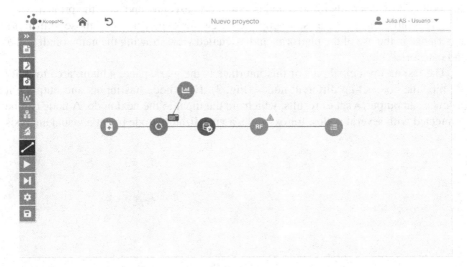

Fig. 3. Pipeline example different tasks involved in the process.

4.2 The Focus Group

The focus group is a qualitative technique that involves a group of participants for discussing on a topic directed by the researcher. Through a focus group, we can learn about users' attitudes, beliefs, desires, and reactions to concepts [22]. It provides valuable assistance to the specification of the interaction and visual design concept of the product under consideration [23].

The objective of the focus group is identifying the design requirements and testing the digital prototype. The focus group was organized fully online to facilitate user participation and to meet the social distancing measures established by the COVID-19 health crisis [24, 25]. We used Zoom as communication tool because not only support grid view, but also allows remote control. During the focus group we gave remote control to some of the participants to perform some tasks within the digital prototype.

The participants in the focus group were the three types of users previously identified:

- CE1: A cardiologist with some knowledge of ML.
- CE2: A cardiologist and researcher involved in ML projects.
- CE3: A cardiologist with a positive attitude towards ML.
- DE1: A physics and data scientist.
- DE2: An industrial engineer and data scientist.
- DE3: A software engineer and data scientist.
- S1: A computer science student working on a ML project related to cardiology.

The focus group was in Spanish, it took 60 min, and it was moderated by three women researchers related to software engineering and HCI. The roundtables were divided into two phases. A first phase in which we introduce the platform and explained the user access and roles; and a second phase in which participants answered different questions related to the main parts of the digital prototype (the personal area and the workspace).

There were common questions for each screen:

- Can you identify briefly what can be done on this screen?
- Can you describe it?
- What is your opinion regarding the visual aesthetics of the screen?

After these questions, the moderators shared some specific questions for each part. For the personal area (Fig. 2):

- How would you delete a project?
- How would you download a project?
- How would you create a project?

Some of the questions also involved the interaction of a volunteer with the digital prototype using the remote-control tool. For the workspace with a new project:

- How would you start a ML pipeline?
- Do you know how to continue the workflow from this first node?
- How would you modify a previous/already created project?

Later, we showed a workspace with a ML pipeline example (Fig. 3):

- Could you describe what you see on this screen?
- Once you have the ML pipeline defined, how would you get the results?
- How would you explore the results of the ML pipeline?

Finally, some general questions:

- Have you been able to see how to navigate between screens?
- What positive aspects of the platform have caught your attention?
- What negative aspects of the platform have caught your attention?
- What tasks would you like to perform with the platform?

5 Results

The analysis of the focus group was focused on identified positive and negative aspects across the different screens. Moreover, we identified a set of suggestions.

5.1 Positive Comments

The ML experts and cardiologist has similar opinions about the workspace. Both indicate that it is an intuitive interface (CE3), notably the first step for uploading data to begin a pipeline (CE2, DE3) and the interaction to add nodes into the pipeline (CE2). Furthermore, CE1 highlight the general order of steps suggested by the category organization in the toolbar. All user groups have underlined the tools to facilitate the use of the platform for users with basic knowledge of ML, such as the tooltips (DE3) and the information about errors and recommendation associated to our pipeline (CE2).

Likewise, domain and ML experts emphasize the design. CE1 indicates that the look & feel is good, and DE3 likes the appearance with few well-organized buttons and with plenty of white space to get started.

Cardiologists pay more attention to pipeline execution. CE1 and CE2 comment the option of executing each node step by step and seeing results from initial stages without waiting to get the final results of the pipeline.

On the other hand, ML experts pay more attention to flexibility. The platform allows creating pipelines with few (or many nodes) connecting them in any order (DE1, DE3). Moreover, DE2 remarks that the platform allows adding different ML models and visualizing many interim results.

Finally, the participants highlighted several general positive aspects of the digital prototype. Both ML experts and cardiologists emphasized the interface design, the navigation, and the simplicity of the tool. Moreover, the ML experts point out that the tool is quite scalable.

5.2 Negative Comments

Regarding the negative aspects, we have identified the following:

- The way the toolbar is expanded is not intuitive. (DE1).
- The "save data" category of nodes causes confusion about their function. (CE1, DE1, DE3).
- Not fully self-explanatory. It is not clear how to proceed to create and join nodes the first time you use the tool if you have not used a similar tool before. Invites you to follow a trial-and-error strategy. (CE1).
- It is not clear which tasks are in progress and which have been completed during the pipeline execution. (DE3).

5.3 Suggestions

Throughout the focus group, the participants suggested several improvements to reduce the identified negative aspects:

- Support new users with the platform indicating which are the first elements of a ML pipeline (DE3) and a set of guidelines or instructions to start the definition of the pipeline (DE3). According to CE1, it would be useful an example (initial simulation) showing how the platform works.
- Improve the toolbar with tooltips (CE1) and using the expanded view as default (CE2).
- Provide a set of short video tutorials on how to use the tool, illustrating basic operation and more concrete things (CE1, DE3).
- Restrict the options for defining the pipeline to beginners and allowing full flexibility for experts (DE3). For example, a default pipeline structure for people with basic ML skills, so they can start a project with two clicks and learn how to do it (DE2).
- Changing the name of the subcategory "save data" to "download or export data" (DE3).
- Add a visual help to know how to join the nodes within the pipeline (CE1).
- Enable execution not only from the toolbar, but also using the right mouse button because this is a common interaction with this type of tool (DE3).
- Include an execution mark to indicate whether the execution of the node within the pipeline was successful or there was a problem (DE1).

6 Conclusions

The health sector produces a huge amount of dataset with useful information to support decision-making processes and complex common activities. However, physicians are not deeply trained in data science although they have the domain knowledge. On the other hand, ML experts are not usually experts in the domain. This work describes the design process of a ML platform to bridging the data science gaps of physicians while automatizing ML pipelines.

Although there are already different tools that allow users to build and execute ML pipelines, the requirements found in the medical context asked for a customized platform with the goal of offering a tool adapted to the necessities of the end users found in this context: physicians with lack of ML and programming skills that are interested in taking advantage from the application of these algorithms.

In addition, the development of a customized tool opens the path for the integration of other already developed tools for the cardiology department at the University Hospital of Salamanca. By implementing communication mechanisms, it is possible to connect different platforms to foster the creation of a technological ecosystem with data science features specifically adapted to the medical context requirements.

The focus group session has provided a considerable amount of data concerning usability functions and their validation by domain experts and ML experts. It has provided information to understand users' current situation and needs, getting the perspective of multiple users discussing the same requirement or functionality. On the other hand, we have collected the reactions to the digital prototype.

The results of the focus group have served as an input to develop a new version of the digital prototype to solve the main detected problems and improve it including some suggestions.

References

1. Litjens, G., et al.: A survey on deep learning in medical image analysis. Med. Image Anal. **42**, 60–88 (2017). https://doi.org/10.1016/j.media.2017.07.005
2. González Izard, S., Sánchez Torres, R., Alonso Plaza, Ó., Juanes Méndez, J.A., García-Peñalvo, F.J.: Nextmed: automatic imaging segmentation, 3D reconstruction, and 3D model visualization platform using augmented and virtual reality. Sensors (Basel) **20**(10), 2962 (2020). https://doi.org/10.3390/s20102962
3. Izard, S.G., Juanes, J.A., García Peñalvo, F.J., Estella, J.M.G., Ledesma, M.J.S., Ruisoto, P.: Virtual reality as an educational and training tool for medicine. J. Med. Syst. **42**(3), 1–5 (2018). https://doi.org/10.1007/s10916-018-0900-2
4. Abadi, M., et al.: TensorFlow: a system for large-scale machine learning. In: 12th USENIX Symposium on Operating Systems Design and Implementation OSDI 16, pp. 265–283. USENIX Association, Savannah (2016)
5. Anil, R., et al.: Apache mahout: machine learning on distributed dataflow systems. J. Mach. Learn. Res. **21**(127), 1–6 (2020)
6. Bisong, E.: Google colaboratory. In: Building Machine Learning and Deep Learning Models on Google Cloud Platform: A Comprehensive Guide for Beginners, pp. 59–64. Apress, Berkeley (2019). https://doi.org/10.1007/978-1-4842-4470-8_7
7. Frank, E., et al.: Weka-a machine learning workbench for data mining. In: Maimon, Oded, Rokach, Lior (eds.) Data Mining and Knowledge Discovery Handbook, pp. 1269–1277. Springer, Boston (2010). https://doi.org/10.1007/978-0-387-09823-4_66
8. Hall, M., Frank, E., Holmes, G., Pfahringer, B., Reutemann, P., Witten, I.H.: The WEKA data mining software: an update. SIGKDD Explor. Newsl. **11**(1), 10–18 (2009). https://doi.org/10.1145/1656274.1656278
9. Bjaoui, M., Sakly, H., Said, M., Kraiem, N., Bouhlel, M.S.: Depth insight for data scientist with RapidMiner «an innovative tool for AI and big data towards medical applications». Paper presented at the Proceedings of the 2nd International Conference on Digital Tools & Uses Congress, Virtual Event, Tunisia (2020)
10. McCormick, K., Salcedo, J.: IBM SPSS Modeler Essentials: Effective Techniques for Building Powerful Data Mining and Predictive Analytics Solutions. Packt Publishing Ltd., Birmingham (2017)
11. Berthold, M., et al.: KNIME - the Konstanz information miner: version 2.0 and beyond. ACM SIGKDD Explor. Newsl. **11**(1), 26–31 (2009). https://doi.org/10.1145/1656274.1656280
12. Rodríguez-García, J.D., Moreno-León, J., Román-González, M., Robles, G.: Evaluation of an online intervention to teach artificial intelligence with LearningML to 10–16-Year-old students. In: Proceedings of the 52nd ACM Technical Symposium on Computer Science Education. Association for Computing Machinery, pp 177–183 (2021). https://doi.org/10.1145/3408877.3432393
13. García-Peñalvo, F., et al.: Application of artificial intelligence algorithms within the medical context for non-specialized users: the CARTIER-IA platform. Int. J. Interact. Multimed. Artif. Intell. **6**(6), 46 (2021)
14. Vázquez-Ingelmo, A., et al.: Usability study of CARTIER-IA: a platform for medical data and imaging management. In: Zaphiris, P., Ioannou, A. (eds.) HCII 2021. LNCS, vol. 12784, pp. 374–384. Springer, Cham (2021). https://doi.org/10.1007/978-3-030-77889-7_26
15. García-Holgado, A., García-Peñalvo, F.J.: Validation of the learning ecosystem metamodel using transformation rules. Futur. Gener. Comput. Syst. **91**, 300–310 (2019). https://doi.org/10.1016/j.future.2018.09.011
16. García-Holgado, A., García-Peñalvo, F.J.: A metamodel proposal for developing learning ecosystems. In: Zaphiris, P., Ioannou, A. (eds.) LCT 2017. LNCS, vol. 10295, pp. 100–109. Springer, Cham (2017). https://doi.org/10.1007/978-3-319-58509-3_10

17. Carroll, J.: Making Use: Scenario-Based Design of Human-Computer Interactions. The MIT Press, Cambridge (2000)
18. Buitinck, L., et al.: API design for machine learning software: experiences from the scikit-learn project. Paper presented at the ECML PKDD Workshop: Languages for Data Mining and Machine Learning (2013)
19. Scikit-Learn: Choosing the right estimator - Scikit-Learn documentation (2020)
20. Pernice, K.: UX Prototypes: Low Fidelity vs. High Fidelity (2016)
21. Krueger, R.A., Casey, M.A.: Focus Groups: A Practical Guide for Applied Research. Sage publications, Focus group. Usability.gov (2014). https://www.usability.gov/how-to-and-tools/methods/focus-groups.html. Accessed 12 June 2021
22. Kuhn, K.: Problems and benefits of requirements gathering with focus groups: a case study. Int. J. Hum.-Comput. Interact. **12**(3–4), 309–325 (2000). https://doi.org/10.1080/10447318.2000.9669061
23. García-Peñalvo, F.J., Corell, A., Abella-García, V., Grande-de-Prado, M.: Online assessment in higher education in the time of COVID-19. Educ. Knowl. Soc. **21** (2020). https://doi.org/10.14201/eks.23086
24. Fardoun, H., González-González, C.S., Collazos, C.A., Yousef, M.: Exploratory study in iberoamerica on the teaching-learning process and assessment proposal in the pandemic times. Educ. Knowl. Soc. **21** (2020). https://doi.org/10.14201/eks.23437
25. García-Peñalvo, F.J., Corell, A., Rivero-Ortega, R., Rodríguez-Conde, M.J., Rodríguez-García, N.: Impact of the COVID-19 on higher education: an experience-based approach. In: García-Peñalvo, F.J. (ed.) Information Technology Trends for a Global and Interdisciplinary Research Community, pp. 1–18. IGI Global, Hershey (2021)

Virtual Reconstruction of Objects by Point Cloud Capture to Measurement of Density Parameters Using Low Cost Device

Angel Rodrigues Ferreira[1]([⊠]) [iD], Alexandre Carvalho Silva[1] [iD],
and Camilo de Lellis Barreto Junior[2] [iD]

[1] IF Goiano, Campus Morrinhos, Morrinhos, Brazil
angel.rodrigues@estudante.ifgoiano.edu.br,
alexandre.silva@ifgoiano.edu.br
[2] Universidade Federal de Uberlândia, Uberlândia, Brazil
camilobarreto@ufu.br

Abstract. It is studied in this project the viability to implement an application to virtually rebuild objects using a low-cost device. A rebuilding application was developed using ReconstructMe SDK's interfaces and a Kinect as a depth device. An analysis tool working on the Unity engine was also implemented, operating mainly as Editor Scripting with its C# API feature. This tool implements the capacity to obtain the measurement data of volumetric extremes of the virtual objects. The proposal is tested by rebuilding of some specific objects, which are the closest resource; by manually conducting the device. With results, the application faces some problems with the mesh fitting of some objects, however the mesh quality is relatively good. Based on data measured, it is achieved a good level of precision on the extreme measures besides that each rebuilding procedure can be made within a relatively fast time cost, around 25 s.

Keywords: Kinect · Object scanning · Point cloud · ReconstructMe SDK · Virtual reconstruction

1 Introduction

The means of contact that the human being performs with the environment depends on the overall functioning of their biological devices. Among these means, the eyesight is with no doubt one of the most important device's resources.

Being able to view or measure the physical information of specific objects is important for some determined work areas, but the ways to obtain these data are not always efficient. Towards this objective, it's ideal to explore a possibility of a computational solution of technical implementation that fulfills the objects measurement data work's needs and is able to efficiently fulfill the necessary processes.

Through the eyesight resource, still relating them to the human's eyesight capacity, when implemented in computational vision, the ability to collect data from the real world to the computer becomes sophisticated and wide. With the visual aspects implemented

P. H. Ruiz et al. (Eds.): HCI-COLLAB 2021, CCIS 1478, pp. 250–262, 2021.
https://doi.org/10.1007/978-3-030-92325-9_19

in a machine's sense, with a wide array of sensitive capacities due to varied and specific sensors, the machine can even see what human beings cannot see [1, 2].

The computational rebuilding of an object from the real environment in a virtual 3D model allows dimensional proximity contact and the possibility of any consequent implementation with the virtual model, having it at close range and with a measurable prototype. Overall, there's a rising necessity to represent objects in computer models, allowing different ways to obtain data from the objects' shapes [3].

That way, exploring the visual resources with the approach of a potential technology, the point clouds can be sufficient strategies to scan shapes in an environment, with the need of a structure of sensors acting as capture resources.

Based on these needs and potential scenarios, this project has the overall objective to accomplish the scanning of specific objects in a real environment, making their surfaces be rebuilt in a 3D computer dimension. Enabling then in specific objectives a computational model of capturing and rebuilding and a tool model to analyze their dimensional measures, being able to show the objects' length, depth and height. All of that considering the importance of the quality complexities, precision and viability while using a low-cost device.

2 Theoretical Foundation

The following subtopics have the objective to bring the reader closer to some of the technologies used in this project.

2.1 Surfaces' Reconstruction

The surfaces reconstruction is a geometrical model to use point clouds' data to restore the original surfaces from the objects through measurement and acquisition [4]. Processing a point cloud in a fast and economical way to obtain a 3D model of a real object that adapts itself to reality is a tough job [5]. Therefore, it is significant to study the data processing technology of the 3D point cloud on how to guarantee efficiency and precision in the surface rebuilding model [4].

ReconstructMe SDK is a ISO C library for real-time 3D reconstruction procedures for manual operation of RGB-D camera devices. Projected as a library to implement software to provide an easy interface with the developer. It provides an interface for the whole pipeline, from the 3D scanning including the pre and post-processing steps, a sensor data filter and 3D surfaces post post-processing tasks [6]. It supports a wide variety of common RGB-D sensors, such as the *ASUS Xtion*, the *PrimSense Carmine* or the *Microsoft Kinect* series [7]. All its rebuilding is made within the metric space and the result can be exported to various *CAD* formats, like *STL*, *OBJ*, *3DS* and *PLY* [6].

As a middleware library, the *ReconstructMe SDK* encapsulates the communication with popular 3D sensors and abstracts the hardware details as tasks parallelization. It allows the development of apps in a matter of seconds and provides an API based on pure C, without additional dependencies [6].

The *ReconstructMe SDK* provides specific interfaces that expand the possibilities to adapt an application. Some are necessary and/or essential in any software such as context interfaces, sensors, volume and surface. It also has a calibration and a viewing interface as test-oriented alternatives. The default interfaces are created with default values, but they can be configured through an options interface and it is very important. However, these components offer support to the sensor's communication by tracking the camera movement through visual odometry, fusing the scanned data in a world panel and post-processing these said scans [6].

2.2 Capture Device

The *Time of Flight* cameras and the laser scanners are the chosen tools and have their applicability studied on jobs that require real-life model computational measurement under time efficiency consequences [8].

The *Kinect* sensor is capable of precisely reconstructing a 3D object and determine the objects' volume and if compared to other range sensors used for 3D mapping, the *Kinect* allows a much cheaper way to record point clouds [9, 10].

Works like [9, 11–13] point the model's range of diverse areas with the evaluation and/or extension of the *Kinect*'s applicability (as a depth sensor), covering fields that involve computational vision, mapping and 3D modeling, robotics among others (which allow their implementation in the modern technology).

As a kind of hybrid/composite device [8, 14], with low resolution and high scanning frequency (around 30 FPS) [8], the *Kinect* is a RGB-D sensor that provides RGB image sync and depth of image [10]. It grasps various advanced detection equipment, which of these are a traditional RGB camera and a depth sensor that is made of a near infrared (NIR) laser patterns projector combined with an infrared camera (IR, a complementary monochromatic sensor made of metal oxide – CMOS) [14, 15].

By directing the detection definitions to the *Kinect* sensor, the infrared camera is used to observe, decode the infrared projection's pattern to triangle the 3D scene [14]. Geometric relations between the projector and the camera are calculated to capture depth extents through an offline calibration procedure. The projector displays an IR light pattern on the 3D scene, the IR camera captures the pattern's stains in a given surface and corresponds between the local extents' patterns observed in the images and the calibrated patterns of the projector's extents [10].

The relative geometry between the infrared projector and the infrared camera, as well as the projected infrared pattern's extent are acknowledged and if it's possible to combine an observed point in an image and a point in the projector's pattern, it is made possible to rebuild them in a 3D environment by using triangulation [15]. While registering the consecutive depth images, it is possible to obtain an increased points' density and create a complete point cloud of a scene environment, possibly in real-time [12].

The sensor's performance can be affected by a series of factors, be them external (the environment) and/or from the capture's scene as well as specific from the device that influence its precision and depth resolution. Some factor may be the environment's light level, material's kind, color, presence of infrared light emitted by other sensors, temperature variations, air flow and the distance from the sensor to the capture's contact [8–10].

3 Related Works

Works like [16] and [17] study the potentials from the point cloud's rebuilding technologies while proposing them as an efficient solution on work areas which need some measurement with objects of interest. In [16], a *FARO Photon 120* sensor was used and a *Velodyne VLP-16* in [17]. In [18] a whole processing structure is implemented and configured, showing important resources for a reconstruction application. Generally, these resources will exist in reconstruction applications, prioritizing the quality and efficiency of the reconstruction with subsequent processing over the point cloud. A relation between these works is made in Table 1.

Table 1. Observations about the technologies used, implemented in the related works.

Works	Handling	Point cloud	Mesh
Liu et al. [16]	Heavy and difficult	Scattered	High detail
Pérez-Ruiz et al. [17]	Easily handling	Horizontal lines	Detail lines
Xu et al. [18]	–	Pre-processed	Efficient

Discussions were followed towards some potentials and advantages in these projects. The device used in [16] has an impressive capture capacity with the drawback of having a robust shape which requires a lot of operational effort in its control and operation. The device used in [17] also shows interesting capacities, however, since it's a stationary device, the capture points cannot describe the whole object's surface. Both of these said devices are relatively expensive. As demonstrated in [18], the specific processes to dedicate in a sequential development structure of the essential rebuilding processes, it is interesting and resourcefully important to make use of a library that abstracts the processes and that allows the research's direction.

4 HCI and Study of the Technological Application

This section has a plus approach, it tries beginning a relationship with the Human-Computer Interaction (HCI) topic in relation to the technologies in this work, discussing a possible scenario of technological application. One of the needs to resort to the virtual reconstruction was identified, as when in a work area is necessary to obtain measurement data about interesting objects. In areas as explained, they are usually using rudimentary (traditional) or sophisticated (modern technology) instruments of work, but when it comes to the manual/traditional way of performing, a case study of the referred technological application was explored.

As a proof of concept, can be searched about the necessity to obtain measurement data, when it is manually performed. As which one that usually resort to these techniques, the Zootechnical implementations for the analysis characteristics of the horses can be mentioned; where the specialist takes the surface measurements of specific parts of the animal, analyses the data, and thus he/she can classify and rate its efficiency basing on the relationship of competence in specific factors iterable by its characteristics. Works as [19–21] value the importance of knowing the factors that influence the morphometric measurements of horses, since the shape of the body defines the limits and the ability of the animals to perform movements [19].

To take the horse measures, manual measurement is usually used, in this case it is done by using specific instruments, in close contact with the animal (needing proximity for measures), while it demands technical disposition to measure all the demanding parts of interest of the animal, and more, there are risks for the operator as the horse is a strong animal compared to a human. The work [20] mentions the present search for devices and technologies that enable the correct, practice and economical quantification of the dimensions of the different anatomic and zootechnical parts of the horses. Therefore, in this context, it is possible to identify the adequacy capacity of the technology applying to the referred area, in a matter of insertion of technology.

4.1 Discussion on the Scenario and Theme

Exploring a scenario of the approximated technological application (under discussion), the virtual reconstruction of objects for the activity area of measurements and morphometric analysis of horses, a main advantage was identified, it could be about the capacity to get the object to the virtual environment, the horse, as a 3D virtual object model for the work studies, providing the use of computational interface and analysis methods and software to perform the necessary services, and also, specially about at low cost of the device implementation (carrying low cost). However, it is necessary to evaluate the application scenario well, and from this assessment, the specific needs for the technological adaptation are observed to achieve viability in the area's adherence to technological application. Concluding that in a scenario like this, the technical interaction regarding device manipulation and software system should be studied.

In this context, the issues of system autonomy may be important, in terms of automation and parametrization of process (could be adapted a specialized semi-automatic device driving technological structure), as well as exploring technical authority's capabilities on computational processes of evaluation and classification (the zootechnical professional of the action could have authority to use the captured data and interact in the results, if necessary). Do not eliminating the human part of the service, but adapting this integration, it keeps the employee in his/her work (perhaps requiring a training with the technology) and a certain confidence in the results of processes that use the proposed technology.

In this perspective, it would be possible to provide security to the professional technician involved in the performance of service (eliminating aspects of proximity to the interesting object) and improve the efficiency of the captures (with parametric and automated capabilities) and as well the data evaluation process (by specialist computer system and integrator), and yet perhaps it might even also be possible to achieve results not realized by the human.

By here, there is a scenario that is possibly viable for the referred application of reconstruction technology, even though also exists other scenarios that can be explored, from this and other interesting and interested areas of work. However, aspects of HCI and technology adherence, are factors that must be evaluated, as the need for technological adaptation may be important, if there is potential, to increase this adherence in a favorable way to the desired and interested application area.

5   System's Architecture

The solution that is proposed in this project aims at the implementation of two applications: the first is for the reconstruction processes using the capture device's resource by acquiring data from a point cloud and the second is a tool to visualize the dimensional information of an object's virtual model. The implementation's architecture can be observed in Fig. 1.

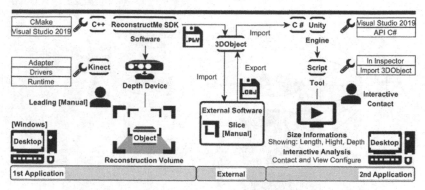

Fig. 1. Representation of the system architecture implemented.

The *Unity* engine provides an integrated development environment, allowing the interaction between the mouse and scripts' edition, as well as the ease to create and import 3D objects [22]. In this project, *Unity* was only used as an editor's engine with the sole purpose to develop scripts, working on the 3D visualization in its editor's mode, being developed a tool that appropriates the analysis of measurement attributes of the objects' virtual models.

Specifications are noticed from the system's architecture (Fig. 1). The reconstruction application is implemented with the functionalities' resources from the APIs that integrate the *ReconstructMe SDK* (v. 2.4.1016), developing with C++. The *CMake* (v. 3.16) tool is utilized to make the assembly/configuration of the development environment, working with the *Visual Studio 2019*. A *Kinect* (1414 model) is used as a depth sensor, requiring a specific power source and the installation/configuration of the *Runtime* and its drivers on the *Windows* OS. The *Unity*'s integrated analysis tool is implemented in C# scripts that customize and extend the *Unity*'s editor.

5.1   System's UML Diagrams – Use Case Diagrams

The functionalities of the reconstruction application (1st Application – Fig. 1), as a software, under resources of the *ReconstructMe SDK* can be visualized in a UML diagrammatic view, through Use Case diagram, in Fig. 2. The system must offer the user specific configuration capabilities, about the "options" files related to the reconstruction performance by the *ReconstructMe*. There are user configs (*userSets*), through the application interface, as well as the programmer configs (*preSets*), of the research, inline code. The configurations on "options" files must be loaded to be used. If the user starts a reconstruction process, after this, there are options to restart or conclude it, if conclude then it generates the surface model from the captured data in the reconstruction volume, able to apply post-processing operations; once having a concluded surface model, it can be saved to a 3D object model.

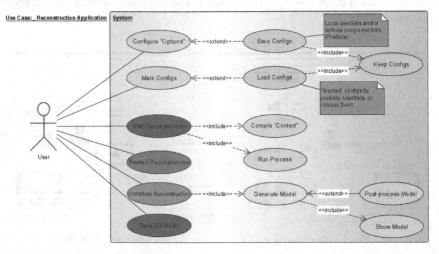

Fig. 2. Use case UML diagram referring to the first application (1st Application – Fig. 1).

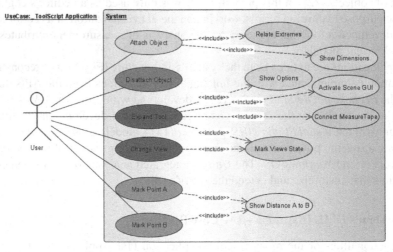

Fig. 3. Use case UML diagram referring to the second application (2nd Application – Fig. 1).

The functionalities of the measurement analysis application (2nd Application –
Fig. 1), as a tool, integrating in the environment of the *Unity*'s editor, also was showed
through the Use Case UML diagrammatic view, in Fig. 3. In this case, at first, the main
activities of the tool must provide resources for the analysis of measurements of extreme
dimensions and interaction of parametric views. It is possible to attach an object, and
then visualize the extreme measures of this object, by an extreme box attached to the
object under the tool performances. The tool can be expanded, and then the user has also
interactions with the scene of the *Unity*'s environment, which at first must work with
a control of perspective modes, viewing the object in scene; but it could be extended
further on the operation as a measure tape component, to measure the distance between
two points in the scene on virtual object.

6 System's Functioning and Implementation

By studying the *ReconstructMe SDK*'s documentation, it was possible to develop and
adapt the algorithm's working logic. Changes were made on some default configuration
options. The kept changes were: a reduction on the reconstruction volumetric edges
regarding the maximum and minimum orientations of a 0,5 m-sided box; an automatic
sync to medium quality (with volume resolution parameters, with a value of 512 for the
x and y axis, 256 for the z axis and 9.766 as a truncation value); and a reduction of the
faces' number limits (as post-processing).

In order to develop the analysis tool, subsides are made on the documentation and
learning pages of *Unity*, specifically interested in the *Editor Scripting* terminologies.
The basic functioning of the developed scripts is made in two code classes. The first
one (*ToolScript*) integrates the *Unity*'s runtime line of processing. The second one
(*ToolScriptEditor*) customizes the *ToolScript* when instanced, as an Inspector interface
and also working over the editor's scene space runtime.

6.1 Functioning

The *Kinect* device must be connected. In general, when the reconstruction application
is started it is created and related to the *ReconstructMe SDK*'s essential functioning
interfaces. It begins the reconstruction process and the predefined rebuilding configurations are loaded, the sensor is opened and loads its default configurations and defines its
position related to the reconstruction's volume as in its front. Then the real time reconstruction process is started, always trying to determine the sensor's position at the scene
and relating subsequent positions, trying to update the debugging's view and volume.

After finishing the reconstruction, the object's surface model is generated, processed
by reducing its number of faces and saved under the *PLY* format. This file must be treated
on an external 3D software to crop the scene with the object and then convert it to *OBJ*
format in order to import it to *Unity*.

In *Unity*, with the analysis tool, the user must import the object's virtual model in
"Assets" and instance it on the tool's "Import" space (as in Fig. 4); the script will work
a collision box's instance that limits itself at the edges of the object's volumetric surface
edges; then, this said volume's measurement information are presented at the Inspector's

component interface and in the editor's scene space with the dimensional information for the x, y, and z axis (as in Fig. 4). The tool also offers an interactive functioning extension for future implementations, however, it already does the resource of managing the default visualization perspective of the object in scene (as in Fig. 4).

Fig. 4. Object in a virtual environment with the analysis tool composing in Unity.

6.2 Limitations and Usage Difficulties

It was noted among the found hardships: a commercial user license for *ReconstructMe SDK* was not enabled, so a reconstructed 3D model always will be saved with the insertion of distinct shapes; the environment's space used for reconstruction processes is relatively small and thus the chosen objects will also be proportionally small; be using the rebuilding application on a desktop computer so the portability with the device in the environment becomes proportional to the cable's length; the manual operation with the post-rebuilt 3D model (in an external software), forcing its resizing through default definitions, causing scene crops and discrepant shapes.

7 Tests to Obtain Results

At this level, functioning and application tests of the proposal are carried out, therefore reconstructing some objects with the intends resources (explaining details of the realizations); also, analysis and evaluations of the results obtained and considerations about the potential with the range of the proposal were carried out. To the point where it becomes interesting to highlight the formation level of the people involved in this work, it is explained that this work was made by a graduation student in Computer Science, under guidance of a professor who is a master, with an emphasis on Computer Graphics. With the obtained results this work is consolidated (the same is finished), as soon the results are satisfactory and sufficient, as in a scientific initiation project. However, future considerations and pretensions still exist and are made (just below next chapter), as a formal idea to give continue and improve to the studies involved here.

In order to test the app's reconstruction functionality, a scanning environment was prepared using a specific-sized platform to place the object. The chosen objects (according to those of closest resource) were: a rectangular box and a round box, both aiming at the importance of their shape; and a plastic gallon as an asymmetrical object.

The reconstruction for each object was made by manually conducing the device, trying to keep its positioning around 0,6 m from the object and assuming circular movements around the target, also capturing it from vertical angles. However, due to the lack of environmental space, it was not possible to complete a full circle around the objects, so at least horizontal angles close to 270° were assumed. Still, the rebuilt surfaces' final generation, even with post-processing, is generally made within 25 s. The resulting 3D models passed through manual processes on an external 3D software. They can be seen in Fig. 5.

The reconstruction of the objects A and B (Fig. 5) will feature low conservation of the edges and shape deformities, but object C shows a superior quality compared to the others, conserving its shape with a good level of precision; since it has a larger shape and no sharp angles, the surrounding keeps the reference points' gathering on the reconstruction's volumetric object, easing the localization's orientation. That way, it is important to highlight location problems at the scene that are related to the device and the reconstruction's volumetric object. During the scanning process, the application showed the need for points of reference on the volume, that way, the bases were the main parts to orient this aspect. Yet, even under this condition, some shapes detached themselves at the scene, however, the mesh results seemed satisfactory.

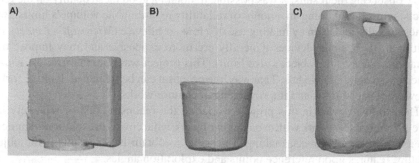

Fig. 5. Virtual results of the reconstruction processes, where it got A, B, C (*virtual objects*).

The measurement conservation of the virtual objects' volumetric extremes in comparison to their real life counterparts can be observed at Table 2. The virtual data come from the Unity's integrated analysis tool developed in this project.

Table 2. Relationship between size in meter of the object's volume in x, y, z axis, respectively.

Object	Real measures	Virtual measures	Error
A (Fig. 5)	0,21; 0,18; 0,05	0,22; 0,19; 0,06	0,01; 0,01; 0,01
B (Fig. 5)	0,15; 0,13; 0,15	0,16; 0,14; 0,16	0,01; 0,01; 0,01
C (Fig. 5)	0,19; 0,29; 0,13	0,20; 0,29; 0,14	0,01; 0,00; 0,01

Based on data from Table 2, the proposal's capacity is remarkable despite its lesser reconstructive capacities with objects *A* and *B* (Fig. 5), which are small, the extreme volume's conservation error is minimal and furthermore, the object *C* (Fig. 5) even with its asymmetrical features was able to present the full capacity of the reconstruction proposal.

8 Conclusion and Future Works

Despite the application's obtained results not always achieving a precise fit of the surfaces during the rebuilding process, this project was able to implement and study the applicability of a low-cost sensor in a point cloud reconstructive process and even study the implementation/configuration aspects regarding the capacity of the resources provided by *ReconstructMe SDK*.

Related to the capture and reconstruction's errors, arguments are proposed that the reconstruction's application may be studied and improved regarding the configuration aspects offered by the development interface from *ReconstructMe SDK* and it's still possible to highlight a factor that may influence on the sensor's capture quality. Related to the overall distance, the minimum capture distance was not ideally followed since the used environment couldn't provide this aspect for the reconstruction processes.

By observing the results, it was possible to obtain a good mesh quality on the rebuilt objects, while maintaining an amount of reliability regarding the volume's limits. Based on these results, and even by making use of a low-cost device (*Microsoft*'s *Kinect*), once traditional 3D Scanner devices generally are more expensive and may impose many limitations (such as the object's size limit). This project was able to prove the *Kinect*'s capacity to rebuild 3D models. That way, the proposal can be sustained, looking forward to new implementations and improvements for future works.

The capture device in this project works on the reconstruction of relatively large objects, being able to work with even larger objects, what covers the solution's applicable dimension to specific areas, making it possible to obtain better results if the object's structure features good reference points and exploration angles.

The developed analysis tool (*ToolScript*) working with the *Unity*'s engine made an excellent job of analyzing the objects' dimensions in a virtual space. In future projects, its interactive analysis feature can be further developed, bringing to this tool interactive measurement resources where the user would pass the mesh's points of interest and an equivalent value of the distance between the points would be shown.

In according to the section discussed about, "HCI and Study of the Technological Application" (Sect. 4), it's possible, of a parallel to the application sector, with what was studied and developed int this work, approximate this technological model (about the reconstruction) to a viewing of a scenery of the application field, when it was validated a sensor and an algorithmic that work. Clearly, it becomes possible to develop a scenery of the application of virtual reconstruction for horse Zootechnical analysis and classification. An approach of this work could interest the field of application, as well as it could propose to the sector the adaptation of the technology, resorting to the interest of this sector in the technological application, being able to reach or encourage it.

As a complement to a future project, more than applying implementations to the reconstruction application's sophistication, the insertion of other research-comparative analysis devices, like easy-obtainable devices with more adherence, can be explored. It's also interesting to develop an application to classify the 3D model's data, but focusing on parametrizing and displaying the specific and important features of the captured data, with the objective of sophisticating the analysis of specific objects. Bringing to the rebuilding procedure an automatic conduction can also be an interesting resource to this proposal. Bringing the developed project to a field test is also an important objective, since it will propose and test the implemented solution at the sophistication of a workplace that requires the acquisition of measurement data from specific objects, easing the analysis of measured data and rendering the interest's classification with the specific objects something objective.

Acknowledgments. Acknowledgments to the "Instituto Federal Goiano (IF Goiano)", especially to the Morrinhos institution campus, and the science initiation program "Programa Institucional Voluntário de Iniciação Científica (PIVIC)", who value and provide opportunities for all engagement and performance on this work as a research project, and that contribute to the state of this paper.

References

1. Gonzalez, R.C., Woods, R.E.: Digital Image Processing, 4th edn. Pearson, New York (2018)
2. Alves, G.T.M.: A study of techniques for shape acquisition using stereo and structured light aimed for engineering. Thesis, Pontifícia Universidade Católica do Rio de Janeiro, Rio de Janeiro, Brazil (2005)
3. Vasconcelos, C.N.: Image processing and computer vision algorithms for graphics cards parallel architectures. Thesis, Pontifícia Universidade Católica do Rio de Janeiro, Rio de Janeiro, Brazil (2009)
4. Haibo, Y.: Industrial design applications of surface reconstruction algorithm based on three dimensional point cloud data. In: 2017 International Conference on Robots & Intelligent System (ICRIS), pp. 178–181. IEEE (2017)
5. Zhang, R., Wang, Y., Song, D.: Research and implementation from point cloud to 3D model. In: 2010 Second International Conference on Computer Modeling and Simulation, pp. 169–172. IEEE (2010)
6. Heindl, C., Bauer, H., Ankerl, M., Pichler, A.: ReconstructMe SDK: a C API for Real-time 3D scanning. In: 6th International Conference and Exhibition on 3D Body Scanning Technologies, pp. 185–193. Hometrica Consulting - Dr. Nicola D'Apuzzo, Ascona, Switzerland (2015)
7. Chikurtev, D., Rangelov, I., Chivarov, N., Karastoyanov, D.: 3D modelling for object recognition with depth sensors. Probl. Eng. Cybern. Robot. **70**, 35–42 (2018). Accessed 07 Sept 2020. http://www.iict.bas.bg/pecr/index.html
8. Rafibakhsh, N., Gong, J., Siddiqui, M.K., Gordon, C., Lee, H.F.: Analysis of XBOX kinect sensor data for use on construction sites: depth accuracy and sensor interference assessment. In: Construction Research Congress 2012, pp. 848–857. American Society of Civil Engineers, Reston (2012)
9. DiFilippo, N.M., Jouaneh, M.K.: Characterization of different microsoft kinect sensor models. IEEE Sens. J. **15**, 4554–4564 (2015)
10. Han, J., Shao, L., Xu, D., Shotton, J.: Enhanced computer vision with Microsoft kinect sensor: a review. IEEE Trans. Cybern. **43**, 1318–1334 (2013)

11. Andersen, M.R., Jensen, T., Lisouski, P., Mortensen, A.K., Hansen, M.K., Gregersen, T., Ahrendt, P.: Kinect depth sensor evaluation for computer vision applications. Aarhus Univ, pp. 1–37 (2012)
12. Khoshelham, K.: Accuracy analysis of kinect depth data. In: ISPRS Workshop Laser Scanning, pp. 133–138 (2011)
13. Khan, W., Phaisangittisagul, E., Ali, L., Gansawat, D., Kumazawa, I.: Combining features for RGB-D object recognition. In: 2017 International Electrical Engineering Congress (iEECON), pp. 1–5. IEEE (2017)
14. Smisek, J., Jancosek, M., Pajdla, T.: 3D with kinect. In: Fossati, A., Gall, J., Grabner, H., Ren, X., Konolige, K. (eds.) Consumer Depth Cameras for Computer Vision, pp. 3–25. Springer, London (2013)
15. Zhang, Z.: Microsoft kinect sensor and its effect. IEEE Multimed. **19**, 4–10 (2012)
16. Liu, H., Zhang, X., Wang, S., Chen, L.: The reconstruction of three-dimensional tree models from terrestrial LiDAR. In: 2011 IEEE International Conference on Computer Science and Automation Engineering. pp. 371–374. IEEE (2011)
17. Pérez-Ruiz, M., Tarrat-Martín, D., Sánchez-Guerrero, M.J., Valera, M.: Advances in horse morphometric measurements using LiDAR. Comput. Electron. Agric. **174**, 105510 (2020)
18. Xu, Q., Wang, J., An, X.: A pipeline for surface reconstruction of 3-dimentional point cloud. In: 2014 International Conference on Audio, Language and Image Processing, pp. 822–826. IEEE, Shanghai (2014)
19. Donofre, A.C., Puoli Filho, J.N.P., Ferreira, I.E.D.P., Mota, M.D.S.D., Chiquitelli Neto, M.: Equilíbrio de cavalos da raça Quarto de Milha participantes da modalidade de três tambores por meio de proporções corporais. Ciência Rural. **44**, 327–332 (2014)
20. Lage, M.C.G.R., Bergmann, J.A.G., Procópio, A.M., Pereira, J.C.C., Biondini, J.: Associação entre medidas lineares e angulares de equinos da raça Mangalarga Marchador. Arq. Bras. Med. Veterinária e Zootec. **61**, 968–979 (2009)
21. Santiago, J.M., Rezende, A.S.C., Fonseca, M.G., Abrantes, R.G.P., Lage, J., Lana, Â.M.Q.: Comparação entre as medidas morfométricas do rebanho atual de machos Mangalarga Marchador e dos campeões da raça. Bol. Indústria Anim. **70**, 46–52 (2013)
22. Pasternak, M., Kahani, N., Bagherzadeh, M., Dingel, J., Cordy, J.R.: SimGen: a tool for generating simulations and visualizations of embedded systems on the unity game engine. In: 21st ACM/IEEE International Conference Model Driven Engineering Language System Companion Proceedings, Model, pp. 42–46 (2018)

Author Index